Irish Booksellers and English Writers 1740–1800

Irish Booksellers and English Writers 1740–1800

Richard Cargill Cole

Mansell Publishing Limited

Humanities Press International, Inc.

First Published 1986 by Mansell Publishing Limited
(A subsidiary of The H. W. Wilson Company)
6 All Saints Street, London N1 9RL, England
First published 1986 in the United States by
Humanities Press International, Inc.,
Atlantic Highlands, New Jersey 07716

British Library Cataloguing in Publication Data
Cole, Richard Cargill
Irish booksellers and English writers 1740–1800.
1. Book industries and trade—Ireland—History—
18th century
I. Title
338.4 '7686 '09415 Z331.3

ISBN 0–7201–1808–5

Library of Congress Cataloging-in-Publication Data
Cole Richard Cargill, 1926–
Irish booksellers, and English writers, 1740–1800.

Includes bibliographies.
1. Booksellers and bookselling—Ireland—History—18th century. 2. Reprints (Publications)—Publishing—Ireland—History—18th century. 3. Copyright—Unauthorized reprints—Ireland—History—18th century. 4. Englsh literature—Publishing—Ireland—History—18th century. 5. Book industries and trade—Ireland—History—18th century. 6. Book industries and trade—United States—History—18th century. I. Title. II. Title: Irish book sellers and English writers. 1740–1800.
Z331.1.C64 1986 070.5 '09415 85–21488
ISBN 0–391–03432–4

Printed in Great Britain by
Whitstable Litho Ltd., Whitstable, Kent

To Florence, Celia, and Paul
and our Irish sojourns

Contents

Preface

The Irish book trade in the eighteenth century provides materials for an interesting tale that has been told only in part. James A. Phillips has done the only extensive study of Irish publishing in the eighteenth century, "A Bibliographical Inquiry into Printing and Bookselling in Dublin from 1670 to 1800," but this book-length work, a 1952 doctoral dissertation for Trinity College, Dublin, has not been published. Phillips's pioneer work gives an account of such aspects of book production in eighteenth-century Dublin as printing, bookselling, bookbinding, paper, ink, presses, type and imprints, while also exploring the copyright problem. My study focuses on a dimension of the Irish book trade not dealt with by Phillips, the significant contribution by Irish booksellers to the dissemination of the major British writings of the time. In articles for the *Paper of the Bibliographical Society of America* in 1975 and 1981, I showed how Irish booksellers reprinted London editions of the works of Tobias Smollett and Samuel Johnson and sold them at home and abroad, but the extension of British culture, learning, and literature by Irish booksellers deserves a broader and more systematic treatment. The thesis of the present study is that Irish booksellers through cheap reprints disseminated the works of the major British writers of their time and augmented the audience for these writers not only in Ireland but in Britain and the United States of America. The circulation in America of Irish reprints of these writers was enhanced by the transfer of at least 101 members of the book trade from Ireland to the American book trade between

1750 and 1820. Many of these Irish booksellers in America both imported cheap Irish reprints of the British writers from their former colleagues and issued their own cheap reprints of these writers as they had either done or been trained to do in Ireland. These Irish booksellers in America would continue issuing their reprints of British writers for an American audience after their parent reprinting industry in Ireland had been destroyed by the Union of 1800.

The Irish book trade in the eighteenth century was essentially a reprint industry. Irish booksellers or their agents in London obtained first copies of London editions of English writers or, better yet, sheets from printing-houses and reprinted them within a month or two in Ireland at lower prices. More often than not their practice was to acquire the printed sheets surreptitiously and without paying the copyright holder or securing his permission. Naturally, the London book trade regarded the Irish booksellers as pirates and regularly denounced the Irish editions as piracies. To the late twentieth-century reader the charge seems well deserved, but the issue is more complex than it appears. Irish reprinting practices were not illegal; the British Copyright Acts of 1709 and 1739 did not prohibit Irish reprints sold only in Ireland. Furthermore, few people in Ireland thought the practice ethically questionable or that it needed a defense. Almost all Irish booksellers saw the practice as the only way they could make money and did not pursue any ethical implications, but a few defended it with vigor and with a certain cogency. This tiny group of apologists, like the pirates of books and sound and video recordings in our own day, were most apt to argue that they provided cheap books to poor people in Ireland who could not afford the expensive original editions. If the Irish booksellers had been content with this modest and even laudable goal, they probably would not have aroused the ire of British writers and publishers. But the Irish booksellers were aggressive and ambitious, more out of necessity than of greed, and they catered to both a domestic and foreign market. By 1796 the Irish booksellers could testify before the Irish parliament that they sold more cheap reprints to Americans than to Irishmen.

Even in the late twentieth century the profusion of eighteenth-century Irish reprints of the English writers in the institutional libraries of the English-speaking world is a remarkable phenomenon. Since the Eighteenth-Century Short Title Catalog has not been completed, the next best evidence of the Irish reprints is the *National Union Catalog, Pre-1956 Imprints* (London: Mansell, 1968–81) in 754 quarto volumes for the libraries of the United States of America and Canada. Irish reprints of the works of two famous eighteenth-century British writers who have entered the main stream of Anglo-American literature and culture are good examples. Eighteenth-century Irish reprints of Oliver Goldsmith's works appear in thirty-seven institutional libraries almost entirely in the United States with a total of 153 copies. The *National Union Catalog, Pre-1956 Imprints* locates eighteenth-century Irish reprints of Samuel Johnson's works in forty-one libraries almost entirely in the United States with a total of 120 copies, and for both these writers there are other copies of Irish reprints owned by rare book dealers and private collectors in the United States. Needless to say, eighteenth-century Irish reprints are numerous in British and Irish libraries; collections at Trinity College, Dublin, the National Library of Ireland, and Cambridge University are especially outstanding. Though these copies for the most part were not acquired by these libraries in the eighteenth century, the fact that they have survived in such numbers suggests that their publication was extensive and that they were valued and preserved by their original purchasers in the eighteenth century.

The Irish reprint industry was a viable and at times a prosperous one for most of the eighteenth century. The London book trade saw it as a threat to its profits by 1734, and the rise of the novel after 1740 and the growth of the reading public in the English-speaking world compounded the threat. It flourished during the last two decades of the century until a series of developments both inside and outside Ireland brought it to an end and with its demise the near collapse of the Irish book trade which depended so heavily upon it. This Irish reprint tradition was continued in the United States after 1800, however, by scores of its practitioners who had taken their bookmaking skills with them from Ireland to such publishing centers as Philadelphia, New York, and Baltimore. Unique in the annals of publishing, this massive transfer from one national book trade to another helped to make early nineteenth-century America a reprint center far surpassing its Irish model. Among these Irish booksellers in

America were Mathew Carey, who would become the leading publisher in the United States, and fifteen others who would earn places in the *Dictionary of American Biography* for their achievements in publishing and related fields.

This work examines in chapter one how booksellers in Ireland 1740–1800 reprinted the English writers of their time, and in chapter two who bought these Irish reprints of English writers in Ireland itself. The third chapter is concerned with two kinds of exports to the United States: (1) Irish reprints of English writers, (2) the first two phases of emigration of Irish bookmen before and immediately after the American Revolution. Chapters four through seven provide documentation and illustrations of the general points made in the first three chapters by examining reprints by Irish booksellers of works by eight major British authors. These eight writers have become part of the literary, intellectual, and cultural tradition of the English-speaking world, and perhaps the most significant achievement of the Irish booksellers was to disseminate their works and works of other major writers through cheap reprints. Chapter four deals with reprints by Irish booksellers of the four chief novelists of the eighteenth century, Samuel Richardson, Henry Fielding, Tobias Smollett, and Laurence Sterne. Chapter five views Irish reprints of the many and varied works of Samuel Johnson and his biographer James Boswell. The only Irishman in the group, Oliver Goldsmith, whose extensive publications in the drama, verse, fiction, and history were all reprinted by his countrymen, deserves a chapter of his own. For readers of the Irish reprints one of the most popular types of writing was history, and chapter seven explores historical writings of Goldsmith, Smollett, and Edward Gibbon in their Irish dress.

The eighth chapter shows how the combination of the Union of 1800, the greatly increased paper duty, and the new British and American reprints destroyed the reprint industry in Ireland itself. At least sixty-two booksellers then transferred from the book trade in Ireland to the American book trade to join the thirty-nine already there and to continue the Irish reprinting practices that their former colleagues in the Irish book trade could no longer engage in. Foremost among these sixty-two was Patrick Byrne, a leading Dublin printer–bookseller who figures throughout this work as the quintessential Dublin–Philadelphia reprinter of English writers. Chapter nine examines Byrne's publishing career in Dublin and Philadelphia in detail along with the careers of two predecessors in Dublin and Philadelphia, Robert Bell and William Spotswood. The tenth and final chapter explores the varied impact of Irish booksellers and their reprints of British writers on Irish, British, and American culture and society.

I have conducted much of the research for this study in a number of Irish archives, but primarily in the National Library of Ireland and the Library of Trinity College, Dublin. Since these two great libraries are only a block apart, their holdings essentially represent a union library which contains the finest collection of eighteenth-century Irish editions and Irish newspapers in the world. I also found important research materials in other Dublin archives: the Dublin Public Library in Pearse Street, the Public Record Office, the Royal Irish Academy, the Registry of Deeds, the Marsh Library. Elsewhere in Ireland other archives afforded useful information: the Linen Hall Library, the Public Record Office of Northern Ireland and the Library of the Queen's University in Belfast; the Armagh Public Library (Church of Ireland); and in Cork, the University College Library and the Public Library. I examined a few eighteenth-century Irish newspapers in the Colindale branch of the British Library that are not available in Ireland. Late in my study I checked editions of the eight writers in the Bradshaw Collection of Irish Books at Cambridge University and the many additions after the Bradshaw catalogue was published in 1916. As rich as this collection is in Irish editions in general, however, it contains almost no editions of the eight writers that are not to be found in Dublin. I found all staff members of these libraries and record repositories courteous and helpful. I am especially indebted to Miss Mary Pollard of the Trinity College, Dublin, Rare Book Room, and Mr. W. G. Wheeler of the Queen's University Library, Belfast, for many helpful suggestions.

In the United States I have conducted most of my research in the several libraries of Yale University, which as part of its massive eighteenth-century archives has an outstanding collection of Irish editions of the eight writers; the Yale collection includes several editions not available in Dublin and many copies autographed by their eighteenth-century owners. Mr. Herman

W. Liebert, Director Emeritus of the Beinecke Rare Book Library at Yale, generously made his private collection of eighteenth-century Irish editions of the works of Samuel Johnson available to me along with helpful comments. The Mathew Carey papers in the American Antiquarian Society, Worcester, Massachusetts, and the Historical Society of Pennsylvania, Philadelphia, provide the most detailed evidence of the Dublin–Philadelphia book trade. I am grateful for the assistance rendered by staff members of these archives in the United States. Dr. Hugh Amory of the Houghton Library, Harvard University, made especially valuable recommendations about my project.

I am deeply appreciative of the numerous summer stipends I have received from my own institution Davidson College, Davidson, North Carolina. I am also grateful for research funds from the American Council of Learned Societies, the Procter and Gamble Fund, the Piedmont University Center of North Carolina, and the Board of Higher Education of the Presbyterian Church in the United States. For permission to use material from six articles published by me I am indebted to the following publishers of scholarly journals: the New York Public Library for "James Boswell and the Irish Press, 1767–1795," *Bulletin of the New York Public Library*, 73 (1969), 581–98; the University of Chicago Press, Journals Division, for "Oliver Goldsmith's Reputation in Ireland, 1762–1774," *Modern Philology*, 68 (1970), 65–70, "Community Lending Libraries in Eighteenth-Century Ireland," and "Private Libraries in Eighteenth-Century Ireland," *Library Quarterly*, 44 (1974), 111–23, 231–47; the Bibliographical Society of America for "Smollett and the Eighteenth-Century Irish Book Trade," *Papers of the Bibliographical Society of America*, 69 (1975), 345–63, and "Samuel Johnson and the Eighteenth-Century Irish Book Trade," *PBSA*, 75 (1981), 235–55; comments on the Smollett article by Guilland Sutherland in *PBSA*, 71 (1977), 494–97, have proved helpful.

In this book I use eighteenth-century Irish editions almost entirely from the National Library of Ireland, the Library of Trinity College, Dublin, and the Yale University libraries. These three together make up a collection of the eight major authors that is probably 90 per cent complete, a collection that includes editions not listed in the *New Cambridge Bibliography of English Literature*, II (Cambridge: Cambridge University Press, 1971) or the *National Union Catalog, Pre-1956 Imprints* (NUC); *NUC* copies that I have not examined but whose existence I have confirmed are identified in endnotes, as are a few Cambridge University copies. Most copies in these libraries are autographed by their eighteenth-century owners, who may usually be identified in the various editions of *Burke's Landed Gentry*; in identifying owners I cite only sources not readily available. Since I refer so often to these libraries, I use their initials in endnotes, NLI for the National Library of Ireland and TCD for Trinity College, Dublin.

1
The Irish Reprint Industry 1740–1800

Irish booksellers were neither the first nor the last to reprint new books without authorization, but they were among the most successful and among the very few that made such reprints the heart of the book trade. Their story begins with the English Copyright Act of 1709, which with all its verbosity and complexity may be reduced to two statements: (1) The author of a book already printed or the bookseller who had bought his copy should have the exclusive right of publication for twenty-one years; (2) The author of a book not yet published should have the sole liberty of printing it for fourteen years from its publication and for an additional fourteen years if he were still alive. The failure of the Act to mention Ireland offered the Irish booksellers an opportunity which they quickly took advantage of. Since they were not bound legally to pay copyright, they could quickly reprint London editions and sell them for much less. At first, the Irish booksellers aimed their reprints at their own people, but it was not long before they saw they could increase their sales by exporting some of their production to Britain and, after the American war especially, to America. Journals of the British House of Commons show that complaints by London publishers against what they saw as Irish piracies of their editions began to come to the attention of the government as early as 1734. A committee report in March of that year to the British House of Commons cited examples of London editions which were reprinted in Ireland without payment to the London publisher and then sold in England at a price well below the price of the London edition. Rev. Dr. Samuel Clarke, Dean of

Salisbury, had sold his sermons to his London publisher for one thousand pounds, and the London edition of ten volumes sold for forty shillings in sheets. The Irish printed edition in two volumes folio sold for only twenty-six shillings. Charles Rivington reported that his London edition of the *Gardener's Dictionary*, whose copyright he had purchased from the author, sold for twenty-five shillings, but he had bought the Irish piracy in York for twenty-two shillings. Rivington had also bought the copyright of *Revelation Examined with Candour* and sold its London edition for seven shillings only to find the Irish piracy selling in England for 5s.5d. Other London publishers had similar tales of woe about such major works as Clarendon's *History of the Rebellion* and Burnet's *History of His Own Time*. James Crockatt had personally observed a large shipment of Irish piracies arriving at a bookshop in Preston, Lancashire, and he had bought the Irish pirated edition of Burden's *Complete Farrier* from the batch. Though the Irish were the main culprits, the House of Commons also heard complaints about Dutch pirated editions of English books.[1]

After several years of agitation an act was passed by Parliament and signed by King George II on 14 June 1739 "prohibiting the Importation of Books reprinted Abroad, and first composed or written, and printed in Great Britain."[2] Although the law made the Irish reprints subject to seizure in British ports by agents of the Commissioners of Excise, some Irish exports continued. The details of how they were smuggled into Britain are unknown. The Irish smuggling trade was large, but most of it was concerned with spirits, tea, and tobacco smuggled into Ireland; little was smuggled into Britain from Ireland, though Irish ships were regularly used to smuggle goods into England from the western coast of France.[3] Evidence is sparse for the continued export of Irish editions until 1759, prior to which there is some evidence from Welsh sources that a Welsh clientele for the Irish reprints continued after the 1739 law. One Welshman in 1751 was warned that books ordered by him from Ireland would be confiscated by officials looking for them, but at about the same time Welshmen in Anglesey were ordering catalogues from Dublin booksellers, and some were sending books to be bound in Dublin.[4]

The earliest incontrovertible evidence of the success of the Irish booksellers in evading the law of 1739 is the scheme of the London booksellers in 1759 to prevent the sale in England of Irish reprints of English writers. A prominent London bookseller John Whiston wrote two letters in April 1759 to John Merrill, bookseller in Cambridge, explaining that the London booksellers had agreed that "No one, after the first day of May next, shall sell any Scotch or Irish editions of books first printed in England ... or shall purchase or take in exchange, or bring in by any means whatsoever, such Scotch or Irish books." Merrill is to send to London immediately all his Scotch and Irish editions, and James Fletcher in Oxford is doing the same. The London booksellers will sue any bookseller who sells these editions, and they have raised £3,150 for court costs and to pay agents to inspect bookshops in "all parts of England" for the presence of these editions. Claiming perpetual copyright, the London booksellers made no distinction between the Irish reprints of current books protected by copyright and the Scotch reprints of old books for which copyright had expired. Even better proof of the success of Irish reprints in England is the letter of 2 November 1759, by John Wilkie, chairman of the committee of London booksellers, to all booksellers in England. Having lost heavily because of the Scotch and Irish reprints, the London booksellers have agreed "to prosecute, by due course of law, all such persons as shall be detected in either printing or vending piratical editions of the books which are their property." Some English booksellers are already being prosecuted for selling these reprints in their shops.[5] A month later Ireland's most famous printer and bookseller, George Faulkner, advised Samuel Derrick that he was sending his reprint of Swift's *Works* to England, but these books were liable to seizure.[6]

In spite of these vigorous measures the London booksellers in 1759 failed to keep the Irish reprints out of England just as they had failed in 1739. After 1759 the continued success of the Irish reprints in England is best reflected in the great controversy of 1785 over commerce between Britain and Ireland. Two British pamphlets prior to this controversy, however, indicate that the Irish reprints were still available in British bookshops. An Edinburgh writer in 1769 was of mixed mind about the Irish reprints of the English writers as he noted with approval that their presence in British bookshops made it possible for "people of middling fortune" to buy the significant English writings; he cited especially Robertson's *History of Charles V* just published at three pounds for the London edition and fifteen shillings for the Irish reprint. But the writer further observes that William Blackstone's famous *Commentaries on the Law of England* "has been reprinted in Ireland, copies have been smuggled over to Britain, and a good many of them ... were seized some time ago by the Doctor's agents in the port of London"; the writer wonders why Blackstone does not "sue the Irish printers for piracy, robbery or theft since he took the trouble to have "those pirated copies" confiscated.[7] The Dublin reprint of Blackstone was also sold in Philadelphia and along the Atlantic coast by Mathew Carey and his agents in 1796 at double the Dublin price but still under the London price.[8] The well-known political writer Catharine Macaulay in 1774 also had doubts about the Irish reprints of her fellow English writers, but at the same time she was glad that they were available in London bookshops as a check on the excessively high prices of the London editions; customers who didn't want to pay the high prices of the London editions had "recourse to the Irish ..., who would furnish them with as many editions of the authors as they pleased."[9]

In 1785 the London booksellers made their last attempt before the Union of 1800 to keep the Irish reprints out of British bookshops. A notice appeared during the first week of March 1785 in the *Daily Universal Register* and *Lloyd's Evening Post* and undoubtedly in other London papers: "The piracies so daily practised by the Irish booksellers, call aloud for redress, as there is scarce a production of merit brought out on this side of the water, which they do not contract into a smaller work, and publish at a lower price, which soon finds its way here, to the great detriment of men of genius and science." A few days later four prominent London booksellers testified before a committee of the British House of Commons: "There is no Doubt that there is a great clandestine Importation of Books from Ireland into this Country. There have also been many Seizures made, and lately a very considerable One at Edinburgh, of such Books where the CopyRight still subsists under the 8th of Queen Anne." Their testimony was reprinted in the *Journals of the House of Commons of Ireland*[10] and in such newspapers as *Lloyd's Evening Post* for 21–23 March 1785 and the *Dublin Evening Post* of 31 March 1785 and undoubtedly many others. In like vein the Master Printers of Edinburgh complained in the *Edinburgh Evening Courant* of 11 April 1785 that "the Irish would destroy their trade," and their protest was conveyed to the British House of Commons on April 20th.[11]

Edinburgh newspapers, however, do not appear to have recorded the large seizure of Irish pirated editions in Edinburgh mentioned in the House of Commons testimony, although there are frequent notices of seizures of the favorite smuggling goods, spirits, tea, tobacco, by the Commissioners of Excise during 1784 and 1785.

These protests against Irish reprints of the English writers emerged because of the extensive debates in 1785 in the parliaments of both Britain and Ireland and in the newspapers over the need for new commercial agreements between the two countries in the light of the legislative autonomy won by Ireland in 1782. Of the twenty resolutions concerning commerce first proposed by William Pitt, the Lord Chancellor, and then passed by the British Parliament, though never passed by the Irish Parliament, the seventeenth resolution essentially tried to extend the 1709 Copyright Act to Ireland. Opposition to the seventeenth resolution came from many powerful groups in Irish society. Although the Irish Parliament was receptive to some of the resolutions, it was strongly opposed to a measure which it believed would destroy the Irish book trade. Edmund Pery, Speaker of the Irish House of Commons, said on 27 May 1785: "The seventeenth resolution, relative to books, would put an end to the printing business in this country, without serving Great Britain. It would transfer that business from Ireland to Holland or some other foreign country."[12] The Dutch booksellers were Ireland's main competition in supplying cheap books to British readers. The many complaints to Parliament about the threat of the seventeenth resolution to the burgeoning American trade will be discussed in chapter three on the Irish reprints sold in America. Pampleteers in Dublin responded to the threat; of the several pamphlets that survive from the 1785 debates, *The Account Settled! or A Balance Struck Between the Irish Propositions and the English Resolutions*, published and probably written by Patrick Byrne, is perhaps the most cogent. Patrick Byrne, one of the many Irish booksellers whose latter years would be spent in the American book trade, believes that the seventeenth resolution is a plot by the London booksellers to stop the sale of the Irish reprints in Ireland, Britain and America. The Irish book trade would no longer exist if the act passed, but the London booksellers would gain nothing since the resolution could only have the "effect of throwing the trade into the hands of the Dutch, who already enjoy the advantage of publishing almost all French books which are prohibited."[13]

Three leading Dublin newspapers in numerous articles also reflect the well nigh universal opposition to resolution seventeen. The *Dublin Evening Post*, the *Dublin Journal*, and the *Hibernian Journal* in April, May, and June 1785 agreed that only the Dutch would benefit if the resolution passed. Two of these papers should be quoted at length because they represent the kind of apologia for the Irish reprints that the more articulate Irish booksellers were wont to offer. The *Dublin Journal* for 14 April 1785 dismisses the claims of the London booksellers to be harmed by the Irish reprints:

> The English booksellers, when they have purchased any copy which they esteem valuable enough to enter at Stationers'-hall, publish an edition of it in such a size and at such a price as compensates for the whole of their purchase; and the sale of this valuable edition is not confined to England, but every buyer as well in Ireland as elsewhere, who is able to purchase, gives the splendid edition the preference. The Irish editions, which afterwards appear, are only published with a spirit of accommodation, and are suited to men who love literature, but cannot afford the expence.

The *Dublin Evening Post* had made essentially the same argument on April 5th and concluded that if the London booksellers won, reading in Ireland would become too great a luxury and would "as in the days of barbarous ignorance be confined solely to the cloister — or the castle of the insolent and haughty Baron." Furthermore, "If the price of books are enhanced — they are placed beyond the purchase of the poor, who must remain in that state of lamentable ignorance, which alas has so long degraded the mass of our people." What these writers and other apologists for the Irish reprints failed to say was that there were customers in Britain and especially in America in 1785 and that the Irish audience, like audiences everywhere, was made up largely of the landed and professional classes, as succeeding chapters will show.

Among the few Irish supporters of the seventeenth resolution extending the 1709 Copyright Act to Ireland was the Rev. Dr. Thomas Barnard, Bishop of Killaloe. The *Freeman's Journal* appears to be the only Irish newspaper to give the Bishop's speech in the Irish House of Lords sympathetic coverage, claiming that he spoke for authors rather than the interests of the Irish booksellers.

For other Irish newspapers the Bishop was a traitor to his country since copyright would destroy the profitable reprint industry and the jobs of the many people who were employed in it and in related industries like paper and leather-making. A complaint of this time by an Irish writer against an Irish reprint of his book is a further example of the conflicting interests of the writer and the publisher indicated by the *Freeman's Journal*. Thomas Sheridan of the famous Irish literary family protested that his *Dictionary* first printed in London was pirated by Dublin booksellers. Sheridan's warning against the Dublin piracy in the *Edinburgh Advertiser* for 6 July 1784 tells much about the threat posed by the Irish reprints in general: "Whoever shall discover any person vending, or exposing to sale, any book or books, of the above pirated edition, in Scotland, or elsewhere in Great Britain, shall, upon conviction of the delinquent, receive the sum of Ten Pounds from the author, over and above the penalty by act of parliament, to be paid by Mr. Alexander Johnston, writer [i.e. lawyer] in Edinburgh." The two Dublin booksellers Patrick Byrne and Patrick Wogan, whose reprint of Sheridan's *Dictionary* sold for less than a fourth of the price of the London edition, replied in the *Dublin Journal* for 13 July 1784, that Ireland was an independent kingdom and they were only doing what was done in Holland and elsewhere in reprinting the book in a cheaper format without paying royalties. Better writers than Sheridan, such writers as "Gibbon, Robertson, Hume, Doctor Johnson," had not complained of the practice. As did the more articulate Dublin booksellers, Byrne and Wogan affirmed that they were enlarging the audience for the English writers by printing cheap editions. As Roman Catholics suffering from British penal laws in Ireland, Byrne and Wogan undoubtedly saw copyright as another example of British oppression. Like scores of their fellows in the Irish book trade, Byrne, his two sons and his son-in-law, after the collapse of the Irish reprint industry at the Union of 1800 would emigrate to the United States to continue reprinting the English writers. Byrne's career in the Dublin book trade 1779–1801 and in the Philadelphia book trade 1801–14 will be discussed in chapter nine as one of the more successful among the 101 persons who left the Irish book trade to work in the American book trade. Sheridan's efforts to prevent the sale of the Irish reprint of his work in Britain may have been successful, but Americans wanted the cheap edition, as Mathew Carey, formerly of the Dublin book trade, now of the Philadelphia book trade, wrote to Byrne in 1788.[14]

Not all Irish writers shared the opinions of Bishop Barnard, Thomas Sheridan, and the *Freeman's Journal*. Ireland's greatest writer of the century Jonathan Swift was sympathetic to the Irish bookseller's position, even though Swift himself suffered financially. He protested against London publishers' flooding Ireland with books and defended the right of the Irish to reprint London editions for sale both in Ireland itself and in Britain. He wrote to his London publisher Benjamin Motte on 25 May 1736: "I would encourage our Booksellers here to sell your authors Books printed here, and send them to all the Towns in England, if I could do it with Safety and Profit; because (I repeat it) it is no Offence against God or the Laws of the Country I live in."[15] Another famous writer and also a Lord Lieutenant of Ireland Lord Chesterfield urged George Faulkner on 17 September 1748 to print a cheap edition of Bower's *History of the Popes* because the London edition was too expensive.[16] On the other side of the Atlantic, Benjamin Franklin was another writer with some sympathy for the Irish reprints. He wrote to Benjamin Vaughan in London on 21 April 1785 that cheap Irish reprints should be available to English readers: "If books can be had much cheaper from Ireland (which I believe, for I bought Blackstone there for twenty-four shillings, when it was sold in England at four guineas), is not this an advantage, not to English booksellers, indeed, but to English readers, and to learning."[17] The future "Liberator" of the Roman Catholics in Ireland, young Daniel O'Connell certainly agreed with Franklin when he wrote from London on 11 March 1794 to his uncle in Ireland asking for Irish reprints of Blackstone and other law books.[18]

Since Swift, Lord Chesterfield, and Franklin were not dependent on income from authorship, their views on the Irish reprints are perhaps atypical. Their position can be matched by three other writers who had to leave Ireland, as most Irish writers had to do, in order to earn a living from authorship. In June 1747 a debating club at Trinity College, Dublin, of which Edmund Burke was a member, debated the subject of copyright. Andrew Buck introduced a resolution "for ye better Regulation of ye Press, & ye Prevention of Piracy." William Dennis was opposed to the resolution because Irish booksellers could not exist without reprinting English writers. Burke maintained that the interest of writers was more important than the interest of booksellers. On being put to a vote the Buck proposal won.[19] Another professional writer, either John Courtenay or Robert Jephson, both of whom used the sobriquet *Jeoffry Wagstaffe*, and both of whom were soon to emigrate to London, lamented in the *Dublin Mercury* for 14 September 1771 that Irish writers had to exile themselves to make a living. Wagstaffe does not identify the Irish booksellers as the cause, but it is clear that he holds them responsible for the flight of Ireland's many gifted writers because they reprint London editions rather than pay Irish writers for original works. The grievances of another Irish writer in exile, Oliver Goldsmith, against the booksellers of his native land will be discussed in chapter six on Irish reprints of Goldsmith's works.

Although few original works were published in Ireland, reprinting the English writers kept a large number of printers, booksellers, and bookbinders busy. In 1760 there were thirty-three printers and forty-six booksellers in Dublin.[20] The peak year for printers was 1787 with fifty-three, but the new British and American reprints at the end of the century, the Union of 1800 with Britain and the consequent extension of British copyright laws to Ireland, and emigration to the United States cut the number in half. The number of bookbinders dropped from forty-two in 1768 to nine at the Union. The number of booksellers decreased from sixty-five at the peak about 1790 to forty-three at the Union.[21] The best known booksellers were also printers, such men as Swift's publisher George Faulkner and his nephew, the Hoeys, the Griersons, the Ewings, the Wilsons, the Exshaws, Robert Marchbank, William Sleater, James Williams, James Potts, Patrick Byrne, and John Chambers; the latter two would continue these activities in the United States. Many of these printer–booksellers also published newspapers and magazines that provided them a means of advertising and reviewing their reprints of the English writers, and these are publishing endeavors that many Irish bookmen would resume in the United States. George Faulkner published the *Dublin Journal* from 1725 until his death in 1774 when he was succeeded by his nephew. The younger James Hoey published the *Dublin Mercury* 1766–73 and was a leading Roman Catholic bookseller as his father had been. Three prominent printer–booksellers who published the two leading magazines were James Potts, who had the new *Hibernian Magazine* 1771–75 until replaced by another prominent printer–bookseller Thomas Walker, and John Exshaw, who with his father had the *Gentleman's and London Magazine*, commonly called *Exshaw's Magazine*, for over sixty years. As leading publishers both of periodicals and of reprints of London editions, Faulkner, Hoey, Potts, Walker, and Exshaw skillfully used their periodicals to encourage their readers to buy their reprints of the English authors. These were the giants, but others combined the two roles on a smaller scale, Patrick Byrne of the *Universal Magazine*, Dillon Chamberlaine of the *Dublin Library or Irish Magazine*, Thomas Henshall of the *Minerva Magazine*, Richard James of the *Dublin Gazette*, Thomas M'Donnell of the *Hibernian Journal*, James Moore of the *Dublin Magazine* 1798–1801, William Spotswood of the *Dublin Chronicle*, Eugene Swiney of the *Corke Journal* and the *Cork Evening Post*, and Peter Wilson of the *Dublin Magazine* 1761–64.

Some of the booksellers had large shops since most sold not only books but stationery and in the last two decades of the century tickets for the Irish state lottery. Lawrence Flin's catalogues from 1761 until 1770 list over eight thousand volumes, and his *Hibernian Journal* advertisement for 18 May 1778 notes that his shop has twenty thousand volumes. Luke White, perhaps the most prosperous of all Irish booksellers, issued in 1786 the first *Complete Dublin Catalogue of Books*, most of whose several thousand Irish reprints were available in his shop; White reprinted some of the most significant English works of the time such as Edward Gibbon's *Decline and Fall of the Roman Empire* in twelve volumes, the Hume-Smollett *History of England* in thirteen volumes, and Samuel Johnson's *Lives of the English Poets* in three volumes. George Draper in 1791 reissued White's catalogue as *A General Catalogue of Books in all Languages, Arts, and Sciences, That Have Been Printed in Ireland and Published in Dublin, first published in 1786 and again in 1791.* These two catalogues enabled booksellers in Britain and especially in America to order Irish reprints of specific English writers.[22] John Archer in the *Hibernian Journal* for 29 March 1793 claims thirty-thousand volumes in his shop, and three years later his customers subscribed for one hundred sets of the noted Dublin reprint of Smollett's *Don Quixote*. Archer's catalogues for 1789 and 1793 reveal a large stock and a building sufficiently commodious that over his bookshop he could set up a "spacious room" where in the words of the *Dublin Evening Post* for 27 November 1788 the "literati" could "be secured from intrusion of the vulgar, and the indiscriminate intercourse, which a shop is liable to."

Besides printers, booksellers, engravers, and bookbinders, the Irish reprint industry needed agents in London to supply London editions, or better yet the sheets from London printing houses, as quickly as possible for reprinting in Ireland. One of the eight major British authors used in this study and also a renowned printer in the London Samuel Richardson wrote on 14 September 1753 in his *Address to the Public* that "he had heard an Irish Bookseller boast, some years ago, That he could procure from any Printing Office in London, Sheets of any Book printing in it, while it was going on, and before Publication." The story of the reprinting of Richardson's novel the *History of Sir Charles Grandison* will be told in Chapter four, but some details here help to show how some Irish reprints, piracies to their London publishers, came into being. Two of Richardson's employees sold printed sheets of *Sir Charles Grandison* to London agents of Dublin booksellers just as they had some years earlier sold sheets of Richardson's popular novel *Pamela*. One of the employees Thomas Killingbeck had formerly been a printer in the Dublin shop of the famous George Faulkner, who had always had him print from copies "clandestinely obtained from England." Killingbeck also said that Faulkner was well known among London printers for his "great diligence in London" in obtaining sheets from printing houses surreptitiously, as he had for his pirated edition of *Pamela*.[23] The Dublin pirates were so successful that the pirated edition of *Sir Charles Grandison* was published before the London edition, and Richardson reported his fear that the Dublin pirates would charge him with piracy!

This example of *Sir Charles Grandison* points to another aspect of the Dublin reprints. Although Faulkner got most of the bad publicity, he had actually arranged to pay Richardson seventy guineas for the right to print and sell the novel in Ireland just as he had paid Richardson for rights to *Clarissa*, though not to *Pamela*. The real pirates were three other Dublin booksellers, John Exshaw, Henry Saunders, and Peter Wilson, who had obtained the sheets from Richardson's printing office and were publishing their own edition of *Sir Charles Grandison* in competition with Faulkner's. Faulkner stopped his presses, but as reprints of the eight major authors will show, competing Irish reprints were not uncommon. In spite of their claim to provide cheap books for Ireland's poor and untutored masses, some Dublin booksellers were willing to make money not only at the expense of the British oppressors but at one another's expense. The custom in the Dublin book trade through its Guild of St. Luke the Evangelist was that the bookseller who first announced publicly his intention to reprint a London edition was to have no competition, but as the newspapers show, this custom was honored both in the breach and the observance. No mean pirate himself according to London publishers, Faulkner often in his newspaper charged his fellow Dublin booksellers with piracy. When he was reprinting the London edition of the *Universal History* in eight volumes, he had this grievance on 7 February 1744:

> It is humbly hoped, that if any Attempts should be made by any Persons whatever to pirate this Work, that they will be discountenanced and treated with the Contempt and Abhorrence suitable to their vile Intentions, which is done with a View only to hinder the Subscriptions to this Work, by endeavouring to impose upon the Publick by printing Proposals to publish it in sixteen Volumes Octavo; whereas, it is impossible to bring it into forty in the Letter our Edition is printed in, or a Character that can be read with Pleasure; but, if they should succeed in such a Scheme, by acting as Agents for people Abroad, whose Intention is to destroy Printing in this Kingdom … we are sure, there are Patriots enough in this Kingdom, to confound such horrid Devices, and who will countenance me in this Work.

He wrote years later in his newspaper for 8–12 August 1758 while charging the Ewings with pirating his *Swift* that he had lost fifteen hundred pounds when his *Universal History* was pirated in Dublin in 1744. The few Irish writers who were willing to have their work published in Ireland were also wary of piracy. An accountant in Dublin Joseph Middleton obtained 752 subscriptions to have his *Correct Book of Interest* printed by Robert Marchbank of Dublin in 1778. Middleton warns his readers at the end of his book that every copy of the Marchbank edition has Middleton's signature in his own handwriting "in order to prevent Piracies."

Some Dublin booksellers and printers like Robert Bell boldly proclaimed the right of all Irish booksellers to reprint new British books without permission. Bell was one of over a hundred Irish bookmen to transfer their publishing activities to America as the Irish book trade declined. In 1767, the last year of his Dublin career before emigrating to Philadelphia to resume his career in publishing, Bell reprinted Alexander Donaldson's *Some Thoughts on the State of Literary Property* cited above. Bell's own introductory and concluding remarks represent an apologia for Irish reprints. Dublin booksellers cannot accuse one another of piracy, for all are pirates; the pot cannot call the kettle black. All Dublin booksellers "are daily loaded with the odious appellation of pirates from the other side of the water." Dublin booksellers "neither give copy money to authors, nor to British booksellers," and it is no "invasion of the property of another to reprint all or any of the books published in Great Britain." Any Dublin bookseller is completely free to reprint any London edition; he does not need to consult certain Dublin booksellers who are trying to monopolize the reprinting business "to the prejudice and injury of all the people of Ireland." One of the most articulate, brash, and colorful of the Dublin and Philadelphia publishers, Bell would offer a spirited defense of American and Irish reprints in 1771 after his arrival in Philadelphia, as will be discussed in chapter three on Irish booksellers in America.

Not all Irish reprints were unauthorized, however. Some Irish booksellers worked out arrangements with the copyright holder, normally the London publisher. Two examples have already been cited, George Faulkner's payments to Samuel Richardson for *Clarissa* and *Sir Charles Grandison*. Patrick Byrne's extensive collaboration with John Debrett of London will be discussed in chapter nine on Byrne's successful career in the Dublin and Philadelphia book trades. Some Dublin booksellers also sold London editions especially at mid-century or before. Giles Barber has shown by an analysis of the Customs records in the Public Record Office of London that book exports to Ireland from London from 1701 until the end of the records in 1780 reached a peak value of £3,841 in 1743 and then declined intermittently to lows of only £256 in 1777 and £202 in 1778.[24] Barber's figures and those from the Irish Customs House Books 1764–80 are comparable in that both reflect a significant decline in British book exports to Ireland, and these exports continued to be low through the next decade according to Irish records while export of Irish books especially to America steadily increased.[25]

The two decades 1780–1800 represent the golden age of the Irish reprint industry, and British book imports were low, but the new London reprints towards the end of the century brought about an increase in British book imports, as will be discussed in chapter eight on the decline and fall of the Irish reprint trade. After mid-century most Irish readers, and the Irish library owners discussed in chapter two offer solid evidence, seem to have followed the bookseller's frequent appeals in newspapers to "Buy Irish." Faulkner's appeal of 18 November 1758 is typical. Faulkner will be reprinting the *Universal History*, and he hopes "that Gentlemen will suspend entering into any Engagements in Favour of FOREIGN Editions, especially as such Engagements cannot tend to their Advantage, but may possibly prove detrimental to themselves, and very injurious to the Trade of this Kingdom in general, as to the Printing and Paper Manufactures in particular." Although there appears to be no newspaper evidence of public ire against sellers or buyers of British books as there is for other British goods such as woolens and shoes, buyers and sellers of books after mid-century do seem to have supported the local industry for the most part.[26]

The domestic audience to which this Irish reprint industry catered will be analyzed in detail in the second chapter, but generalizations on its size and composition are relevant here. Illiteracy was high in Ireland primarily because the Roman Catholic majority consisting largely of tenant farmers and farm laborers were exluded by the penal laws from any regular and systematic schooling; some of these farm workers were not illiterate but read and wrote Irish rather than English. In a 1745 pamphlet George Faulkner and George Grierson estimated that of the Dublin population of about 100,000, 20,000 were illiterate. They saw a large group of 40,000 literate people who, nevertheless, were not able to read serious books, and a group of 40,000 nobility, clergy, gentry, and professional men who could be an audience for literature but would not be.[27] The *Hibernian Journal* of Dublin in its protest of 13 April 1785 against the campaign of the London booksellers to extend British Copyright Laws to Ireland asserted there were over 2,300,000 illiterates in Ireland, who needed every available opportunity for education and cheap books. This figure is high since the hearth and money collectors for that year set the entire population at 2,845,932, but a modern scholar has revised this up to 4,019,000.[28] As late as the census of 1841, after public education had been instituted, half of the male population in the four provinces of Ireland were illiterate. This illiteracy figure is substantially higher than the figure for England in 1841 when less than one-third of the adult male population were illiterate.[29] The estimate, partly tongue-in-cheek, by Faulkner and Grierson in 1745 that 40 percent of the Dublin population were potential readers of literature was probably exaggerated. In the first systematic census of Dublin taken in 1798 by James Whitelaw and published in 1805, only 37,305 of a population of 182,370, or about 20 percent, were assigned to upper and middle classes. In a later work done after the Union with Britain in which Whitelaw was joined by John Warburton and Robert Walsh, the middle and upper classes in Dublin were identified as thirty-five peers, thirteen baronets, five Members of Parliament, 288 Clergymen, 1,851 lawyers, 204 physicians, 1,484 gentry, 4,911 businessmen, and two hundred military officers, and their families; this figure multiplied by four for families is close to the 1798 number in spite of the exodus from Ireland after the Union.[30] The audience in Ireland itself for Irish reprints of the major English writers was drawn largely from these groups and their counterparts outside Dublin, as an analysis of owners of private libraries, book subscribers, and patrons of community libraries will show in chapter two. These groups in the most important of the county towns, Belfast, Cork, Limerick, Waterford, and Kilkenny would be much smaller, and in the smaller towns and countryside smaller still.

George Faulkner seems to have been the Irish bookseller who was the most vociferous about the lack of literary taste in Ireland, even though he was the best known and one of the wealthiest members of the Irish book trade. His long publishing lists in most issues of his newspaper the *Dublin Journal* from 1730 until 1774 suggest the hope of a wide audience, but the lists may be less an index of demand than evidence of books unsold in Ireland. Faulkner wrote to Samuel Derrick on 16 November 1758: "You know that Dublin is the poorest Place in the World for Subscriptions of Books. It is much easier to get a hundred Dinners, with as many dozen Bottles of Claret, than a single Guinea for the best author, few or no People here caring to subscribe, Reading not being the prevailing Taste at present."[31] In his edition of Swift's *Works* in 1768 Faulkner wrote in his preface of the "very small" demand for books in Ireland and that "the State of Learning ... is now at a low Ebb in Ireland." A similar statement comes from the pen of an Irish poet, essayist, and civic leader William Preston, who in the preface to his own *Poems* published in 1793 observes: "The Irish, with a number of good qualities, are yet, collectively taken, an unlettered people. We have few readers among us, and, of the few that do read, a very small proportion are capable of thinking, or of judging for themselves." Of the several comparable evaluations from English visitors to Ireland, George Montagu's are the most colorful. Montagu wrote to Horace Walpole in 1762 that there were no readers in Dublin, and he quoted his friend Sir William Hamilton as saying, "He never found a book or a whore in any one's house since he came to Dublin." In another letter to Walpole he said there was no point in sending Walpole's *Anecdotes of Painting* to Ireland because only Lord Charlemont and the Bishop of Derry could understand the book and for the rest of Dublin it was "pearls before Swine."[32]

The audience for the Irish reprints was a small and relatively elite one in Ireland itself, as these observations suggest and as a more detailed analysis confirms. Ireland's poverty also made it necessary for Irish booksellers to look outside Ireland for some of their customers and after the American war increasingly to America. The typical Irishman, a Roman Catholic farm laborer, if he earned a money wage at all, earned less than a shilling a day whether the wage was 10½d. as declared by the English writer Thomas Newenham,[33] or the sixpence as asserted by William Preston in an influential paper read before the Royal Irish Academy in 1796 and later published by them.[34] A popular novel like Fielding's *Tom Jones* sold in 1749 for eighteen shillings in the London edition and 8s.8d in the Dublin reprint. The typical Irishman would require well over a week's earnings to purchase the Dublin reprint and well over two week's earnings to purchase the London edition. This typical Irishman probably could not read English. If he could read English, and the famous hedge schools insured that some members of the peasant class could read English, he probably read newspapers. The stamp duty records show an average weekly circulation in Dublin of 45,000 newspapers over the eleven year period 1775–85, with an average of two thousand outside Dublin.[35] An important newspaper outside Dublin the *Belfast News-letter* printed 3,225 issues weekly in 1794, and these were read by 19,300 persons according to the *Dublin Journal* for 4 July 1794; six readers for one newspaper was regarded as the usual ratio in Ireland. The *Dublin Evening Post* for 1 October 1785 boasts the sale of 1,516 copies for each issue or 6,064 copies weekly. These figures suggest that there were probably some working-class readers in Ireland for the least expensive of the Irish reprints.

How many people read the Irish reprints inside and outside Ireland is hard to determine. Demand for several Irish editions as was true of most works by the eight major authors of this study suggests a large audience, but information about the size of an edition is lacking. Records for the Irish booksellers comparable to those of William Strahan, William Bowyer, or John Nichols in London do not survive. Some help on the size of an edition is provided by an analysis of 194 books published in Ireland by subscription, most of them reprints.[36] Dominated by religion, these works represent most literary genres adequately except the serious novel in English, and they include five works by authors used in this study, Oliver Goldsmith's *History of the Earth and Animated Nature*, two editions of Samuel Johnson's *Dictionary*, Samuel Richardson's novel *Clarissa*, and Tobias Smollett's translation of *Don Quixote*. Subscriptions range in number from a low of twenty-six for the *Life of James Freney*, a tale of a popular outlaw, to a high of about three thousand for the Irish reprint of Dr. Kennicott's *Universal Family Bible*. Only twenty-three of the 194 titles have over a thousand subscriptions, and only three over two thousand, with a mean of but 539.

That the small size of the typical subscription edition is representative of the Irish editions in general is suggested by other reports on the size of editions. In an advertisement at the end of his edition of James Simon's *Essay towards an Historical Account of Irish Coins* in 1749 the Dublin bookseller S. Powell states that his edition of the *Analogy of Divine Wisdom* has sold over a thousand of its 1,050 copies. The Irish cleric Rev. Thomas Campbell says in his Philosophical *Survey of the South of Ireland* that in 1775 Dublin booksellers agreed that "500 copies of any work, except of a novel or political pamphlet, overstocks the market."[37] As will be shown in chapter nine, Patrick Byrne published two thousand copies in two editions of Edmund Burke's *Letter to Sir Hercules Langrische* in 1792. The Dublin bookseller J. Milliken gave at least three sales reports in the *Dublin Journal* around the end of the century. On 12 November 1796 Milliken announced that he had sold seven hundred sets of William Belsham's *Memoirs of the Kings of Great Britain* since July 1st, and on 27 June 1801 that the first edition of 1,250 copies of Musgrave's *History of the Late Rebellion in Ireland* was sold out, "a Sale hitherto unprecedented in this Kingdom." By 6 April 1802 Milliken had sold out the second edition of eleven hundred copies. The Irish cleric Rev. Edward Ledwich informed Bishop Percy on 16 August 1806 that the two Dublin editions of his *Antiquities of Ireland* had sold 2,300 copies.[38] A final testimony to the small size of the typical Irish edition comes from an anonymous Irish book collector in about 1820 who had inherited a library from his father and added to it for fifty years. Few books published in Ireland, even if they reached a second or third edition, exceed two thousand copies.[39] On the basis of these reports, sparse though they are, and the figures from the subscription editions, it seems fair to conclude that the typical Irish edition was well below a thousand copies and probably closer to five hundred.

This estimate makes the Irish editions roughly similar in size to the London editions that most of them reprinted. D. F. McKenzie has shown that very few books published in London during the eighteenth century exceeded the figure of 1,250–1,500 copies for an edition set in 1587 by the Stationers' Company.[40] William Strahan's ledgers, that give perhaps the most precise evidence about eighteenth-century publishing in London, show that during his long career from 1738 until 1785 he printed 514 books, of which only forty-three ran to two thousand copies or more. The most common number for an edition was five hundred, and 428 books were printed in one thousand copies or less.[41] To be sure, McKenzie points out the dangers of setting norms, and there are startling exceptions like T. Dyche's *Guide to the English Tongue*, whose nineteenth edition was ten thousand in 1733 and whose thirty-fifth edition was five thousand in 1747, but it is highly doubtful that a comparably large edition was ever published in Ireland. Richard Altick finds five hundred as the usual first printing for fiction and 500–1,000 for non-fiction in eighteenth-century England.[42] Lawrence C. Wroth estimates 300–500 copies in an edition published in the American colonies.[43]

Subscription editions are also valuable because they identify subscribers by name and title and sometimes by occupation and residence. The readership for the five subscription works by Goldsmith, Johnson, Richardson, and Smollett will be discussed in the appropriate chapters. Although subscribers to these 194 subscription editions are almost entirely from the Irish landed and professional classes, some of the lists give British and American subscribers. American subscribers will be discussed in chapter three, but typical examples of Irish subscription editions with British subscribers may be given here. The 1791 Dublin reprint of the English translation of the *Lusiad* lists thirteen British subscribers who presumably preferred it to the more expensive London edition and who were willing to risk confiscation by the Commissioners of Excise. As it was by a number of American subscribers, the 1791 Dublin reprint of *Shakespeare's Dramatic Works* in three volumes edited by Samuel Ayscough was chosen over the 1790 London edition by booksellers in Wales, Chester, and Shrewsbury for a total of eighteen sets, by four Londoners, by one subscriber from Norfolk, and one from Bourdeaux; the price was "one-third less" than the London edition which had to pay royalties. London booksellers subscribed for fifty copies of the 1800 Dublin reprint of Francis Xavier de Feller's *Philosophical Catechism.* Henry Boyd's 1785 translation of Dante's *Inferno* was more attractive to thirty British subscribers, one of whom subscribed for twenty sets, than the London edition of the same year; this edition by Patrick Byrne was issued jointly with the London publisher. To the 1791 reprint of the Rheims-Douai Bible nine British residents subscribed, nine from Newfoundland, four from Lisbon, and one from Rome. The 1801 Dublin reprint of John Brown's *Dictionary of the Holy Bible* in two volumes lists thirteen sets for residents of the Isle of Man. In London the famous Shakespearean scholar Edmond Malone was a frequent subscriber to Dublin reprints like the 1775 Johnson's *Dictionary* and the Dublin *Dante* cited above, and he had 148 Irish editions in his library, many of them multi-volumed and most of them reprints.[44]

Not only are the subscription editions interesting for what they tell about the number of readers and their identities but for what they tell about editing in Dublin. To save time and money most

Dublin printers simply reproduced the London text without changes or corrections. Their London critics like Richard Twiss saw the Dublin reprints as "vile editions" produced as cheaply as possible and "saving the expence of a corrector of the press."[45] Though most of the Dublin subscription editions were piracies in the eyes of the London booksellers owning the copyrights, some of the Dublin booksellers used the money from subscribers to make improvements in the London editions. All five subscription editions being emphasized in this study are good examples and will be discussed in the appropriate chapters, but there are others. John Morris edited a number of reprints, usually of Roman Catholic works, and he says of the beautifully bound 1775 subscription edition of Alban Butler's *Moveable Feasts, Fasts, and other Annual Observances of the Catholic Church* that "He has not only given it Page by Page from the London Copy, but has corrected carefully the Typographical Errors of the English Printer." The Dublin editor of John Brown's *Dictionary of the Holy Bible* cited above says he has omitted certain definitions in the London edition "as were solely calculated to maintain the particular doctrines of a Sect, and no way serviceable in elucidating Scripture truth"; he also notes that engravings have been added at "a very great expence." In the preface to the 1791 *Shakespeare* cited above William Jones declares that he has surpassed the London edition by adding commentary and notes by Samuel Johnson and other editors and a "highly finished Head of Shakespeare" by an Irish artist. His edition is aimed primarily at readers from the "middling and lower ranks," but those who already own expensive editions of Shakespeare can carry the Dublin edition "into a post-chaise, for amusement in a journey" or consult it quickly if a Shakespearan allusion crops up in conversation. Jones claims "to omit nothing which may serve to render Shakespeare intelligible to every capacity, and to every class of readers." In Philadelphia John Bioren would prefer to reprint this Dublin edition by Jones rather than the original London editions.[46]

An edited Dublin reprint of particular interest because of its American connections is William Guthrie's extraordinarily popular *Modern Geography*. John Chambers, who would emigrate to the United States at the turn of the century like so many other Irish bookmen, reprinted the work in 1789 for 807 subscribers. In the preface to this fine quarto edition Chambers maintains that he published the work "not more with a view to profit than to prove that this country has spirit, when encouraged, not only to undertake literary publications on an English scale of liberality, but even to attempt improvement thereon." His Irish editors, whom he does not identify, have consulted sources not used by Guthrie and added significantly to the account of Ireland. The Carey Letter Books show that Mathew Carey, only recently arrived in Philadelphia to continue the publishing activities that he had begun in Dublin, sent Guthrie on 15 November 1788 special material on America by Jedidiah Morse to be included in the Dublin edition. Chambers in turn sent copies of his Dublin edition on 8 November 1789 to Carey to sell in Philadelphia, and Carey published an excerpt from it in his *American Museum* for January 1790.[47] A few years later Carey developed his own American edition that became one of the most popular books in the United States.

The main business, then, of the eighteenth-century Irish book trade was reprinting London editions usually without authorization from the author or publisher holding the copyright and without paying royalties. Irish booksellers repudiated the judgment of British authors and publishers that Irish reprints were piracies since there was no copyright law in Ireland and no violation of British copyright law as long as Irish reprints were sold only in Ireland. It is clear, however, that Irish booksellers did sell some copies of their reprints in Britain, and these copies may be viewed as piracies. Although the Irish reprint trade claimed to be interested primarily in supplying cheap reprints to Ireland's poor and untutored masses, its clientele in Ireland itself was the landed and professional classes for the most part, supplemented by at least some readers in Britain and perhaps exceeded by Americans as the century neared its end. The Irish reprint industry flourished from about 1780 until about 1800 when a series of developments culminating in the extension of British copyright law to Ireland in 1801 would bring it to an end.

2
Irish Readers and Irish Reprints

Through most of the eighteenth century Irish booksellers aimed their reprints primarily at Irish readers, though they always sold some reprints in Britain and America, and in the last two decades of the century there was a significant increase in American readers. Evidence about British readers is interesting but sketchy,[48] as suggested in chapter one, and evidence about the large number of American buyers will be presented in the third chapter. The large number of auction catalogues of private libraries that have survived from eighteenth-century Ireland and the many advertisements in Irish newspapers about community libraries give us detailed information about Irish buyers of the Irish reprints. Almost all the private library owners can be identified by name, occupation, family background, and usually by education, as can the eighteenth-century owners of Irish editions surviving today in the libraries of Trinity College, Dublin, the National Library of Ireland, and Yale University. Similarly, most of the subscribers to the Dublin editions of Richardson's *Clarissa*, the 1775 and 1798 editions of Johnson's *Dictionary*, Goldsmith's *History of the Earth and Animated Nature*, and Smollett's *Don Quixote* may be identified and will be discussed in the appropriate chapters. We should look first at 203 private libraries in eighteenth-century Ireland; for the most part these owners bought Irish reprints rather than the original British editions.[49]

As table 1 indicates, the landed class represents the largest group among the 203 library owners, with nine peers, four baronets, and fifty-four gentry. Ireland was predominantly agrar-

Table 1. 203 Owners of Private Libraries in Eighteenth-Century Ireland

Profession (number)	*Median number of books*	*Education at Trinity College, Dublin*	*In DNB*
Land (67)			
Peers and baronets (13)	1,360	1	3
Gentry (54)	781	5	0
Church (64)			
Protestant (39)	651	28	10
Roman Catholic (25)	376	0	1
Law (36)	1,130	21	12
Government (12)	983	3	6
Arts and Letters (11)	970	7	6
Medicine (5)	670	2	0
Commerce (4)	1,490	1	1
Military (4)	1,043	0	2

ian, and most members of this class lived on estates in the country, but some lived in town houses on the great squares of Dublin such as Merrion or Rutland Square. The group is headed by the Duke of Leinster; the Earls of Charlemont, Clanbrassil, Londonderry, and Mornington; Viscount Wicklow; and Lords Clonbrock, Farnam, and Moore.[50] Most members of this class were involved in the affairs of their estates or other private interests, but several were active in political life, and Lord Mornington, father of the Duke of Wellington, was a professor of music at Trinity College, Dublin. All peers were members of the House of Lords by virtue of their positions, but the Duke of Leinster and the Earls of Charlemont and Clanbrassil were not merely nominal members. Members of the Irish House of Commons included Alexander Stewart of Newtown and Mount Stewart; Philip Doyne of Wells, who was also a well-known poet; and James Grattan of Tinnehinch, eldest son of the great Henry Grattan. Many of the gentry were magistrates or sheriffs of counties; Wogan Browne of Castle Browne, County Kildare, is perhaps the best known. The internationally renowned name in the group is that of Lord Charlemont, active member of the Irish House of Lords, member of Samuel Johnson's Literary Club, patron of literature, collector of rare books, the general of the Irish Volunteers in 1782, and first president of the Royal Irish Academy in 1785. His was the great library of Ireland, with many rare editions from the Renaissance including Shakespeare's *First Folio*, but he also owned books by five of the eight contemporary writers, usually in Dublin reprints. As a member of the Literary Club, he knew personally four of the eight writers— Johnson, Boswell, Gibbon, and Goldsmith— and many of their works were in his library, though, strangely enough, nothing of his fellow Irishman Goldsmith. These owners could certainly afford London editions but usually bought the cheaper Irish reprints whether out of patriotism or parsimony.

Clergymen make up the second largest class of the 203 owners of private libraries, thirty-nine Protestant and twenty-five Roman Catholic. All the Protestant clerics belonged to the Church of Ireland, as the Anglican Church in Ireland was called, except Sinclair Kelburn, a Presbyterian pastor in Belfast. Almost all the Protestant clergy were from Anglo-Irish families, and most were graduates of Trinity College, Dublin (TCD). Few of the thirty-nine, however, were simple parish priests like Goldsmith's village preacher in *The Deserted Village*, "passing rich with forty pounds a year." John Brinkley and John Kearney achieved bishoprics in the early nineteenth century but were professors at Trinity College during the eighteenth century. Eight were higher clergy of various types, six besides Brinkley and Kearney were professors at Trinity College, and two were schoolmasters. Ten had careers of sufficient distinction to admit them to the Dictionary of National Biography (DNB);[51] and part of this recognition stemmed from their publications. Although the median number of books owned by the thirty-nine clerics was 651, there were six large libraries of more than two thousand titles. All the libraries were heavily oriented toward divinity, but all were represented adequately in other intellectual disciplines. No one seems to have owned works from all eight major authors, but most had works from three to five of the major authors, two had works from six, and two from seven; most of these works were Dublin reprints. Though several of the Anglican clergy were writers of note, their comments on any writers outside the field of divinity seem not to have survived.

The Roman Catholic clergymen are more shadowy figures.[52] Because of the penal laws against Roman Catholics during the eighteenth-century, these priests had obtained their education in the several Irish colleges on the Continent, and thus their libraries ran heavily to Latin and French, Italian, Spanish, or Portuguese, depending on which Irish college they attended. The French Revolution resulted in the closing of the Irish colleges on the Continent, and a new theological college for Roman Catholics was opened at Maynooth, County Kildare, in 1795. In the eighteenth century only Anglican houses of worship were called churches, while Roman Catholic houses of worship were called chapels and were permitted only on back streets. Most of the twenty-five priests whose libraries we know about were in charge of rude chapels on back streets in Dublin. Martin Hugh Hamill, for example, was priest-in-charge of the Francis-street Chapel in Dublin, now the Carmelite Church off Grafton Street, when he bought the new Dublin quarto edition of Johnson's *Dictionary* in 1798; he had studied at the Irish College in Rome until 1778 when he came to the Francis-street Chapel as assistant priest. The only Roman Catholic cleric among the library owners to be included in the *Dictionary of National Biography* is Rev. Dr. John Troy, Archbishop of Dublin from 1784 until his death in 1823, whose library of 1,089 titles included, in addition to the dominant Roman Catholic divinity, Johnson's *Rambler* essays and *Dictionary* in Dublin reprints, Smollett's translation of *Don Quixote* in the fine four-volume Dublin edition of 1796, and Goldsmith's *History of Rome* and his *Grecian History*, both Dublin reprints. Like most of the clerics, Anglican and Roman Catholic alike, and many of the laymen, Archbishop Troy had no novels or poetry in his library

Another Roman Catholic leader among the library owners was Rev. Dr. Patrick Joseph Plunkett, Bishop of Meath from 1779 until his death in 1827. In 1779, on his way back to Ireland from Paris, where he had been a professor in the Irish college, the ship on which he was a passenger was seized by John Paul Jones, the American naval hero, and Plunkett's books were not returned to him until Benjamin Franklin intervened on his behalf. His library of 525 titles was almost exclusively Roman Catholic divinity, and the only work he had of the eight major authors was Smollett's *History of England*, the most popular in Ireland of Smollett's many works. Rev. Dr. Michael Blake, who won renown in the nineteenth century as president of the Irish College at Rome and then as Bishop of Dromore, was a theological student in Rome in 1790 and then an assistant priest in the chapel of St. Michael and John in Dublin. His library of 1,088 titles in 1825 had eighteenth-century Dublin reprints of Boswell, Fielding, Goldsmith, Johnson, Richardson, and Smollett. The largest library belonged to Rev. John Barrett of Francis-street Chapel in Dublin, whose library at his death in 1823 contained 1,822 titles, including eighteenth century Irish reprints of Fielding, Goldsmith, Johnson, and Sterne. The smallest library belonged to Rev. John Wickham, a parish priest in County Wexford. He had studied at Louvain in 1751, and of his hundred books only twenty-five were in English, one of these being Smollett's *History of England*. As with the Protestant clergymen, the Catholic priests bought and presumably read the important books of their day usually in Irish reprints but did not write about them. Undoubtedly, many clergymen bought the cheaper Irish reprints out of necessity.

Lawyers make up a third sizable group of library owners after the landed proprietors and the clergy. A writer in *The Flapper* of Dublin for 16 February 1796 observed that the only people who read much in Ireland were lawyers. Certainly many lawyers owned large and well-planned libraries, if this group of thirty-six is at all representative. The average library was large, and there were six with more than two thousand titles. All the libraries were well supplied with legal books, which was a speciality of the Irish booksellers but all were also well represented by the humanities. Only the great libraries of the Earl of Clonmell and Viscount Avonmore had all eight authors, but most had three to five. In Ireland, as in Britain and elsewhere, the law was a popular avenue to fame and fortune, and several of the lawyers achieved high places in the judiciary. There were three Lord Chief Justices of the King's Bench, a Chief Baron of the Court of the Exchequer, and seven other judges of the higher courts. Among the politicians John Foster was Speaker of the Irish House of Commons, and Daniel O'Connell, in the eighteenth century a young barrister in Dublin reading Gibbon, Johnson, and Boswell in the public library, became the "Liberator" of the Roman Catholics in the nineteenth century. O'Connell, James Devereux, and Martin Lynch were Catholic barristers who were leaders in the new movement at the end of the century for Catholic Emancipation; prior to the Catholic Relief Act of 1792, Roman Catholics could not enter the legal profession. Among the library owners the lawyers were the most prominent, with twelve of their number attaining recognition in the *Dictionary of National Biography*.[53] The lawyers were also the most articulate of all the library owners about the significant books they had purchased for their libraries. Eight of them commented on one or more books by the major authors of this study,[54] some of them at length, and their evaluations will appear in the appropriate chapters. Like the landed class, the lawyers could afford London editions but usually bought the Irish reprints.

As table 1 indicates, 167 of the 203 library owners or about 82 percent were landowners, clergymen, or lawyers, but the five small groups of library owners should be mentioned briefly. Many of the twelve statesmen and civil servants were also landowners, but they were much more directly involved in carrying out government responsibilities than the large group of sixty-seven. Political figures recognized in the *Dictionary of National Biography* included John Beresford, holder of many positions in Irish government, sometimes known as the "King" of Ireland at the end of the eighteenth century; Denis Daly, a leader in the Irish House of Commons; Henry Grattan, the leading Irish statesman of the eighteenth century; Wills Hill, Marquess of Downshire, a sometime secretary of state in England and Benjamin Franklin's host in Ireland; Lord Macartney, an Irish Chief Secretary and holder of many diplomatic posts, and Archibald Hamilton Rowan of the United Irishmen. There were several large libraries in the group, and all eight of the major writers were represented in the library of Lord Fitzgerald, though most libraries had three to five, usually in Dublin reprints.

A fifth group of library owners consists of eleven men more directly involved in arts and letters than the other groups: writers, artists, scholars, and teachers. *Dictionary of National Biography* entrants include Francis Bindon, the painter; Ambrose Eccles, the Shakespearean scholar; James Gandon, the architect, who though of English birth spent the last forty-two years of his life in Ireland; William Preston, poet and critic; Richard Kirwan, philospher and scientist; and Henry Ussher, the professor of astronomy at Trinity College. There were several large libraries in the group, and William Preston and Paul Twigg of the Royal Hibernian Academy of Painting had works of all eight major writers, mostly in Dublin reprints. Although these library owners had a professional interest in literature and the arts and presumably were most apt of all groups to read the books in their libraries, only William Preston's comments on books in his library survive.

Little needs to be said about the three remaining groups beyond what table 1 offers. There is no record of comments by any of the physicians or military officers on the many Irish reprints in their libraries. Two of the soldiers, General Vallancey and Colonel Keatinge, are recognized in the *Dictionary of National Biography*, in part because of their writing, but they apparently did not write about the eight authors, represented in their libraries mostly in Dublin reprints. The small commercial group consists of two bankers, one merchant, and a civil and mining engineer. Christopher Dillon Bellew deserves special mention as the owner of a great library and as a representative of a new Roman Catholic middle class, which, exluded by the penal laws from the professions, had turned with marked success to commerce. The Bellew family made a fortune in flour milling during the eighteenth century, and this Bellew was heir to an estate in county Galway worth more than £5,000 a year. The Bellew library of nearly 3,800 titles contained all eight authors except Gibbon, who was anathema to Roman Catholics and many Protestants because of the famous fifteenth and sixteenth chapters against the Church in the *Decline and Fall of the Roman Empire*. Sir Richard Griffith was also from a wealthy merchant family, but he earned the fame that got him into the *Dictionary of National Biography* as a civil and mining engineer. Griffith represents the third generation of a distinguished Anglo–Irish family, the first of whom was a well-known Irish writer and friend of Sterne, and the second a prosperous merchant. The first Richard Griffith, who started the library and acquired the Dublin 1774 reprint of Sterne's *Works* in seven volumes, wrote of Sterne's *Tristram Shandy* on several occasions.

These Irish library owners — largely landed proprietors, clergy, and lawyers — stocked their libraries with the masterpieces of yesteryear but also bought the significant books of their own time in respectable numbers, usually in Irish reprints. As shown in table 2, Dr. Samuel Johnson's famous *Dictionary* was the only work by a leading contemporary writer bought by a majority of the library owners. Of the 113 libraries, forty-fou had the best known of the several Dublin reprints of the work the Thomas Ewing two-volume quarto edition published by subscription in 1775, and fifteen of the library owners were among the original subscribers to the work; twenty-four had the 1798 Dublin reprint also published by subscription. Of the eight authors Samuel Johnson was clearly

Table 2. Works by Eight Major Authors, 1740–1800, in 203 Irish Private Libraries

1.	Johnson's *Dictionary*	113
2.	Johnson's *Lives of the Poets*	74
3.	Gibbon's *Decline and Fall of the Roman Empire*	67
4.	Sterne's *Works*	54
5.	Johnson's *Rambler*	49
6.	Gibbon's *Miscellaneous Works*	48
7.	Boswell's *Life of Johnson*	45
	Smollett's *History of England*	45
8.	Johnson's *Works*	43
9.	Smollett's *Don Quixote*	41
10.	Goldsmith's *History of the Earth*	37
	Sterne's *Tristram Shandy*	37
	Sterne's *A Sentimental Journey*	37
11.	Fielding's *Tom Jones*	34
	Goldsmith's *Roman History*	34
	Johnson's edition of Shakespeare's *Plays*	34
12.	Boswell's *An Account of Corsica*	31
	Richardson's *Clarissa*	31
	Sterne's *Sermons*	31
13.	Johnson's *Journey to the Western Islands of Scotland*	29
14.	Fielding's *Works*	28
	Smollett's *Roderick Random*	28
15.	Goldsmith's *History of England*	27
16.	Smollett's *Gil Blas*	26
17.	Boswell's *Tour to the Hebrides*	25
18.	Goldsmith's *Grecian History*	24
	Goldsmith's *Vicar of Wakefield*	24
19.	Fielding's *Amelia*	23
	Johnson's *Rasselas*	23
20.	Johnson's *Letters*	22
21.	Fielding's *Joseph Andrews*	21
	Goldsmith's *Citizen of the World*	21
22.	Richardson's *Pamela*	20
	Richardson's *Sir Charles Grandison*	20
	Smollett's *Humphry Clinker*	20
	Smollett's *Peregrine Pickle*	20

the favorite. His *Dictionary, Lives of the Poets, Rambler* essays, and his collected *Works*, rated first, second, fifth, and eighth in popularity with them, and Boswell's *Life of Johnson* was seventh. Other works by Johnson owned by at least ten percent of the library owners were his edition of Shakespeare's *Plays*, his *Journey to the Western*

Islands of Scotland, his *Rasselas*, and his *Letters*. Nearly 80 percent of the library owners bought at least one book by Johnson, usually in a Dublin reprint rather than the London edition.

Edward Gibbon's two major works were bought in significant numbers, but works of Oliver Goldsmith, a native Irishman, were the most widely owned of the eight writers after Johnson; over half the library owners had at least one of his many books, usually in a Dublin edition. His books bought by at least 10 percent included, in order of popularity, *History of the Earth*, the *Roman History, History of England*, the *Grecian History*, the *Vicar of Wakefield*, and the *Citizen of the World*. The striking fact about these six works is that only the latter two have stood the test of time, while Goldsmith's historical writings are often regarded today as hack work. As well as for his novel and essays, Goldsmith is valued today for his poems and plays, but only fifteen of the library owners bought the collected edition of the *Poems and Plays* and the collected *Poems*. Judging from the number of Irish editions of Goldsmith's writings, Goldsmith was the most widely read of the major authors; his *Vicar of Wakefield* with ten Irish editions in the eighteenth century was more often reprinted in Ireland than any single book by a major writer, and his histories of Rome and England rated second and third. The purchasers of the *Vicar of Wakefield*, however, were not the library owners or the landed and professional classes that they represented. For these groups Goldsmith was a historian; working class readers of the Irish reprints apparently anticipated posterity's judgment that the *Vicar of Wakefield*, along with the poems and plays, were Goldsmith's greatest works.

The four novelists — Richardson, Fielding, Smollett, and Sterne — fared poorly, except for Sterne. A fourth of the library owners bought Sterne's collected *Works*, but this was not necessarily because of his novels, since the *Sermons* were bought as often as either of the novels. Smollett to the library owners was primarily a historian and translator of *Don Quixote* and *Gil Blas*, while the three novels for which he is known today — *Roderick Random, Peregrine Pickle*, and *Humphry Clinker* — were bought by few. Nevertheless, some book by Smollett was in 125 libraries. Fielding's three major novels — *Joseph Andrews, Tom Jones*, and *Amelia* — were bought by at least 10 percent, but they ranked well below the non-fiction works of Johnson and Gibbon. Richardson's three novels were bought by at least 10 percent but they are low on the list, and the famous *Pamela* was owned by only twenty.

The library owners apparently preferred works of discursive prose, works represented by such genres as lexicography, history, biography, and the essay. Many of these were essentially reference works, which would be consulted by one seeking particular facts rather than for entertainment. History rated especially high; included in the top ten were histories by Gibbon, Smollett, and Goldsmith, and three other histories of Goldsmith were not far behind, almost always in Dublin editions. Novels and other types of prose fiction were not purchased in any numbers except for Smollett's *Don Quixote*, usually in the 1796 Dublin edition, and part of Sterne's *Works*. It was not simply novels that the library owners did not buy in large numbers, but other examples of *belles lettres* such as poems and plays. No contemporary poems were read by as many as 10 percent of the library owners, except possibly a few by Johnson included in his complete *Works*. Plays by contemporaries were also bought by few; Johnson's edition of Shakespeare was bought by thirty-four, but this was probably for Shakespeare rather than Johnson.

Other evidence about Irish readers of the Irish reprints suggests the same small, elite group. The subscribers to the 194 subscription editions were from the landed and professional classes by and large, as were the eighteenth-century owners of the many Irish editions that survive today. Nevertheless, there were numerous libraries open to the public in eighteenth-century Ireland; presumably these libraries reflect a larger audience for the Irish reprints than the landed and professional classes. Irish booksellers not only advertised their books for sale, but, especially during the last two decades of the century, many of them also noted their books for hire. Little information is given on most of these circulating libraries usually maintained by booksellers in Dublin, Belfast, and Cork, but advertisements in the newspapers are numerous. The well-known publishing family of Hoey in Dublin, in addition to its printing and bookselling activities, was associated with circulating libraries for more than thirty years. In 1737 James Hoey, Sr., established "a large Collection of Histories, Romances, Novels, Memoirs, etc." that could be rented for eightpence for a large book and sixpence per week for a small one. This appears to be the first circulating library in Ireland. Whether the library existed continuously from 1737 is uncertain, but James Hoey, Jr. advertised his circulating library in 1775, and Peter Hoey his in 1778. Other early circulating libraries in Dublin according to the newspapers were Richard Watts's in 1754, Thomas Armitage's in 1762, James Williams's in 1765, and the Butler Circulating Library in 1774. Watts, Armitage, and Williams were prominent booksellers in Dublin, like the Hoeys, and I have found only two proprietors of lending libraries in Ireland who were not booksellers. The newspapers give no details except to mention Williams's rental fee or 16s.3d. yearly of sixpence weekly, fees that became standard in Dublin in later years.[55]

During the last two decades of the century circulating libraries in Dublin increased in number and prominence, and their advertisements occupy an increasing amount of space in the Dublin newspapers. The four leading libraries seem to have been the Apollo Circulating Library, Colbert's Circulating Library, Jackson's Circulating Library, and the Universal Circulating Library. The earliest of these the Universal Circulating Library appears at different times to have been called the Essex Gate Library or Spotswood's Circulating Library. Its name first appears in 1775, and its catalogue was announced by William Spotswood, one of the leading Dublin–Philadelphia booksellers of this study, in 1779 and again in 1782. Spotswood reported in 1783 that his charge of 16s.3d. was the same as the charge at the famous circulating library at Bath, and he also observed that circulation in the Dublin area had been extensive. Like all circulating libraries of the commercial type in Ireland it seems to have been stocked primarily with popular novels, some Dublin reprints but often London reprints which were now becoming available as copyrights expired; Spotswood still urged his customers, however, to read Irish editions. Spotswood had more than ten thousand volumes in 1784, mostly novels, but he added his own reprint of the *Beauties of Sterne* before joining the Philadelphia book trade the same year.[56]

Colbert's Circulating Library in Dublin, sometimes called the Established Circulating Library, seems to have led a somewhat longer existence. It was founded in 1778 by Samuel Colbert, a Dublin bookseller, with initial stock of three thousand volumes that had declined by 1780 to four hundred volumes. Its main stock in trade was new novels, many imported from London, even though Colbert, like all Dublin booksellers, reprinted London editions. Colbert helped Spotswood to reprint *Beauties of Sterne* for his circulating library as he had reprinted *Beauties of Johnson* in 1782. By 1786 Samuel Colbert was dead, and his widow Harriet Colbert was running both the bookshop and the circulating library. In that year she sold the Dublin reprint of Mrs. Piozzi's *Anecdotes of the late Samuel Johnson* in her bookshop, and she also added it to her circulating library.[57]

Another important circulating library of the latter years of the century in Dublin was T. Jackson's, advertisements of which may be found in Dublin newspapers from at least 1786 through 1799. Like his rivals, Jackson charged 16s.3d. per year and advertised mainly the latest novels. On 18 April 1786 Jackson claimed that he had the largest circulating library in Dublin and that he had just added three hundred new titles to his collection, one of which was the Dublin reprint of James Boswell's *Tour to the Hebrides*. Like the other libraries he lent new novels primarily, but on 7 July 1794 he made an announcement that boded ill for the Irish book trade. Because perpetual copyright had been overturned by the courts, London publishers could now reprint the older novels cheaply, and Jackson said he was importing cheap London reprints of the novels of Richardson, Fielding, Smollett, Sterne, Goldsmith, and Johnson.[58]

The last important commercial lending library in Dublin was the Apollo Circulating Library founded by Vincent Dowling in about 1792. Dowling issued a catalogue in 1794 of two thousand volumes, which is probably the only catalogue of an eighteenth-century commercial lending library in Ireland to have survived to the present day. Unfortunately, the copy listed in the catalogue of the National Library of Ireland, a unique copy as far as I can determine, has been lost since 1973. The undated catalogue consisted of 117 pages and was dated circa 1800 by the staff of the National Library, but it may have been the one issued in 1794. Dowling seems to have specialized less than his rivals in the latest novels, and among a number of nonfiction works cited in his announcement of one thousand new books on 18 October 1792 was the Dublin reprint of Boswell's *Life of Samuel Johnson*, one of the masterpieces of the century but apparently not to be obtained from Dowling's rivals. His advertisement of 22 January 1794 in the *Hibernian Journal* stresses how different his rental collection is from the others: "This Collection is by no Means confined to mere Novels and Romances, the usual Furniture of Circulating Libraries, but includes the best Authors in History, Biography, Natural History, Philosophy, Chemistry, Poetry, Dramatics, Politics, and Belles Lettres." Dowling in the same paper reported on 13 June 1794 that he had formerly managed the British Library in London; in 1805 after the collapse of the Irish book trade Dowling, described by an admirer as "a fellow of infinite jest," would return to London as a newspaper reporter and bookseller.[59]

Four other commercial lending libraries in Dublin near the end of the century did little advertising in the newspapers. Charles Brown advertised his library intermittently from 1784 to 1794.[60] The General Book Repository set up in 1788 by John Archer, discussed in chapter one as a bookseller, may have been a literary society rather than a lending library, but it was a large room above his bookshop where intellectuals could gather for discussion and apparently have access to the books below. Another Dublin bookseller Bernard Dornin announced on 9 May 1794 in the *Hibernian Journal* a reading room and library where one book at a time would be lent out between 7:00 A.M. and 10:00 P.M. for a fee of one guinea a year; this fee was somewhat higher than the 16s.3d. charged by his competitors. Dornin modestly added: "The above Plan for acquiring a Fund of entertaining and useful Information, being the most reasonable one ever set on Foot in this or any other country, the Proprietor hopes for public Patronage." The last circulating library to be set up during the century was Thomas Hope's Circulating Library, identified in the *Dublin Evening Post* for 19 and 31 May 1796 as a new circulating library; Hope also published with John Magee *Magee's Weekly Packet or Hope's Lottery Journal of News, Politics and Literature*. These last two proprietors of lending libraries, along with William Spotswood of the Universal Circulating Library, would be among the 101 Irish bookmen to transfer to the United States book trade as the result of the decline and fall of the Irish reprint industry. William Spotswood would join the Philadelphia book trade in 1784 and later the Boston book trade, Bernard Dornin the New York book trade in 1803 and later the Baltimore book trade, and Thomas Hope the Philadelphia book trade in 1805, and these will be discussed in chapters three and eight on the mass transfer of Irish book craftsmen to America.

John Archer's General Book Repository cited above was probably the predecessor of the Dublin Library Society founded in 1791. The Library was open only to the 311 members who paid a guinea annually to read in the Library itself since no lending was permitted. Its 319 titles included works of Boswell, Johnson, Gibbon, and Smollett, mostly in Dublin editions, which the Society was required to purchase if available. The library in 1792 had no novels, poems, or plays, but had plays and poems by 1806. In tastes and in background the members reflect the 203 owners of private libraries.[61] One atypical member was the young Daniel O'Connell, the future "Liberator," who on 6 December 1796 subscribed for two guineas with the intention of reading four days a week there until 10 P.M.[62]

Cork also had libraries open to the public. Founded in 1792 as a proprietary library, the Cork Library Society was open only to those proposed by two members and voted on by the Society. For their half guinea entrance fee and their one guinea annual fee they could read each day except Sunday and borrow one book at a time. All eight major writers were represented in the Library usually in Dublin editions.[63] Like his colleagues in Dublin, John Connor specialized in current novels in his lending library, though some histories and travel books appear in his list in the *Hibernian Chronicle* of Cork for 17 August 1795. Also a printer, Connor lent his own reprints of novels such as Fanny Burney's *Camilla*, which he announced in the *Dublin Evening Post* for 7 September 1796, and he presumably lent his own reprint of Goldsmith's *Roman History*. The *Hibernian Chronicle* for 12 April 1787 mentions the opening of A. Edwards's Circulating Library of six thousand volumes from both London and Dublin. A fourth lending library in Cork was the English, French and Italian Circulating Library, whose catalogue of 1803 survives but shows few works in English.[64]

The Belfast Society for Promoting Knowledge established in 1788 had only 137 titles in its lending library in 1793. The library was not permitted to have novels or plays, but it did have such masterpieces of the later eighteenth century as Boswell's *Life of Samuel Johnson*, Gibbon's *Decline and Fall of the Roman Empire*, the massive Hume–Smollett *History of England*, Johnson's *Works*, and his *Lives of the Poets*, probably in Dublin editions like those in the other proprietary libraries. The admission fee was two guineas with a monthly fee of a shilling. The eighty-nine members in 1798 were the city leaders, bankers, physicians, merchants and clergymen.[65] Two commercial lending libraries existed in Belfast even before the Belfast Society. The Belfast printer and bookseller John Hay announced his circulating library in the *Belfast News-letter* for 12 September 1775, issued a catalogue shortly afterward, and charged only thirteen shillings a year compared with the standard fee in Dublin of 16s.3d. and the fourteen shillings charged by Connor in Cork. Another Belfast printer and bookseller Hugh Warrin opened his circulating library in Belfast in 1772, and it existed until at least 3 January 1792, when he announced his twentieth anniversary in the *Belfast News-letter*.

The three proprietary libraries of Dublin, Cork, and Belfast catered to the group represented by the owners of private libraries, but presumably the commercial lending libraries in Dublin, Cork, and Belfast reflect a larger audience in Ireland for the Irish reprints. Clearly the fees for these libraries eliminated a substantial part of the population, and those who could not pay lending fees certainly could not purchase the Dublin reprints, cheap though they were in comparison with the London editions. The clientele for these lending libraries remains unknown, but there is a borrowing record that survives from the Armagh Public Library.[66] With the endowment left by the Archbishop of Armagh who started the public library with his own collection contemporary literature was purchased, and the manuscript catalogue of 1815 lists among the nearly five thousand titles many works by the eight major writers of this study except for Richardson and Sterne.[67] There were more London editions represented than Dublin reprints, but there was clearly no prejudice against the Dublin reprints, and sometimes there are both London and Dublin editions of the same work. Boswell's *Account of Corsica* was available both in the London edition of 1768 and the Dublin reprint of the same year. This was true also of Gibbon's *Decline and Fall of the Roman Empire* and Johnson's *Dictionary*, his *Lives of the Poets*, and his edition of Shakespeare's *Works*. Although there were few novels in the library, there was no rule against them as there was in the Marsh Library, the Dublin Library Society, and the Belfast Society for Promoting Knowledge.

The borrowing record of the Armagh Public Library does not begin until 1796, and how many readers used the Library as a reading room or as a reference library rather than as a lending library is unknown. Since the cost of borrowing was so high, the number of actual users probably exceeded the number of borrowers. A study of the borrowing record from 1796 through 1802 reflects the same small, elite clientele.[68] The high level of education and culture of those who did borrow books is shown by the fact that all but three of the thirty-three borrowers during this period of seven years read at least one of the significant works of the later eighteenth century. The favorite work of the thirty-three borrowers was Gibbon's *Decline and Fall of the Roman Empire*, in both London and Dublin editions, which was checked out either in separate volumes or as a whole eighteen times during the period of seven years. Boswell's *Life of Johnson* was a close second at fifteen; Smollett's translation of *Don Quixote* was third, at eleven. Other books by major contemporary authors that were taken out several times during the seven-year period included Johnson's *Lives of the Poets*, checked out eight times; and several works taken out four times: Boswell's *Tour to the Hebrides* and Johnson's *Fugitive Pieces, Idler, Rambler,* and *Rasselas*; some of these works were in London editions and others in the Dublin reprints.

The borrowing system of the Armagh Public Library was different from that of other lending libraries in Ireland or in the British Isles as a whole. There is no evidence of a set fee such as the 16s.3d. usually charged by Dublin circulating libraries. Rather, the borrower had to deposit a sum equal to and sometimes in excess of the cost of replacing the book; in fact, the borrowing record is called a "book of deposits." For example, George Pepper deposited £5.2.4 in 1798 to check out Gibbon's massive *Decline and Fall of the Roman Empire*, while the Dean of the Armagh Cathedral Rev. Dr. Hugh Hamilton deposited £5.13.9 in 1797 to borrow Boswell's *Life of Samuel Johnson*. Needless to say, this heavy fee eliminated most people as borrowers. It should also be noted, however, that though heavy deposits were required, the library was a free public library, since the borrower got his money back when he returned the book and apparently paid no fees of any kind as he would have done in Dublin, Belfast, and Cork. The thirty persons who read the major writers consisted of seventeen landed gentry, seven British army officers, three Anglican clerics, and three surgeons.

The patrons of the Armagh Public Library had little opportunity to read novels, the staple fare of circulating libraries in Ireland, but they did not borrow in any number even the few that were available to them. Fielding's *Amelia* was borrowed only twice during the seven-year period, and unspecified sections of his complete *Works* were borrowed twice. Nothing by Goldsmith, not even his popular novel *The Vicar of Wakefield*, which went through ten Irish reprints in the eighteenth century, was ever checked out. Of works of prose fiction in general, only Smollett's *Don Quixote* and Johnson's *Rasselas* were borrowed by this upper-class group of readers. Like the 203 owners of private libraries which they so closely resembled in background and in tastes, they preferred to borrow the great works of discursive prose such as those by Boswell, Gibbon, and Johnson when they wanted to read literary works, and other borrowed books that were not specifically literary were also works of discursive prose. Aside from the contemporary masterworks, they preferred to read, as did readers elsewhere in the English-speaking world, travel books, history books, sermons, often in Dublin reprints. As Irishmen, they read works of specifically Irish interest and quite often combined their interest in religious writings with their interest in Irish books in such a work as Mervyn Archdall's *Monasticum Hibernicum*.

Although this survey of public libraries in eighteenth-century Ireland has turned up few readers other than those of the landed and professional classes, it is a reasonable assumption that there were some working-class patrons of these libraries in the three major cities and hence for the Irish reprints in general. Some evidence of working-class readers is provided by subscription lists to a few Roman Catholic books published in Ireland. Working-class subscribers to Hugh Fitzpatrick's Dublin reprint of the Rheims–Douai Bible in 1791 included the following: five carpenters, three bricklayers, two wheelrights, a shoemaker, baker, brazier, hosier, seedsman, chandler, tailor, saddler, tanner, beam maker, and button maker. A subscription list like this is rare, but other Catholic works listing skilled craftsmen among the subscribers are the 1796 Dublin reprint of Josephus's *Works* and the 1797–1802 Dublin reprint of Alban Butler's *Lives of the Fathers, Martyrs, and other Principal Saints*. These Catholic subscribers were from a group of Catholic tradesmen that numbered 1,250 in Dublin by 1778,[69] and though their piety may have led them to subscribe for Catholic Bibles and devotional works, some of them probably bought other Dublin reprints and patronized the circulation libraries. Books containing subscriber lists sometimes include book clubs or reading societies among the subscribers. For example, one of the few original works published in Ireland William Crawford's *History of Ireland*, published in Strabane, County Tyrone in 1783, lists among subscribers the Ballyaston Book Club, the Patrick Library, and the Doagh Book Club. The 1800 Dublin reprint of Clement Cruttwell's *New Universal Gazetteer* includes among the subscribers the Banbridge Reading Society and the Galway Amicable Society. That there were some working-class readers in these groups is suggested by a letter to Dr. William Drennan, a prominent physician and leader in the United Irishmen. Dr. Drennan wrote to his friend the Rev. Dr. William Bruce of Belfast on several occasions in 1785–86 about activities of the Newry Book Society, Newry, County Down, a group in which both men were active.[70] Mrs. McTier, Dr. Drennan's sister, wrote to him on 28 October 1792 from Belfast that two reading societies there like the Newry Book Society had been collecting for three years sets like the *Encyclopaedia Britannica* and the *Parliamentary Statutes*. These societies had been organized by people of the working class, and there was no one of higher social position than "McCormick the gunsmith" or "Osborn the baker."[71] These working-class readers probably would not have had their personal copies bound, and hence these copies do not survive.

Readers of the Irish reprints in Ireland itself, one may conclude, tended to be from the landed and professional classes leavened by a few tradesmen. These Irish readers supplemented by the British readers for the Irish reprints suggested by the London book trade's vigorous efforts to keep Irish reprints out of Britain made up a sizable clientele, but perhaps a larger clientele for the Irish reprints by the end of the century was across the Atlantic in the new United States of America where thousands of Irish emigrants were to be found and large numbers of Irish booksellers to cater to their reading needs and to those of other readers who wanted cheap Irish reprints rather than expensive London editions of the English writers.

3
Irish Booksellers in America Phases I and II, 1750–1794

Probably Irish reprints did not make their way across the Atlantic in large numbers until the end of the American revolution. Since 1663 when the Navigation Acts had been passed, Ireland had been forbidden to export anything directly to the American colonies except horses, provisions, servants, and after 1705 linen; these severe restrictions on Irish trade were not dropped until 1780 as the result of pressures on the British Parliament generated by the American Revolution. There was a large and flourishing trade between Ireland and the American colonies before the war, but the Irish exports were food products and linen which were allowed by law in exchange for American flaxseed and naval stores. Such important American merchants as the Jacksons, Lees, and Hancocks of Boston, the Browns of Rhode Island, the Trumbulls of Connecticut, the Beekmans of New York, and the several Charleston, Philadelphia and West Indies merchants appear to have gotten their food products and linen from Ireland and their books primarily from London.[72] American booksellers for the most part also seem to have obtained their books from London before the war. Benjamin Franklin's voluminous correspondence reveals that he got most of his books for his bookshops and his private use and also for the new Library Company of Philadelphia from the well-known London bookseller William Strahan, and in a letter to Strahan on 1 May 1764 Franklin indicates that private persons in Philadelphia also bought their books from London booksellers.[73] Other sources indicate that Philadelphia bookshops and private individuals with their dependence on London suppliers for the most part were probably representatives of the American colonies as a whole.[74]

Nevertheless, there is evidence that Irish reprints of the English writers were smuggled successfully into the American colonies before the restrictions on trade were removed in 1780. The earliest testimony comes from America's premier printer himself Benjamin Franklin, who complained on 29 July 1747 to his London bookseller William Strahan that he could have sold more sets of the London edition of the *Universal History* if an Irish ship had not brought in twenty sets of the cheap Irish "piratical Edition."[75] Among the subscribers to the 1758 Dublin reprint of Thomas Stackhouse's *Life of our Lord and Saviour Jesus Christ* was Captain George Weston, Engineer, "in America," who subscribed for twenty-one copies. The Dublin bookseller David Hay, for whom London editions of works by Goldsmith and Smollett were reprinted, among others, seems to have been especially active in smuggling books to the colonies. He sent two boxes of books worth £85 to New Castle, Pennsylvania, for David Hall's bookshop in Philadelphia in October 1764, and he wrote to the Bradford book firm in Philadelphia on 13 April 1770 that he was sending them four boxes of books worth £190.3.4 and added, "I have frequently dealt with your city in this trade and have often found very good Acct. from it."[76] Hall also ordered Irish reprints from Alexander Kinkaid in Dublin and James Magee, Belfast's best-known printer and bookseller. Like David Hall and the Bradfords, William Young ordered stock for his Philadelphia bookshop from both London and Dublin. In the same year as David Hay's letter to the Bradfords the Dublin reprint of Sir James Steuart's *An Inquiry into the Principles of Political Economy*, in three volumes, had subscriptions from fifteen South Carolinians including one for six sets, from a New Yorker for three sets, and from eight high-ranking British army officers in America. This Dublin reprint was also in the 1789 catalogue of the Library Company of Philadelphia. In New York James Rivington, though an agent of his family firm in London, also imported Irish reprints and sold them to other booksellers such as Henry Knox in Boston during 1773 and 1774.[77] Rivington, for example, told Knox on 15 May 1773 that he had cheap Irish reprints of Johnson's *Dictionary*, travel books, histories, novels like Fielding's *Tom Jones*, plays of Goldsmith, Bickerstaffe, Kelly, Cumberland, and Garrick, and Jacob's *Law Dictionary*, which is "much better than the London edition." Rivington's invoice to Knox of 15 June 1774 lists large numbers of plays in Irish editions, a dozen copies of Goldsmith's *She Stoops to Conquer*, a dozen of Hugh Kelly's *False Delicacy*, for instance. Catalogues of few circulating libraries in the American colonies survive, but one that I have seen by John Mein of Boston lists nine Irish reprints in 1765, three of them novels.

The Irish book trade sent both its cheap reprints and eighteen of its members to the American colonies before the war. The emigration of these eighteen Irish bookmen was the first of three such emigrations to America.[78] By the early years of the nineteenth century at least 101 Irish printers, booksellers, bookbinders, and engravers would have transferred from the Irish to the United States book trade with far-reaching consequences for both Ireland and America. This first large transfer of Irish bookmen included three who would become the second, sixth, and twelfth most productive printers in America, John Dunlap, Hugh Gaine, and Robert Bell.[79] The most vociferous member of this first emigration was the Dublin bookseller Robert Bell, cited in chapter one for his reprint of Alexander Donaldson's *Some Thoughts on Literary Property* and his own addenda to Donaldson. Bell left the Dublin book trade in 1767 and opened up his shop in Philadelphia. He issued at least thirty-six catalogues during the years 1768–84, most of which do not survive, but the ones I have seen do not list the place of publication for his books.[80] Bell remained in Philadelphia what he had been in Dublin, an outspoken apologist for unauthorized reprints, Irish or American, of London editions. In 1771 Bell issued specimens for his own Philadelphia reprints of works by Blackstone, Hume, and Robertson. In the fifth part of this work, "Address to Subscribers," Bell argues that the British Copyright law does not extend either to Ireland or to the American colonies; the Irish and the Americans are perfectly free to reprint any London edition without authorization or payment. London publishers are "Bibliopolists" and "Monopolists," seeking to deprive both Irishmen and Americans of the educational opportunities provided by cheap books.[81] Bell's colorful career in Dublin and Philadelphia will be discussed in detail in chapter nine.

A second candidate for the *Dictionary of American Biography* was Matthew Lyon, who after a two-year apprenticeship to a Dublin printer emigrated to New England in 1765.[82] After brief stints as a printer in Connecticut and New Hampshire and service as a regimental commander in the Continental Army, he set up a printing shop, a bookshop called Voltaire's Head, a newspaper, and a paper mill in Fair Haven, Vermont. Lyon is usually regarded as the first person to make paper from wood pulp rather than from rags; he printed his newspaper, the *Farmer's Library*, and such reprints as Franklin's *Works* on his own paper. Lyon's prosperity and local leadership got him elected to Congress from Vermont as it did later from Kentucky, but the many controversies he became involved in because of his radical political views encouraged him to leave Vermont for Kentucky with a large following. In 1802 Lyon wrote from Kentucky to Mathew Carey, formerly of the Dublin book trade, now of the Philadelphia book trade: "I have sold a Vast many more books I am sure than all the merchants below the Kentucky river."[83] Like many Irish bookmen in the United States Lyon was succeeded by a son. James Lyon, who had been an apprentice in Franklin's printing shop in Philadelphia, worked in his father's many publishing activities in Vermont and Kentucky and continued them after his father's death. As a printer and newspaper publisher in fifteen communities in nine states James Lyon was in the words of one well-known historian of the book trade "the most widely roving printer of his day."[84]

A third candidate for the *Dictionary of American Biography* Hugh Gaine served his apprenticeship with the leading printer and bookseller of Belfast James Magee, as did Andrew Steuart, and both apprentices emigrated before the war, Gaine to New York and Steuart first to Philadelphia and then to Wilmington, North Carolina. A newspaper publisher, printer, and bookseller like Matthew Lyon, Gaine, the sixth most active printer in the American colonies with 307 publications 1764–83, advertised in his many catalogues after the war "books lately imported from England, Ireland, and Scotland." Gaine's catalogue of 1792 lists more than five hundred titles published in Ireland.[85] Continuing the reprint tradition in which he had been trained in Ireland, Gaine in New York issued his own reprints of London editions of Addison, Robert Blair, Bunyan, Burke, Lord Chesterfield, Defoe, Dryden, Josephus, Pope, Shakespeare, Richard and Thomas Sheridan, and Edward Young among major writers, and such extraordinarily popular works as Thomas Dyche's *Guide to the*

English Tongue in the forty-first edition.[86] Though Steuart's stay in Philadelphia was brief, he trained the well-known printer Joseph Cruikshank and developed a reputation for piracy. His contemporary Isaiah Thomas said Steuart "was not over nice as it respected the publications of others," and unlike most of the Irish printers in America who were happy to pirate London editions but usually not works by American authors, Steuart pirated American works on occasion such as Francis Hopkinson's *Science, a Poem* in 1762.[87] His 140 imprints of 1758–1769, however, seem to have run more heavily to almanacs and publications on local affairs than to reprints of London editions.

Another Irishman emigrating to New York and also one whose notable career as printer, bookseller, and newspaper publisher 1773–95 would bring him recognition in the *Dictionary of American Biography* was Samuel Loudon. Loudon's 218 publications show his heavy involvement in the American Revolution and local affairs later on in his career but not many reprints of London editions. Many Irish bookmen in America were succeeded by family members in the book trade, and Samuel Loudon was succeeded at least in his newspapers by sons John and Samuel.[88] Other Irish bookmen who emigrated to New York before the war were Oliver Templeton and Alexander Stewart, who worked together as book auctioneers from 1769 until at least 1782, and both were active in the Society of the Friendly Sons of St. Patrick.[89] Little is known about David Flanagan born in Dublin in 1759, but he fought for the colonists in the Revolution and conducted a bookselling business after the war until his death in Bedford, New York, in 1806.[90]

Well over one hundred thousand Irish emigrated to America in the half century before the American Revolution, and most of these were from the Presbyterian northeast.[91] Their most popular destination was Philadelphia, and among these emigrants were four from the Irish book trade, William Dunlap and his nephew John Dunlap from County Tyrone, James Adams from County Londonderry, and John Dean from Belfast. William Dunlap published 110 works 1754–67, mostly almanacs, sermons, and other religious writings but among his reprints of London editions were such important writers as Alexander Pope, Henry Scougal, and Isaac Watts. John Dunlap began work with his uncle in the Philadelphia book trade but then branched out on his own; his achievement as publisher of the first morning daily newspaper the *Pennsylvania Packet*, as the second most active printer with 424 publications during the years 1764–83, and as the official printer of both the *Declaration of Independence* and the *Constitution*, among other important government documents, would earn him a place with Bell, Lyon, Gaine, and Loudon in the *Dictionary of American Biography*. Among his many reprints of London editions were works by George Colman, Garrick, Goldsmith, Smollett, Sterne, Watts, and John Wesley, and the popular Hawkesworth's *Voyages*. After working for over seven years in Franklin's printing shop in Philadelphia, James Adams headed south to become the first printer in Wilmington, Delaware, where he conducted his printing and bookselling business from 1761 until his death in 1792. Adams trained three sons to take over the business and at least two other apprentices who became well-known printers in New Jersey, Isaac Collins and Shepard Kollock. Primarily known as the official printer for Delaware and as a newspaper publisher, Adams also reprinted a number of religious works and London editions of such important writers as Lord Chesterfield, John Locke, and Isaac Watts and the popular *New Guide to the English Tongue* by Thomas Dilworth. He prospered and left the business and money to his three sons and twenty pounds to a nephew back in Londonderry. His obituary commended him for the "regularity, neatness and correctness of his printing."[92]

John Dean learned bookbinding both in Belfast and Dublin and practiced that trade along with bookselling in Philadelphia in 1765 and from 1775 until 1779.[93] Also trained as a bookbinder in Dublin, Philip Brooks was binding books in Philadelphia in 1773 and worked in the same capacity in the New York book trade from 1775 until at least 1783 according to the *New York Gazette*.[94] He also sold stationery and published the *New York Mercury* 1779–83 along with other works. Less is known about the training of two brothers from Ireland, Samuel and William Dellap, who were in the Philadelphia book trade by 1771. Samuel was a printer, bookbinder, auctioneer, and bookseller until his death in 1793, and among the London editions that he reprinted were the popular *Lecture on Heads* by George Stevens and *Abelard and Heloise*; he also sold some "obscene books," according to his contemporary William McCulloch. His brother William had his own small bookshop.[95] McCulloch also knew John Reader from the Irish book trade.

Reader was a papermaker both in England and in James Blow's firm in Belfast before joining the Philadelphia book trade in 1768. McCulloch called him the best papermaker of his time but regretted his deficiencies in character.[96] Of Lewis Nicola much more is known. Of Huguenot background, he was educated in Ireland and was in Philadelphia by 1765 as a bookseller, publisher, and proprietor of a circulating library. In 1769 he was publishing the *American Magazine*, in which he included transactions of the American Philosophical Society and materials acquired because of an earlier association with the Royal Dublin Society. These were activities of his early career, however, and he made the reputation that admitted him into the *Dictionary of American Biography*, as a soldier and public official.[97]

Until the end of the century New York and Philadelphia were the magnets for members of the Irish book trade because they were the publishing centers, but at least two Irish bookmen went elsewhere. John Douglas Macdougall spent a short time in Philadelphia but also worked as a printer, bookbinder, and bookseller in Providence, Rhode Island, and in Boston during the war years. Among his sixteen imprints were reprints of Captain Cook's *Voyages*, George Lillo's *London Merchant*, Pope's *Essay on Man*, and Lord Chesterfield's *Letters*, the latter following the Dublin edition in its additions, and Courtney Melmoth's *Pupil of Pleasure* in response to Lord Chesterfield.[98] Thomas Howe was apparently the only Irish bookman to go elsewhere in the Americas. He was publishing the *St. Christopher's Gazette* in the West Indies by 1747.[99] Many of these eighteen emigrants from the Irish book trade were selling the cheaper Irish reprints in their shops in the colonies to compete with the London editions for the American market, and in the latter decades of the century many issued their own reprints of London editions just as they had done in Ireland.

During the years 1780–82 there were three important developments that contributed to a vast increase in the export of Irish reprints to the new United States: Ireland won legislative independence, restrictions on trade with America were removed, and the American war for independence ended. The Irish booksellers could now export their reprints legally to the United States, and the growth of this export trade was rapid. The Irish Customs House Books show the beginning of legal book exports to

America near the end of the war, though they by no means give the full story of Irish book exports. For the year ending 25 March 1780 sixty-nine hundredweight (cwt.) or 7,728 pounds of unbound books were exported to America from Ireland, as compared with no legal exports at all up to this time, though there had been considerable illegal exports before the war.[100] The expected increase at the end of the war did not take place immediately since for the year ending 25 March 1783 only seventy-three hundredweight of unbound books were exported to the United States, but the following year there was a spectacular jump to over 951 cwt. or 106,512 pounds or somewhat higher according to British Customs House figures. Book exports to America represent almost the entire legal export trade in books during these years, though the clandestine export of books to Britain and especially to America continued. Thomas Todd Faulkner, nephew and successor of the famous George, observed in his *Dublin Journal* on 18 February 1783 that Irish editions were much in demand in America, and the Whitestone firm announced in the same paper on 23 September 1783 that they were eager to deal with merchants interested in exporting books to America. The publication of the *Dublin Catalogue* in 1786 and in 1791 aided exports since American booksellers knew what was available; Mathew Carey asked for it on 25 November 1794.

As described in chapter one opposition in Ireland to resolution seventeen of the 1785 commercial resolutions which would have extended copyright law to Ireland was well nigh universal, and much of this opposition stemmed from an awareness that the burgeoning American trade in books would end if Irish booksellers had to pay copyright. In the debates in the Irish House of Commons of that year the great Henry Flood stressed that book exports to America would stop if there were a copyright law, and Mr. Ogilvie added that a copyright law would nullify the 1780 removal of restrictions on trade with America, which he termed "the Magna Charta of Irish trade."[101] The London booksellers, who were the primary backers of resolution seventeen, were keenly aware of the Irish threat to their book trade with the United States. Their representatives before the House of Lords Committee on resolution seventeen William Grosvenor and Thomas Vallance told the Committee on 27 June 1785 that Irish book exports to North America and the West Indies were "very considerable," and they voiced their alarm about the significant increase since 1780.[102] Lord Sheffield, of Irish birth though now living in London, shared their concern in his influential and provocative *Observations on the Commerce of the American States*, as he observed that though the London booksellers might be able to capture the American market for school books, the Irish booksellers, unless prevented by copyright law, would take the American market for new books since they paid no royalties and could undersell the London editions.[103] From the other side of the Atlantic Tench Coxe wrote that Lord Sheffield was wrong about both London and Irish booksellers because America had the paper mills, the printing equipment, and the craftsmen to do their own printing;[104] though Coxe was right in the long run, the American reading public would be heavily dependent on British and Irish book imports until the new century.

The year 1785 was also notable for the beginning of one of the most distinguished careers in the history of the United States book trade. Young Mathew Carey founded the only publishing firm in the history of Ireland and the United States to last from the eighteenth century to the present day, in this instance two hundred years. Since Carey's story has been often told,[105] only his relationships with Dublin booksellers and printers need be discussed. Carey had been an apprentice to Thomas M'Donnell, publisher of reprints and the *Hibernian Journal* in Dublin and then founded his own newspaper in Dublin the *Volunteer's Journal*. Political pressure encouraged Carey to make a hasty exit from Dublin disguised as a woman in 1784. In Philadelphia Carey set up with funds from the Marquis de Lafayette, whom he had met in Paris along with Benjamin Franklin, a newspaper, a magazine, and a printing and bookselling firm. Carey's massive correspondence with booksellers in Britain, Ireland, and the United States survives in the Historical Society of Pennsylvania and his accounts in the American Antiquarian Society. Carey probably had more dealings with Patrick Byrne, the important Dublin–Philadelphia printer and bookseller who figures throughout this study, than with any other Irish bookseller. His letter to Byrne on 22 October 1788 reveals much about Irish book exports to America. Noting that "We are deluged with books from England and Ireland," Carey wants Irish editions of Bibles, law books, delphini classics, and dictionaries, but not novels. He claims American readers are better educated than Irish readers; if Byrne hopes "to supply the American market with literary food, let it be of the most solid and substantial kind; history, voyages, philosophy, science, and well chosen school books." For books like these Byrne may "expect good returns."[106] Carey makes the same request of Thomas Carey in Dublin on 9 November 1789. Although Byrne was Carey's main Dublin supplier, the Carey accounts and letter books show that Carey ordered Irish reprints from these other Dublin booksellers: Carey's own brothers Thomas and William Paulet Carey and his cousin the Reverend James Carey, John Chambers, Bernard Dornin, John Jones, William Jones, Thomas M'Donnell, James Moore, John and James Rice, and William Wilson of the well-known publishing family. Of these thirteen Dublin booksellers from whom Carey ordered books, six would join the American book trade, Byrne, William Carey, Chambers, Dornin, John and James Rice, undoubtedly encouraged by Mathew Carey's own example.

Carey's business with Patrick Byrne alone was so extensive that it raises serious questions about the Customs House figures as a reliable index of Irish book exports to America. The Carey accounts show that from 20 February 1793 until 28 September 1795 Carey ordered £2,092.11.5 worth of books from Byrne alone.[107] The Customs House figures for the same period show total export to America of only £534.15.0 of bound books and about 130 cwt. of unbound books worth only £325 by Irish calculation. As late as 8 May 1797 Carey still owed Byrne sixteen hundred pounds for books from Ireland. By July 1798 he had paid Byrne £1,663.6.7 but owed £584.15.7 for additional purchases.[108] In several letters to his Dublin suppliers Carey refers to smuggling of books from Ireland into the United States to avoid import duties, but in the letter to Byrne cited above he describes smuggling as "a disreputable traffic, in which I would not choose to be concerned." Whether Carey was always this scrupulous is unknown, but it is clear that Irish Customs House figures on Irish book exports to America show only the tip of the iceberg. Carey's later orders from Byrne show that he dropped his prejudice against novels; he put in a standing order on 25 May 1793 for several copies of every new work published in Dublin and on 4 November 1794 for a dozen copies of every novel and later that month for thirty to fifty copies of some works.[109]

Two of Carey's orders from William Jones and Carey's old Dublin employer Thomas M'Donnell are interesting for what they show about the magnitude of Irish book imports. On 14 November 1792 Carey acknowledged four boxes of books from William Jones and commented on boxes of books sent by Jones to other Philadelphia bookshops. Carey complained, however, that Irish booksellers were "too grasping" and would lose the price advantage they had over their competitors in London; he also said Irish booksellers should allow American booksellers twelve months to pay as did London booksellers. By 16 November 1795 he had arranged with Byrne to pay each spring for the past spring and each fall for the past fall. On 24 October 1791 Carey ordered one thousand Roman Catholic *Catechisms* from Thomas M'Donnell, who like Carey himself was a Catholic, for the growing Irish Catholic population not only in Philadelphia but in New York City where Carey had sixteen outlets for his books and in Boston fifteen by 1813. Carey also asked his cousin the Reverend James Carey on 9 November 1789 to make arrangements with Catholic booksellers in Dublin like Wogan, Cross, and M'Donnell to send Catholic reprints to Philadelphia. Carey asked his cousin to send Dublin magazines, reviews, and periodical essays, even though he had been publishing his own magazine the *American Museum, a Repository of Ancient and Modern Fugitive Pieces, Prose and Poetical* since 1787. Patterned in many ways after the main Dublin magazines, *Exshaw's* and the *Hibernian*, the *American Museum* reprinted materials from London periodicals and sometimes from Dublin periodicals. As early as 4 June 1793 Carey wrote to Patrick Byrne that he was selling books in nine states and Nova Scotia and the West Indies.[110] Carey's most noted travelling representative was the indefatigable Parson Weems, but America's first super-salesman was by 1800 hawking Carey's own reprints rather than the imported Irish editions.[111]

Mathew Carey was the outstanding member of the second emigration of Irish bookmen to the United States. This group of twenty-one came after the American war when travel across the Atlantic was again possible to swell the large and influential Irish-American book trade community already there. The members of the second migration tended to be Roman Catholic rather than Protestant like the members of the first group of eighteen Irish bookmen before the war. Twenty of the twenty-one in the second group worked in Philadelphia, the heart of the American book trade, though two left at a later date for other American cities. William Spotswood and Christopher Talbot had been in the group of Dublin booksellers that had reprinted Oliver Goldsmith's popular comic poem *The Haunch of Venison* in 1776 and Goldsmith's *Poems and Plays* in 1777, and Talbot had reprinted Samuel Johnson's *Political Tracts* in 1777. Spotswood, as noted in chapter two, had also operated a circulating library in Dublin 1775–84, and he had subscribed for his customers to six sets of the impressive Dublin reprint of Goldsmith's *History of the Earth* in 1777. Like Mathew Carey, Spotswood and his wife and successor Hanna Spotswood, and Talbot emigrated to Philadelphia in 1784, and worked briefly with Carey on four periodicals, the *Pennsylvania Herald*, the *American Museum*, the *Columbian Magazine*, and the *Counting-House Companion*. Like Carey, Spotswood and Talbot published their own American reprints in Philadelphia. Although the United States had a copyright law by 1790, it protected only American writers. As in Ireland London booksellers were fair game, and these three Catholic publishers who had suffered from the penal laws in Ireland as had many of those Irish bookmen who would follow their example presumably had no great love for London booksellers or things English in general. One later emigrant William Duane on 7 October 1805 wrote in his famous republican newspaper the *Aurora* that 99 percent of his fellow Irishmen were republicans. Talbot reprinted at least four well-known Roman Catholic books during the years 1784–87, and he undoubtedly sold Irish reprints in his shop. Spotswood issued his own Philadelphia reprint of the *Beauties of Johnson* in 1787 and the *Beauties of Sterne* in 1789, the latter probably from the edition he had printed in Dublin in 1784. In 1785 Spotswood was in partnership with his fellow Irish emigrant John Rice, and the latter was selling Irish reprints and publishing his own reprints in 1789.[112] Typically Irish is the statement by Spotswood and Rice in their advertisement for 7 October 1789 in the *Pennsylvania Gazette* that their edition of Peter Pindar's *Poems* sells "at less than one quarter of the London price." By 1806 John Rice was selling primarily French books according to the *Aurora*. Except for a brief stint as bookseller and stationer in Boston Spotswood continued in Philadelphia until his death in 1805 when he was succeeded by his wife. Spotswood's publishing career in Dublin, Philadelphia and

Boston will be recounted in greater detail in chapter nine. Spotswood hired John O'Connor, a lawyer and bookseller from Dublin, to edit the *Columbian Magazine* in 1787. O'Connor had probably come to Philadelphia in 1784 just as Mathew Carey, Spotswood, and Talbot had, and in that year he was proprietor and editor of the *American Herald*. Also in 1787 O'Connor translated and edited *Anecdotes of the Reign of Louis the XVIth* for the New York bookseller F. Childs, protegé of Benjamin Franklin. Noting O'Connor's "Superior Genius and great abilities," Childs had written to Franklin in France on 31 December 1786 that he had sent O'Connor to Philadelphia to solicit subscriptions for the book. Childs also ordered Dublin reprints, presumably from the *Dublin Catalogue*, in addition to employing John O'Connor.[113]

The year 1784 also saw the emigration of Andrew Brown and son Andrew to Philadelphia from Dublin where the senior Brown had studied at Trinity College. Among other works the senior Brown published the *Federal Gazette*, later the *Philadelphia Gazette*, from 1788 until his death in 1797 when he was succeeded by his son.[114] Several years after the arrival of the Brown family in Philadelphia, another Irish book trade family arrived, more members of the Carey clan. John Carey was working as a bookseller in Philadelphia during the years 1791–93, though apparently not in his elder brother's firm. Presumably he found the work unrewarding, and he emigrated a second time, this time to London, where he enjoyed the distinguished career as a classical scholar that admitted him to the *Dictionary of National Biography*. John Carey while in Philadelphia also edited Washington's official correspondence after obtaining the permission of Washington and Jefferson. Apparently hoping to benefit from a London publication, he delayed publication until reaching London in 1795, but the work was quickly pirated in Boston, and Carey, whose London edition was in Jefferson's library, later complained to James Monroe that the American piracy had deprived him of any profit.[115]

Another Carey brother found the American book trade more attractive. In 1793 James Carey began his publishing odyssey in the south where he published eight newspapers in Virginia, the Carolinas, and Georgia, while also maintaining bookshops. His books for sale advertised in one of his newspapers, the *Wilmington Chronicle* (North Carolina) include no publishers, but Carey announced on 22 October 1795 that he had been able to continue the newspaper and the bookshop only because he brought sufficient funds and supplies with him, and the latter probably included Irish editions from his brother Mathew and certainly from John Rice in Dublin, as he wrote to Carey on 25 February 1793. James Carey maintained his own shop in Philadelphia for the printing and selling of books from 1796 until at least 1801, and he also published three newspapers and over sixty books, mostly reprints of such widely read English authors as Tom Paine, Bishop Watson, Mary Godwin, Captain Cook, Elizabeth Inchbald, and Charlotte Smith.[116] A fourth Carey brother William Paulet Carey had been employed in the Dublin book trade during the years 1788–94 as a bookseller and as publisher of the *National Evening Star* and had supplied his brother Mathew with a number of Dublin reprints. A United Irishman like many other Dublin booksellers, W. P. Carey was in Philadelphia by 1795 as a bookseller and engraver. W. P. Carey was also a poet, and his poems "The Incantation" and "Damon's Farewell" were published in his brother's *American Museum* in October 1788 and in the appendix to the 1792 volume. Like his brother John, W. P. Carey apparently found the Philadelphia book trade unrewarding and emigrated to London where his fame as an art critic earned him a place in the *Dictionary of National Biography*.[117]

Several other Irish book tradesmen in this second phase of emigration to America are linked together by their membership in various Irish fraternal groups in Philadelphia. Hugh Moore preceded the Browns, Mathew Carey, the Spotswoods, and Talbot by a year to Philadelphia where he joined the Society of the Friendly Sons of St. Patrick and set up a shop for selling law books, one of the specialities of the Irish reprint industry. He died in 1803 when he left his law books to his son who was a lawyer.[118] Later joined by his brother Patrick, Henry Rice came from the Dublin book trade two years after Hugh Moore and opened a bookshop in Philadelphia which lasted until 1805. Henry and Patrick Rice issued four catalogues 1789–96, and at least one that survives mentions a "large and general assortment of books" in 1789 from "the last vessels from London, Dublin, and Glasgow."[119] Their advertisements in the *United States Gazette* for 21, 26, 27 May and 4 June 1795 also indicate Dublin reprints for sale. As late as 1 January 1798 they were capitalizing on their Dublin book trade background when they announced in the *Aurora*: "From the nature of their connections in Dublin, they are enabled to sell Irish editions (as they have hitherto shown) at the very lowest prices." Like most ex-Dublin booksellers in America, the Rice brothers continued to reprint London editions, and few of their eighty-one imprints 1788–1803 are original works; among others they reprinted such major English authors as Henry Brooke, Edmund Burke, Richard Cumberland, Daniel Defoe, William Godwin, Elizabeth Inchbald, Tom Paine, Peter Pindar, Ann Radcliffe, Richard Sheridan, James Thomson, and Edward Young. One of the Rice brothers' Dublin book trade connections was a cousin John Rice, who in 1796 issued Elizabeth Hervey's novel the *History of Ned Evans*, noting in the imprint that the work was "sold by H. and P. Rice, Philadelphia"; John Rice would join the Baltimore book trade in 1803. Henry Rice in 1790 joined the Hibernian Society, which Mathew Carey had been instrumental in founding.

Another Hibernian Society member was Alexander Boyd, who replaced the colorful book auctioneer in Philadelphia Robert Bell in 1784 when he issued auction catalogues, and he continued the spectacle of the Irish book auction until at least 1790 when he joined the Hibernian Society.[120] In the latter year Boyd was joined by Joseph Dean from Ireland. Dean was active as a book auctioneer in Philadelphia until at least 1793 when he joined another group favored by Irish emigrants the Society of the Sons of St. Tammany.[121] Although John Patterson had emigrated from Ireland by 1772 when he joined the Friendly Sons of St. Patrick, he was employed by the colonial government in his early years in America and did not enter the Philadelphia book trade as a printer until 1791.[122] Two years later John Parker came from the Dublin book trade to begin work in Philadelphia as a printer and publisher. In Dublin he had sold the Dublin reprint of Samuel Johnson's *Lives of the Poets* in October 1779 and reprinted the *Beauties of Johnson* in 1782. In Philadelphia Parker took over the *Columbian Magazine* from his former Dublin colleague William Spotswood in 1793 besides publishing three newspapers, and he printed books for Mathew Carey.[123] There were others, perhaps many others, in this second phase of emigration from the Irish book trade to Philadelphia, but they must remain anonymous. Some of them were on the ship *Favorite*, which arrived in Philadelphia from Dublin according to the *Pennsylvania Gazette* of 11

August 1784. Among the emigrants were printers and type founders, but they were redemptioners who would be obliged to serve out indentures. A thorough check of Philadelphia newspapers would undoubtedly turn up many more.

Although Philadelphia was the hub both of the American book trade and of the Irish-American community, it was not the only city that offered better opportunities to Irish bookmen who were astute enough to see that the success of the new British reprints by the early 1780s augured ill for the Irish reprint industry. At least two Irish booksellers started out in Philadelphia but then envisioned better publishing ventures in New England. Barnard Brian Macanulty emigrated from Ireland to Philadelphia in 1785, but he was in Salem, Massachusetts by 1791 as a bookbinder and by 1798 as a bookseller. He was publishing his own books by 1799, most of them reprints of London editions but some of them original works for which he paid copyright. He paid Joseph Story two hundred dollars for the copyright of his poem *The Power of Solitude* in 1802, a copy of which was in Thomas Jefferson's library, and he also paid James Tytler for the copyright of his *New System of Geography*.[124] John Henry emigrated from Ireland to Philadelphia a few years after the others but before the great wave of Irish bookmen at the end of the century. After working in 1795 with his fellow Irishmen Andrew Brown and William Duane on the *Philadelphia Gazette* and serving in the United States Army, Henry published the Windsor, Vermont *Post Boy* in 1806–07 and other works.[125] As the *Dictionary of American Biography* labels him, Henry was an adventurer, and he was soon in Canada on dubious and secret diplomatic missions and then dropped out of sight in France. In this second group of twenty-one Irish book craftsmen only Thomas Kirk had no Philadelphia connection. After completing his printing apprenticeship in Cork, Kirk was in New York by 1790 and was listed as a printer and editor by 1797. By 1803 he was conducting his printing and bookselling busines both in Brooklyn where he published three newspapers and a magazine and in New York where he would soon have the largest bookshop in the city.[126] Kirk published 253 works 1797–1819, many of them only of local interest but also a large number of significant reprints. In his earlier years in Brooklyn and New York he reprinted Richardson's *Pamela* for three different publishers, Hugh Blair's *Rhetoric* twice, an important textbook used at both Harvard and

Yale for many years, Samuel Johnson's *Rambler*, Isaac Watt's *Hymns*, and William Hazlitt's *Eloquence of the British Senate* twice. Among the twenty-eight works he published in 1813 were reprints of such important English writers as Edmund Burke, Shakespeare, Robert Southey, and four works by the popular English moralist Hannah More. The next year Kirk reprinted Fanny Burney's *Wanderer*, Lord Byron's *Corsair* and *Lara*, Maria Edgeworth's *Belinda*, and Dugald Stewart's *Philosophy of the Human Mind*. He began reprinting the most popular novelist of the time Sir Walter Scott in 1815 with the first American reprint of *Guy Mannering* and followed it in 1819 with *Rob Roy*. During these years Kirk reprinted other significant new English works such as Lord Byron's *English Bards and Scotch Reviewers*, *Childe Harold's Pilgrimage* and his complete *Poems*, Coleridge's *Biographia Literaria*, Maria Edgeworth's *Harrington*, and the *Poems* of Thomas Moore three times. Because of the extension of British copyright law in 1801 to Ireland, Kirk's former colleagues in the Irish reprint industry could no longer reprint these new Romantic masterpieces. Kirk and the other Irish booksellers in America, however, continued to reprint new English writing in America as they had done in Ireland. The decline and fall of the Irish reprint industry and the resulting emigration of sixty-two Irish book tradesmen at the turn of the century to join the thirty-nine already employed in the American book trade will be discussed in chapter eight.

The thirty-nine Irish book craftsmen in the first two phases of emigration, most of whom sold Irish reprints and later in their careers issued their own American reprints of London editions, were by no means alone as sellers of Irish editions in America. Published by an Irishman William Duane from 1798 until 1820, the *Aurora* has numerous advertisements by booksellers from Philadelphia and elsewhere of Irish editions during the years 1798–1803. Law books, histories, novels and plays, for example, arrived in Irish editions for the Philadelphia bookseller John Conrad on the ship *Prosperity* from Dublin on 9 April 1801, and on the ship *Favourite* from Dublin on 19 May 1802. The most common advertisements for Irish editions in the *Aurora*, however, are by former members of the Irish book trade such as Duane himself, Patrick Byrne, and Henry and Patrick Rice. Catalogues for the latter years of the century show that a number of American booksellers were selling Irish reprints. In Philadelphia William

Prichard advertised in his catalogue for 1787 "latest importations from London, Dublin, and Glasgow," and this was probably true also of his thirteen other catalogues before 1800 and his circulating library in 1783. Prichard also advertised Irish editions frequently in the Philadelphia newspapers, as did others like Bernard Kilkenny in the *Philadelphia Gazette* for 23 July 1783. Isaiah Thomas of Worcester, Massachusetts, Mathew Carey's only rival as the premier American publisher after the turn of the century, advertised in his catalogue for 1790 and probably also in his seven other catalogues before 1800 "English, Scotch, and Irish editions." The catalogues for 1796, 1797, and 1798, of the Boston bookseller, Paul Joseph Guérard de Nancrede also advertise books "lately imported from London, Dublin, Paris, and other capitals of Europe." Similarly, Barzillai Hudson and George Goodwin in Hartford, Connecticut, announced Dublin editions in their catalogue for 1797.[127] Unfortunately, few catalogues survive before 1800, and even fewer list the place of publication for the books sold. A notable exception is *Samuel Campbell's Catalogue of Books for 1794*. Campbell's list for his bookshop in New York City contained Irish editions of 142 different works. The list includes Irish reprints of London editions and a few original works printed in Ireland. There are Irish reprints of works by five of the eight major authors used in this study, Boswell, Fielding, Goldsmith, Johnson, and Smollett. There is also a generous selection of novels, plays, poems, histories, classics, religious and political works, and the ever present travel books. In his catalogue Campbell informs his customers that he will order books for them from Britain or Ireland. Also in New York the French bookseller Louis Alexis Hocquet de Caritat advertised Dublin reprints "at a discount of from 25 to 40 percent" in 1798. In 1801 he offered a "handsome allowance" in American and Dublin editions "to purchasers by the quantity."[127] American booksellers without previous experience in the Dublin book trade such as Campbell and Caritat probably ordered their Dublin reprints from the *Dublin Catalogue* after 1786. The New York bookseller Thomas Allen, who supplied Irish reprints to Mathew Carey in 1795, also ordered from the *Dublin Catalogue*.[129] Other American booksellers were able to import sheets from the Dublin printer and issue them under their own imprints as did Berry and Rogers in New York in 1787 with Emmerich de Vattel's *Law of Nations*, reprinted by Luke White of

Dublin in 1787.[130] The Irish editions advertised by these shops went to private rather than to institutional libraries. The 1789 and 1807 catalogues of the Library Company of Philadelphia show few Irish editions, and this is true also of the 1795 catalogue for the Loganian Library in Philadelphia and the 1790 catalogue for the Harvard College Library.

Of the 142 Irish editions in Samuel Campbell's catalogue, the largest number are law books, fifty-five. Ironicaly enough, Irish booksellers seem to have made a specialty of reprinting law books, perhaps in response to American demand for cheap law books. George Davis's catalogues for 1792, 1795, 1796, 1799, and 1800 advertise "Law books — latest Irish editions" for his Philadelphia bookshop.[131] Davis's announcements of Irish editions of law books appear as late as 2 January 1801 in the *Gazette of the United States* and 26 April 1802 and 11 January 1803 in the *Aurora*. The Philadelphia bookseller F. Nichols was also advertising Irish editions of law books in the *Aurora* as late as 24 December 1802. By this date, however, the Irish reprint industry had collapsed, and the main supplier in Dublin of reprints of law books to Mathew Carey and others, Patrick Byrne, was in Philadelphia. Byrne's extensive dealings in law books in both Dublin and Philadelphia and his most famous customer Thomas Jefferson will be discussed in chapter nine.

There are several contemporary reports on the prevalence of Irish editions of law books in the United States. One great debater in the Irish Parliament Henry Flood has been quoted on the Irish book exports to America; his main rival Henry Grattan commented enthusiastically in Parliament on 12 February 1796 about Irish book exports and cited law books in particular: "The export trade of books had become a very promising trade. The high price of books in England, and the comparatively low price of books in this Country, joined to the predilection which America had always shewn for dealing with Ireland, had induced very considerable orders from that country, particularly for Law books, and political discussions."[132] Essentially the same observation was made in 1789 by a British writer in the United States Leman Thomas Rede: "Irish books (like Irishmen) have, in everything, a preference throughout this country, and the sale of their books, those on law in particular, is extremely great."[133]

That many books were reprinted in Dublin after 1780 with an American audience in mind subscription editions make clear. John Rice, an ex-Dublin bookseller in Philadelphia, subscribed in 1789 for one hundred copies of the two-volume Dublin reprint of Bishop George Hay's *The Scripture Doctrine of Miracles Displayed*. Also for the growing Roman Catholic population in Philadelphia and elsewhere in the Northeast twenty-five sets were sent to Philadelphia, two to Newfoundland, and one to New York of Alban Butler's massive six-volume *Lives of the Fathers, Martyrs, and other Principal Saints*, reprinted by a Catholic printer and Catholic bookseller in Dublin H. Fitzpatrick and Richard Cross during the years 1797–1802. Fitzpatrick also reprinted the Catholic Bible in 1791, for which nine residents of Newfoundland subscribed. The twenty-five sets for Philadelphia of Butler's *Lives of the Fathers* went to Patrick Byrne's bookshop; Byrne was a Catholic like so many ex-Dublin booksellers. Another Catholic reprint from Dublin was Josephus's *Works*, which included two Philadelphians among its subscribers. Of the Dublin reprint in 1791 of the 1790 three-volume London edition of Shakespeare's *Dramatic Works*, edited by Samuel Ayscough, five sets went to William Prichard's bookshop in Philadelphia, and seven sets went to residents of four towns in Connecticut including a New Haven bookseller. Although he was not a subscriber, Samuel Campbell sold it in his New York bookshop in 1794, and Patrick Byrne sold it in Philadelphia according to the *Aurora* for 2 January 1802. A rare example of an original work published in Dublin by subscription is James Mullalla's *View of Irish Affairs*, one of whose subscribers is 1796 was General George Washington of Philadelphia for the astonishing number of fifty copies of the two-volume set. Whether President Washington was ordering gifts for friends or stock for a Philadelphia bookstore is not revealed in his voluminous correspondence. Another subscriber for fifty sets was the Dublin bookseller John Rice, who would transfer to the Baltimore book trade in 1803.[134]

This American audience for the Dublin reprints is significantly under-represented by the Irish Customs House figures as previously noted in the comparison with Mathew Carey's orders from Dublin, but the pattern of the rise and fall of the exports is probably accurate. The last decade of the century never approached the peak year of the previous decade of about 107,000 pounds of unbound books in 1783–84, although there were good years from 25 March 1791 through 25 March 1794. But the drop in the 1790s may not have been as great as the Customs House figures indicate since Mathew Carey's heavy imports and probably those of his Irish colleagues in Philadelphia are not fully represented. The Customs House figures show significant increases during the period 5 January 1801 through 5 January 1805 followed by a precipitous drop. This increase seems surprising since the British Copyright Law extended to Ireland by the Union of 1800 took effect in July 1801. The Irish booksellers seem to have taken a last opportunity to send their reprints to the United States in large numbers before the Copyright Law could be effectively enforced. Some booksellers like Patrick Byrne, perhaps anticipating the Union, had stockpiled reprints in their Dublin warehouses for later shipment to the United States, and Byrne after his arrival in Philadelphia in 1801 drew on his Dublin warehouses for several years. The Customs House figures for 1802 show £541.5.1 of bound books and 314 cwt. of unbound books or 35,168 pounds exported to America and for 1803 £532.0.4 of bound books and 407 cwt. or 45,584 pounds of unbound books. In the light of Mathew Carey's dealings with Dublin booksellers these figures need to be increased several times to indicate the magnitude of Irish book exports to the United States. The export figures also identify other places in the Americas that received Irish editions in the 1790s, Newfoundland, Antigua, Jamaica, Barbadoes, and the West Indies.

The magnitude of the Irish book trade with the Americas at the end of the century is further suggested by influential reporters in Ireland. During the course of the extensive debates in the Irish Parliament 1795–96 on the proposed duty on imported paper, eight leading Dublin booksellers testified that "a considerable number of the Printers of Dublin were heretofore employed on Editions of Works to be exported to America, which was found to be greater in Amount than the home Consumption."[135] During the same year in a paper read before the influential Royal Irish Academy and published in updated and considerably enlarged form in their *Transactions* for 1803, William Preston observed about the book trade "that a very lucrative channel of business, and capable of great extension and improvement, had been opened,—the printing of cheap editions for the American market." In his book-length essay on Irish manufacturing in general Preston speaks of the heavy demand in the United States for Irish reprints not only of books but of maps, prints, and engravings: "It is incredible with what avidity, the people of America call for cheap editions of printed books; and for all kinds of engravings, which I understand are much fought for by the people of America."[136] What William Preston did not know in 1796 when he delivered his paper before the Royal Irish Academy was that the Americans were no longer content to sell Irish editions in their bookshops but were beginning to issue their own reprints. Preston could not have known in 1796 that by the time his paper was published in 1803 the Americans with scores of tutors from the Irish reprint industry in their midst were becoming the world's most successful publishers of cheap reprints.

4
Irish Booksellers and the English Novel

The gradual increase in the Irish reprints at the middle of the eighteenth century coincided with the arrival of a new literary genre, the novel, in the hands of three of its early masters Samuel Richardson, Henry Fielding, and Tobias Smollett. Reprinting popular English novels as quickly and as cheaply as possible soon became an important activity of Irish printers and booksellers whether in Ireland or America. By 31 January 1741 when they made their announcement in Faulkner's *Dublin Journal*, George Faulkner and George Ewing had reprinted Richardson's *Pamela* published on 6 November 1740 in London.[137] They sold their edition of the first two volumes of the work for 5s.5d. to undersell the London edition at six shillings, and the demand was good enough to warrant another reprinting in March, less than a month after the London reprinting of 14 February 1741. When Richardson added volumes three and four in December 1741 to the London edition, Ewing, Faulkner, and William Smith reprinted them in May 1742 at a lower price and added them to the first two volumes to make a new edition in "four neat pocket volumes" selling for 10s.10d. as compared with the London edition at twelve shillings. Even with its price advantage the Dublin reprint did not sell well, and it was advertised intermittently until at least 2 April 1758, when the edition was probably exhausted. Many Irish readers must have bought the London edition, 1,500 copies of which Richardson sent over to Ireland; they provoked the accusation of the *Dublin Spy* on 5 November 1753 that Richardson was trying to ruin Dublin printing. Roger Spy concludes his tirade against

London editions by an admonition to the Irish people that Irish booksellers often used: "Discourage with hand and heart all editions printed in England, join together and determine, my dear country men, not to buy a book printed in England, since if ye let in so pernicious a custom, ye will be instrumental in ruining Ireland." Since Ireland's elite tended to buy the Irish reprints rather than the London editions, they must have accepted this popular argument by Irish booksellers. In America such graduates of the Irish reprint industry as William Spotswood, Thomas Kirk, and Mathew Carey issued their own reprints of *Pamela*, Spotswood in 1786, Kirk printings for three New York booksellers in 1798, and Carey in 1808. The Dublin reprint of Fielding's *Shamela* announced in the *Dublin Journal* on 2 May 1741 was Dublin booksellers' response to their *Pamela*. Fielding was already well known to theater goers in Ireland and to readers of the Irish editions as a playwright. Of the many plays that Fielding had published in London before being driven from the theater by the Licensing Act of 1737, most had been reprinted in Ireland and would continue to be performed in Ireland until the end of the century. *The Virgin unmask'd* seems to have been his most popular comedy; it was reprinted twice in Dublin and once in Cork, and it was staged frequently in Dublin and thirty-six times in the provincial theaters before 1800. The *Tragedy of Tragedies*, Fielding's most famous play today, had first been reprinted in 1730 and often performed.[138] Irish booksellers' second response to their *Pamela* was *Joseph Andrews*, whose Dublin reprint by Faulkner, G. Ewing, and Smith was announced in the *Dublin Journal* on 11 May 1742 at 2s.8d. just ten weeks after the London edition selling for six shillings.[139] The novel lacked the appeal in Ireland that it had in Britain where it went through three editions and 6,500 copies in thirteen months. The first edition was still being advertised in the newspapers as late as September 1746, but a new edition was needed the following year. The second edition of 1747 was printed for the same three booksellers plus A. Ewing in the same two-volume 12mo. format, but the pagination is different. The Yale copy was presented by "The Revd. Mr. J. S. Monck to Master John Kinkead, May the 1st 1751." A graduate of Trinity College, Dublin, Monck later in his career was Archdeacon of Derry. His pupil made several notations in his book including a frivolous one inside the back cover, "John Kinkead is a Lovely Maid." Nearly a half century later Kinkead would participate in the rebellion of 1798 as a United Irishman.[140] The third edition of 1754 for the Ewings, Faulkner, and W. Smith has the same pagination as the second but the page and type are slightly larger; the copy now at Trinity College, Dublin, was owned in the eighteenth century by the landed family of Nash of Richfield, County Cork. The demand by 1767 for a new edition must have been great, for there were two identical editions of that year with different pagination from the earlier editions; one was printed for the same group and the other for Dillon Chamberlaine and James Potts. Both are prefaced by the life of Fielding prepared by Arthur Murphy for the London edition of the works of Fielding in 1762. One of these was sold by Samuel Campbell in his New York shop in 1794. No further Irish edition was needed until the end of the century in Thomas Henshall's series. In America, however, William Spotswood and William Duane, formerly of the Irish book trade, issued their own reprints of *Joseph Andrews* in 1786 and 1801 respectively.

As was the custom of the Dublin booksellers, George Faulkner had not paid Richardson or Fielding or Fielding's London publisher for publishing rights to *Pamela* or *Joseph Andrews*, but he did pay Richardson seventy guineas for publishing rights to *Clarissa*, and he announced the first two volumes of the novel in his *Dublin Journal* for 22 December 1747 at 5s.5d., just three weeks after the London edition selling for six shillings. The next two volumes followed in May 1748; the preliminary announcement of 3 May reveals something of the audience for the work: "As great Numbers of Nobility and Gentry have had the first and second volumes of *Clarissa* by the Author of *Pamela*, it is requested, that such as are inclined to have the third and fourth Volumes ... will be pleased to send one of them to the Printer hereof, to match these two, that the binding may be alike." Faulkner's notice of 4 June 1748 of the demand for *Clarissa* as "very great" is probably exaggerated, however, since as late as April 1758 Faulkner was trying to sell the complete *Clarissa* in seven volumes at 18s.11d. as compared with the London price of one guinea.

The main problem for readers was the length, as stated in the preface to *An Abridgement of Clarissa* published by William Sleater of the *Public Gazetteer* in 1756 in two volumes for 6s.6d. The National Library of Ireland copy appears to be one of two surviving copies, which are the only examples, as far as I can determine, of a Dublin edition of a major novel published by subscription.[141] It is also the only example of an edited version of a Dublin edition of a major novel, and as an abridgement of *Clarissa* it anticipates the London edition of 1769. The editor, a certain W. M., dedicates the edition to Lady Elizabeth Ponsonby from the family of the Earl of Bessborough and writes in a preface that "he was at once deeply affected and pleased at the amiable, and heavenly Light in which true Virtue and Morality were painted in it [*Clarissa*] and at the same time deterred and shocked at the horrid Appearance of Libertinism, Vice, and Irreligion, and had the Opinion of History in general, that it is written with a fine Intention of propagating Religion, Virtue, and Morality, and might very possibly be the means of reclaiming habitual Vice, and also be highly instructive to the Youth of both Sexes." Having heard complaints about the length, W. M. abridged the novel "to give Numbers of People a Taste of what is written with such a meritorious Design of improving the minds and Morals of almost every Degree and Station of Mankind, with Hopes also that they will not be contented or stop here, but proceed, (by reading the compleat History,) in Pursuit of many other Beauties." W. M. had also heard a "late judicious good Man" in Dublin say of *Clarissa* that it was not only good for youth but "proper to be perused by the Heads or Parents of every Family in Europe." Presumably employed by William Sleater, W. M. was able to locate 377 subscribers for 458 sets. Of the twenty subscribers who purchased more than one set three landed proprietors took thirty-seven sets among them, and two clergymen took seven sets each. The subscribers reflect the same landed and professional classes as the 203 library owners and the subscribers to the other four subscription editions of this study. The largest group 144 subscribers have the title "Esquire," which though ambiguous in Ireland as elsewhere was supposed to be used by persons ranking between gentleman and knight, as a *Dublin Evening Post* article of 2 October 1788 points out. Ninety-six subscribers are designated "Mr.," but thirteen of these are listed as merchants, and judging from other subscription editions in which occupations are specified, probably many others in this group were merchants. There are thirty-three who are peers, baronets, knights, or sons and daughters of these titled classes. The clerical group has only eighteen members and the legal group only three, as compared with the large number of clerics and lawyers among the library owners and the subscribers to the 1775 Dublin edition of Johnson's *Dictionary* and the 1777 Dublin edition of Goldsmith's *History of the Earth*. There are eighteen upper-level civil servants and a scattering of physicians, academics, and military officers. There appear to be no English subscribers unlike most Irish subscription editions, and another striking difference is the presence of 102 female subscribers

W. M.'s hopes that his abridged edition of *Clarissa* would encourage readers to tackle the full seven volumes of the unabridged edition must have been realized since James Potts announced his unabridged edition at 19s.6d. in three Dublin newspapers during May and June of 1765. Demand then dropped off until 1792 when Patrick Byrne, one of this study's primary examples of the Dublin–Philadelphia bookseller, issued a new Dublin reprint followed possibly by still another in Thomas Henshall's series of classical novels. Byrne's edition was received in Dumfries, Virginia, by Timothy Brundige, postmaster, bookseller, and one of Mathew Carey's many agents, on 2 January 1796.[142] Other abridgements were listed in Dublin newspapers in 1766 and 1769, and James Hoey in the *Dublin Mercury* for 16 September 1766 indicated that his abridged edition had "justly obtained an infinite number of admirers, as even though the vehicle of entertainment, it teaches the young, inexperienced heart to govern its passions, and regulate its desires, by shewing that virtue leads to pleasure, tranquility, and honour."

There is better documentation for the response to Irish reprints of *Clarissa* than to *Pamela*. The Trinity College, Dublin copy of the 1748–49 Dublin reprint was originally purchased by Catherine Moutray, mother of John Corry Moutray (1771–1859), of Favour Royal, County Tyrone, who inherited the set from his mother and marked such passages as Clarissa's denunciation of duelling in the second volume. This landed family also owned the copies now at Trinity College of the Dublin reprints of Fielding's *Tom Jones*, Smollett's *Peregrine Pickle*, and Sterne's *Tristram Shandy*. Although many well-known Irish readers, the Earl of Cork and Orrery, Lady Echlin, the Sheridan family, Letitia Pilkington, Dr. Skelton, Anne Donnellan, and the Delanys, responded enthusiastically to *Clarissa*, they were all friends of Richardson's and may have had London editions. Mrs. Delany discussed the novel with Dublin friends who probably did own the Dublin reprint, and Mrs. Delany herself generally followed the popular "Buy Irish" policy, as she noted in her letter of 15 July 1750.[143] The Dublin jurist and patriot John Philpott Curran (1750–1817) owned a Dublin reprint of *Clarissa* and sobbed "almost to suffocation, over the pathetic details of Richardson, particularly the will of Clarissa Harlowe, which he considered a masterpiece of pathos."[144]

Competing with Faulkner's *Clarissa* in the spring of 1748, Richard James brought out his Dublin reprint of Smollett's *Roderick Random* on 1 March 1748, according to the *Dublin Journal*, just five weeks after the London edition, though its price of 5s.5d. was not as much below the London price of six shillings as Dublin reprints usually were. James in *Esdall's News-Letter* for 20 May 1748, exaggerated the London sales figures in an effort to sell the novel: "This Work is so generally liked in London, that they have sold off two Editions (of 5,000 each) in less than three months, and are now printing a third, none of the second being to be had."[145] The National Library of Ireland copy of this first Dublin edition belonged to the sixth Viscount Powerscourt. James did another printing in 1749 called the third edition, although there appears to have been no second edition, and another in 1755 called the fourth edition; as the publisher of the *Dublin Gazette* James had ample opportunity to advertise his reprints. The Yale copy of the third edition was bought in 1759 by J. Samuel Waring of Waringstown, County Down, High Sheriff of Down in 1734, who also owned the Trinity College, Dublin, copy of the 1771 Dublin edition of Goldsmith's *History of England*. The 1768 edition was advertised in the *Corke Journal* for 15 March 1770, by Owen Kenelly as a part of his store of "Country Chapmen's Books." *Roderick Random* and *Gulliver's Travels* were the only books to be sold to readers in rural areas that can be classified as literary. A so-called eighth edition was done by James Williams in 1773 followed shortly by a ninth edition printed for the United Company of Booksellers in 1775 as volume one in its eight-volume *Select Works of Smollett*. In 1791 Richard Lewis, an Irish poet and journalist, prepared and printed his own abridgement of the novel presumably in response to a demand for a one-volume edition. There was still a reading public for the two-volume edition, however, and Thomas Henshall met their need in 1794 with a final eighteenth-century reprint as a part of his Ornamental Library of Classic Novels.[146] Henshall's former colleague in the Dublin book trade, Mathew Carey, now of the Philadelphia book trade, issued his own reprint of *Roderick Random* the same year.

Fielding's second major novel, *Tom Jones*, followed Richardson's *Clarissa* and Smollett's *Roderick Random* by less than a year. The London edition in six volumes was out by 10 February 1749 at eighteen shillings. According to the *Dublin Courant* the first Dublin reprint by John Smith in three volumes in much smaller type was out only a month later at 8s.8d., and a second edition in April with slightly different pagination in the first and third volumes. Since Smith reported on 31 January 1749 that he was printing the work, his agent must have obtained the sheets from the London printing house before publication. Smith's 1750 edition, a copy of which made its way to the Bibliothéque Nationale in Paris, is an exact reprint of his second edition. Few Dublin booksellers bothered to defend their unauthorized reprints, but an argument sometimes given by George Faulkner and others was that they corrected typographical errors in the London text. Dublin reprints of *Tom Jones* offer an easy opportunity to test this argument because the London first edition of 1749 lists on p. lxiii of the first volume fifty-six errata in the first five volumes. The three Smith editions correct none of the fifteen errata in the first and second volumes of the London edition and only four of the twelve errata in volumes four and five of the London edition.[147] Smith may have printed his first volume and part of his second volume from the London printing-house sheets and then obtained the published London edition with the errata list so that he could make corrections in the rest of his second volume and his third volume.[148] The Dublin edition of 1759 by four other Dublin booksellers perpetuates John Smith's failure to correct the errata of volumes one and two and most of three of the London edition. To take one example, "Church military" is not corrected to "Church militant" in Book I Chapter 10, but the same four errata are corrected from the third volume and all the errata continue to be corrected in volumes four and five of the London edition. The fifth Dublin edition of 1766 by the same four Dublin booksellers follows the same pattern.

The sixth Dublin edition of 1767 is a landmark. Printed for four Dublin booksellers not involved in the first five editions, the Hoeys, D. Chamberlaine, and James Potts, it corrects all fifty-six errata;

the "Church militant" triumphs at last. It was perhaps with this correct edition that Thomas Dermody fled County Clare for Dublin in 1785, carrying besides the novel only two shillings and a change of linen. Dermody often said that Tom Jones "determined him on his adventure." In a later poem "To Comic Romance" Dermody paid tribute to Tom Jones but even more to Joseph Andrews, whose Parson Adams, "the gymnastic Parson caught the smile/In cassocked wisdom, but resistless mirth;/Created to inform, and glad the earth." Dermody, who died at twenty-seven with the memorable words, "I am vicious because I like it," may have exemplified the fears of some Irish literary critics that Tom Jones was a poor model for the young.[149] This corrected Dublin edition of 1767 was probably the one James Rivington in New York offered for sale to Henry Knox in Boston in his letter to Knox of 15 May 1773.[150] Presumably the Dublin printer of 1767 used a later London edition which corrected the errata of the first London edition. In 1749 Smith had aimed to get his reprint out as soon as possible to take the market from the expensive London edition at home and perhaps to cut into the market in London itself where George Cockburn bought the copy now at Yale.[151] Still, he made some attempt, even if a half-hearted one, to issue a more correct text. Seventh and eighth Dublin editions followed in 1786 and 1794, the former being bought by the novel-reading Moutray family of Favour Royal, County Tyrone. Also in 1786 William Spotswood, trained in the Irish reprint industry, issued his own reprint of *Tom Jones* in Philadelphia. *Tom Jones* was the favorite Fielding novel among Irish library owners with thirty-four acquiring it, usually in one of the eight Dublin editions. At least two other upper-class families in the Dublin area approved of *Tom Jones*. Emily Fitzgerald of Carton, County Kildare, later Duchess of Leinster, wrote to her husband on 17 August 1761, that their friend Lord Powerscourt was reading *Tom Jones* aloud to them, and that their sons found the novel diverting. Her husband replied on 22 April 1762, that he had just sent Fielding's novels to Carton, and he hoped she would approve of the purchase.[152] Both of these noble families patronized the Irish reprints; the National Library copies of Johnson's *Rasselas* and Smollett's *Roderick Random* in Irish editions of 1748 and 1777 respectively, belonged to the Powerscourt family, and Dublin reprints of Johnson's *Dictionary* and *Lives of the Poets* and Goldsmith's *History of the Earth* to the Dukes of Leinster.

Irish reprints of Smollett's second novel the *Adventures of Peregrine Pickle* did not sell as well as those of his first novel or of Fielding's *Tom Jones*. Robert Main announced his edition in the *Dublin Journal* for 15 March 1751, less than three weeks after the first London edition, at 7s.6d., a price well below the London price of twelve shillings. To stimulate interest in his edition Main reported late in March that the novel in London had made "a great noise in all the polite Assemblies on account of some real Characters being exhibited in that Performance." Main presumably alluded to the "Memoirs of a Lady of Quality," reputedly Lady Vane, and Smollett's satire on characters generally perceived to be Lord Chesterfield, Fielding, Garrick, Lord Lyttelton, and others. No new edition was needed until November 1762 when three Dublin newspapers advertised a second edition "with material alterations" printed for Saunders, Potts, and Dyton in four volumes rather than the three of the first edition, and the third edition of 1768 was the same. The fourth edition printed by the United Company of Booksellers in 1775 is a three-volume 12mo. edition like the first, but the pagination and the size of the page are different. The Trinity College, Dublin, copy of the 1787 Dublin edition was owned by John Corry Moutray of the novel-reading landed family of Favour Royal, County Tyrone, cited in chapter four as owners of Richardson and Fielding. Two sets of this edition were received by Timothy Brundige in Dumfries, Virginia on 2 January 1796, from Mathew Carey in Philadelphia.[153] It was also in Samuel Campbell's bookshop in New York in 1794. This Dublin reprint of the second London edition preserves Smollett's boast in his preface: "A very large impression has been sold in England; another was bought up in a neighbouring kingdom." Unlike Richardson, Smollett was apparently happy to have the publicity generated by the Dublin reprints even if he didn't gain financially, though these sales may have helped him negotiate a more lucrative copyright for his next work. Further demand in the eighteenth century was met by an abridged edition by T. M'Donnell, Mathew Carey's former employer and a supplier of Dublin editions to Carey in Philadelphia, and Thomas Henshall's edition in 1796. *Peregrine Pickle* was in only twenty private libraries in Ireland as compared with *Roderick Random* in twenty-eight and provoked little comment.

The beginning of 1751 saw Smollett's *Peregrine Pickle* in Dublin, and the end of 1751 saw Fielding's *Amelia*. Perhaps encouraged by the reports from London that *Amelia* had sold a thousand copies on its first day, Dublin booksellers announced two competing Dublin reprints of the London edition published on 18 December 1751. Only two weeks after the London edition, George Risk and eight other Dublin booksellers said they would publish in a few days a four-volume 12mo. edition of *Amelia*; their announcement in the *Dublin Journal* included this note: "To satisfy the earnest Demand of the Public, this Work is printing in four Houses; and, for the greater Expedition, will be delivered sewed in blue paper. But in case another Edition should appear before this, 'tis presumed that the Public will suspend the Gratification of their Curiosity for a few Days, when they may be furnished with this, on perhaps easier Terms." The rival edition identified in the note was by John Smith, publisher of *Tom Jones*, and both editions appeared on January 7th. Both editions are four volumes of 12mo. bound into two volumes, but the Smith edition sold for 4s.4d. sewed or 5s.5d. bound while the Risk edition sold for slightly less but both well below the London price of twelve shillings. Smith claimed his edition had a hundred more pages and bigger and better type, and examination shows this to be essentially true, though there are actually only eighty-eight more pages. In rebuttal Risk and his group said: "Notwithstanding what has been insinuated by the Publisher of the other Edition, the Proprietors of this assure the Public, that it is printed verbatim from the London Copy, and that not one single Line is omitted in the whole work." Though both reprint the London edition verbatim, the Risk edition, like the London edition, has new paging for each of the four volumes, though the number of pages is significantly reduced through smaller type and margins, while the Smith edition has continuous pagination for the first two volumes and continuous pagination for the third and fourth volumes. Advertisements for the Risk edition stop after February 1st while the Smith edition is advertised through March 1752 and intermittently through 1 April 1755. Apparently it did not sell well since James Potts was advertising the Smith edition as late as 12 December 1761 and William Flyn in Cork as late as 9 May 1774. Among the Irish library owners, however, seven bought the Smith edition and only one the Risk edition. Other Dublin reprints may have come out in 1777 and in the Henshall series in 1795.

First announced in the *Dublin Gazette* for 3 March 1753, Smollett's third novel *The Adventures of Ferdinand Count Fathom*, lacked the appeal of its predecessors, and a new Dublin edition was not needed for nearly twenty years. The National Library copy belonged to Robert Smyth, a Trinity College, Dublin, graduate of 1778 and a solicitor, who wrote at the beginning of volume two in his set after the Count's loss of nearly two thousand pounds "Money makes the Mare go, Money, Money," presumably quoting from John Wolcott's *Ode to Pitt*. Further evidence of the unpopularity of the work is provided by a *Dublin Journal* report of a bankruptcy sale on 30 August 1755 by a Dublin bookseller whose stock included eight sets of the novel. James Potts tried to promote the sale of his new edition of the novel in 1772 by including excerpts in his *Hibernian Magazine* for December 1771 and the observation that the novel was "written with great spirit and knowledge of the world." The novel was not included in the Dublin edition of Smollett's *Select Works* in 1775 but possibly reprinted near the end of the century; Thomas Henshall in the *Hibernian Journal* for 17 January 1794 listed it as nineteenth in his project for reprinting twenty-eight "classic novels," but the popularity of the new London reprints by Cooke and Harrison may have prevented its publication.

The most controversial of all the novels of Richardson and Fielding was the *History of Sir Charles Grandison* because of the quarrel between Richardson and the Dublin booksellers carried on in pamphlets and in the newspapers of both Dublin and London.[154] George Faulkner had agreed to pay Richardson seventy guineas for publishing rights in Ireland, but three Dublin booksellers, John Exshaw, Henry Saunders, and Peter Wilson, got the sheets from workmen in Richardson's printing house and anticipated both Richardson and Faulkner. Richardson blamed all four Dublin booksellers, and the Irish papers accused Richardson of trying to destroy the Irish book trade by flooding Ireland with books printed in London. The Dublin reprint of November 1753 does not list the Dublin booksellers in the imprint of the first six volumes, but the seventh identifies Saunders though not Exshaw and Wilson. Richardson sent over 750 copies to Robert Main in Dublin to sell, but most of the demand had probably been met by the Dublin reprint which sold for two shillings less than the London edition, already reduced for sale in

Dublin. One of the buyers was Frederic Trench (1720-97), of Moate and Woodlawn, County Galway, father of Lord Ashtown; his autographed copy is now at Yale. By 4 January 1754 the Dublin reprint was also being sold in Belfast by the Joys and advertised in their *Belfast News-Letter.* No new edition was required until the 1765 edition, but in 1779 Thomas Walker envisaged a mass sale of the novel in the provinces by subscription. The first advertisement of many in provincial newspapers but not in Dublin papers appeared in the *Belfast News-Letter* of 24 August 1779: "In order to accommodate the Public in general with the above mentioned most ingenious and elegant Performance, which comprehends a complete System of all the relative and social Duties, and which for important Events, just Reflections, and beautiful Diction, has never been excelled, perhaps never equalled, the Proprietor has been prevailed on by several Ladies and Gentlemen, the Friends and Patrons of Virtue and Science, to publish one Volume monthly." The copies at Yale and the University of Virginia of this sixth Dublin edition of 1780, which was sold in Belfast, Coleraine, Cork, Derry, Kilkenny, Lisburn, and Newry, according to the newspapers, do not contain the list of subscribers that the advertisement goes on to specify; five of the library owners had it. Four sets of this Dublin edition were sent on 6 April 1795 by Patrick Byrne to Mathew Carey in Philadelphia as part of an order for Irish reprints totaling over £541, and Timothy Brundige had received them in Dumfries, Virginia, by 2 January 1796.[155] Carey ordered the Dublin edition from his old colleague, even though he had issued his own reprint of *Sir Charles Grandison* both in 1790 and 1794; William Spotswood, also trained in the Dublin reprint industry, had issued his Philadelphia reprint of the novel in 1786.

Richardson, Fielding, and Smollett were joined in 1760 by Laurence Sterne, whose Irish reprints dominate the sixth decade.[156] Dillon Chamberlaine and Samuel Smith in the *Dublin Journal* for 26 April 1760 gave the first announcement of their reprint of the first two volumes of the London edition of *Tristram Shandy* published only a month before.[157] To attract buyers there was the price advantage, 2s.8d.h. *vs* five shillings, later reduced to four shillings, and the two Dublin booksellers reported that all the London reviews had given the work "the highest Character." To their advertisement of volumes three and four on 14 February 1761 they added a warning to prospective readers: "A pyratical Edition of the above work being advertised to be published in a few Days, (printed in the Hedge or Ballad manner) the Public are requested to take Notice that the only Compleat Edition is printed by Dillon Chamberlaine and Samuel Smith, on a beautiful large Type, ornamented with an elegant Frontispiece of the Christening." Henry Saunders was no more a pirate than Chamberlaine and Smith since all had reprinted the same London edition, and ten days later in *Sleater's Gazetteer* Saunders gave the same price and the claim that his edition conformed completely to the London edition, as examination confirms.

A pioneering step towards a complete edition of *Tristram Shandy* was taken by Saunders in 1765 when he bound the first four volumes of the novel into one with continuous pagination; London publishers had not gotten this far. The same year Saunders published volumes five through eight paged continuously and combined them with his edition of the first four volumes to make the first collected edition well ahead of the London publishers. Saunders had rivals in 1765 because five Dublin booksellers announced in the *Dublin Journal* for 9 February 1765 their edition of volumes five through eight, but they did not publish a two-volume collected edition as did Saunders. According to the *Dublin Gazette* for 2 January 1762 a separate edition of volumes five and six was issued by Robert Bell, the outspoken apologist for Irish reprints and then American reprints cited in chapters one and three. *Tristram Shandy* was complete by 14 March 1767 with the publication of volume nine by four booksellers, now joined by their former rival Henry Saunders, and Kenneth Monkman finds this nine-volume Dublin edition bound in two volumes the "earliest known collected edition of the complete text of *Tristram*: a tribute to Irish piratical initiative."[158] The Yale set of this complete Dublin edition was first owned by a member of the famous London Bluestockings, Elizabeth Vesey, addressed by Sterne himself on 20 June 1761 as "the most penetrating of her sex," as "a System of harmonic Vibrations," and as "the sweetest and best tuned of all Instruments."[159] Mrs. Vesey must not have believed her friend Sterne was harmed by her purchase of the Dublin reprint rather than the London edition. Her response to the edition is not preserved, but the letters of Elizabeth Carter, another of the Bluestockings, indicate that Mrs. Vesey wrote often about Sterne, of whom Mrs. Carter disapproved. Mrs. Carter's letter of 18 April

1768 in reply to Mrs. Vesey's, in which Sterne must have inserted a paragraph, notes: "I thought the tone of one paragraph in your Letter did not seem your own, even before you gave me an intimation that it belonged to the *Sentimental Traveller*, whom I neither have read nor probably ever shall."[160] Other Dublin editions followed in 1776, 1779, 1780, and an undated edition by T. Henshall c. 1795, three sets of which were received by Timothy Brundige in Dumfries, Virginia, on 2 January 1796.[161] The Trinity College, Dublin, set of the 1776 edition was owned by the Moutray family again.

John Exshaw may later have regretted the article in his *Magazine* for October 1760 which called the third and fourth volumes of *Tristram Shandy* "a spurious bantling, without one lineament of the supposed father," since he was one of the Dublin booksellers who reprinted the ninth volume in 1767. Mrs. Delany and her circle were among the Dublin readers in May 1760 for whom the novel was in Burke's phrase in an article widely reprinted in Irish periodicals "a perpetual series of disappointments." Like her husband Dean Delany, she thought works of "*that kind*" ought to be discouraged, though her friend Mrs. Clayton believed the reader should trust her own resources and bid "defiance to any injury such books could do her." Mrs. Delany mentioned another friend who declined to buy the Dublin reprint, even though he heard the Dublin booksellers "cry it up so much."[162] On the other hand, the Rev. Philip Skelton of Fintona, County Donegal, was so amused that he could not "for two or three days attend seriously to his devotions."[163]

One of the 203 Irish library owners gave the most detailed reaction to *Tristram Shandy* in its Irish dress. Richard Griffith of Dublin, whose library, rich in Dublin reprints including the 1774 Dublin edition of Sterne's *Works*, descended to his son Richard Griffith of Millicent, Naas, County Kildare, and then to his son Sir Richard Griffith, on whose death in 1878 it was sold. In the preface to his work the *Triumvirate* (1764), Griffith, using the pseudonym *Biographer Triglyph*, calls Sterne "that anomalous, heteroclite genius," whose principal end was to inculcate humanity and benevolence. But Sterne was writing for the moment rather than for posterity and hence gave his readers "rather *more sauce than pig*." Of volumes five and six, which are better than others, Griffith writes: "There is a good deal of laughable impertinence in it. He has repeated the same *empty humour* there, of an *unlettered* page, and has given us a *carte blanche*, in this last. Whatever is neither quite sense, nor absolute nonsense, is true Shandeic. However, through the whole, there is some entertainment for a splenetic person, though none at all for a rational one."[164] Griffith's narrative itself is of three friends, Andrews, Beville, and Carewe, their marriages, and their lives together, but it uses many devices from *Tristram Shandy*, including the blank pages that Griffith condemns in *Tristram Shandy*. In an appendix at the end of volume one Griffith has three blank pages followed by the comment: "I must here ingenuously resign the palm to *Mr. Shandy*, in the *novelty* of this thought; nor shall I in the least, pretend to dispute any merit with him, before *modern readers*, by hinting that my conceit, though poor, has some little meaning in it." The Dublin bookseller David Hay sent two copies of Griffith's work to the Bradford bookshop in Philadelphia in 1770.[165]

A second reaction by Richard Griffith to the Dublin *Tristram Shandy* was his *Posthumous works of a late celebrated genius, deceased*, published for seven Dublin booksellers in 1770 and dedicated to Lord Charlemont, one of the 203 library owners; it bears the half-title, *the Koran: or, The Life, Character, and Sentiments of Tria Juncta in Uno, M. N. A. or Master of no Arts*. The persona appears to be Sterne; he was born in Clonmell, Ireland, the son of an English officer, with friends from Sterne's writings like Le Fevre. He wrote *Tristram Shandy* "in mere idleness and sport," though there were also "some striking passages" and "many foibles ridiculed, and much charity and benevolence instilled." The first part of the work is an autobiography, rambling, digressive, in the Sterne manner, and the second and third parts 359 maxims called "The Koran," usually citing famous thinkers or historical figures.[166] Robert Bell, formerly of the Dublin reprint industry, reprinted Griffith's *Koran* as Sterne's in 1778 in Philadelphia.

Sterne's second work, the *Sermons of Mr. Yorick*, volumes one and two, was announced in the *Dublin Journal* by four Dublin booksellers only two months after the first Dublin editions of *Tristram Shandy*, and these booksellers had another edition out by 10 March 1761 and still another in 1766. Also in 1766 the third and fourth volumes were advertised in the *Dublin Journal* for 19 April 1766 by fourteen Dublin booksellers including Robert Bell, who transferred to the Philadelphia book trade the next year, with a brief description:

"Truly Shandenian, conveying Knowledge and Instruction in a Manner peculiar to himself, which may have its Use in engaging some in a Discourse where Wit and Morality are intimately connected, who could not think of reading a Sermon." Anticipating the London collected edition by three years, the four volumes were bound into two by 31 May 1766, and a second collected edition was out the next year. Sterne's *Sermons* got no reviews from the Irish press or from individual readers, unlike Charles Churchill's *Sermons*, for example. They did not sell well, and by 19 May 1767 the Dublin booksellers had reduced the price of the collected Sermons as part of a campaign to encourage the purchase of Irish rather than London editions. Sterne's *Sermons* were completed with the announcement of volumes five and six by James Hoey and other Dublin booksellers in Hoey's *Dublin Mercury* for 30 September 1769 and announcements by northern booksellers in the *Belfast News-Letter*, and there were other Dublin collected editions in 1775 and 1785. The *Sermons* were in thirty-one private libraries in Ireland, mostly in Dublin editions. Mathew Carey in Philadelphia and Timothy Brundige in Dumfries, Virginia, were selling the Dublin reprint by 2 January 1796.[167]

Sterne's last work *A Sentimental Journey through France and Italy* was purchased, as was *Tristram Shandy*, by thirty-seven Irish library owners, more than owned any other novel by a major author. The Dublin reprint was out by 16 April 1768 according to the *Dublin Journal*, less than two months after the London edition, and a second edition by thirteen Dublin booksellers was out in August. In Kilkenny Edmund Finn advertised both Dublin editions in his *Leinster Journal*, but in Belfast James Magee listed his own reprint on 28 July 1768, which was also sold in Newry by George Stevenson in August. The second edition met the demand until 1769 when the thirteen issued a third edition that George Faulkner was still advertising in 1773. The second edition, however, was still being sold in 1775 when Mary Houston of the landed family of Orangefield and Roddens, County Down, purchased the copy now at Yale, and Robert Addison bought his copy in England and took it with him to Canada in 1791.[168] Other copies that crossed the Atlantic were those sent by David Hay of Dublin to the Bradford bookshop in Philadelphia on 13 April 1770.[169] Two graduates of the Irish book trade reprinted *A Sentimental Journey* in Philadelphia, Robert Bell in 1770 and William Duane in 1801.

Perhaps to compete with the many reprints of Sterne in the Sterne decade James Hoey advertised Smollett's *Adventures of Sir Launcelot Greaves* more widely than any of Smollett's other works. Hoey's first advertisement in *Pue's Occurrences* for 30 January 1762 contains a brief critique that stresses Smollett's skill at character delineation. Hoey had difficulty unloading his second edition of 1762 and was still advertising it ten years later in his *Dublin Mercury*. Though Hoey's editions were to London publishers piracies like most Dublin editions, Hoey warned his readers in his newspaper in November 1767 of a rival "pyrated edition" without copperplates and abridged in several places. Albeit one of Hoey's writers, Jeoffry Wagstaffe on 27 December 1766 declined to promote the sale of his employer's edition and envisioned Sir Launcelot Greaves sinking in the River of Dulness "under the weight of Don Quixote's armour which he stole." Wagstaffe also envisaged the same fate for Richardson's *Clarissa* reprinted by his employer's rival.

James Hoey had better luck with the *Expedition of Humphry Clinker*, Smollett's last and greatest novel, which he announced in his newspaper with fourteen other Dublin booksellers in July 1771 at 5s.5d. as compared with the London price of 9s.9d. Like other Dublin booksellers who ran periodicals, Hoey used his newspaper to "puff" his reprints:

> Dr. Smollett's reputation is so justly established, particularly in the walk of novel writing that very little need be said to recommend the present performance to the public. The characters are marked with all that strength of colouring, for which Smollett's pencil is deservedly celebrated; and the reader is either continually entertained with some whimsical relation, or what is still better, instructed with some original remarks upon men and things, that do honour to the good-sense and humanity of the author. In fact, this performance is something greatly preferable to most novels; it is a pleasing, yet an important Lesson on life; and that part of it that describes the Scotch Nation, is at once calculated to entertain the most gay, and to give the serious a very useful fund of information.

The Trinity College, Dublin, set of this first Dublin edition was owned by the Montgomery landed family of Conway, County

Donegal, during the eighteenth and nineteenth centuries, several of whose members autographed the set. Dublin editions of 1774, 1781, 1784, 1790, 1793, and 1795, show a continued appeal to readers in Ireland and such places as Philadelphia and Dumfries, Virginia, where Timothy Brundige received sets from Mathew Carey on 2 January 1796.[170] It was also part of the pioneering step taken by Dublin booksellers in 1775–76 to collect four of the five major Smollett novels in the eight-volume *Select Works*, a collected edition that anticipated both the Edinburgh edition of 1790 and the London edition of 1793–94.

For the Irish book trade Smollett was not only a novelist but a translator of major rank. Smollett's translations of Voltaire's *Works* and Fenelon's *Telemachus* in their Dublin editions seem not to have won a large audience, but some copies of the 1793 edition of the latter did cross the Atlantic to Samuel Campbell's New York bookshop in 1794. Since Smollett was so profoundly influenced by Le Sage and Cervantes, his translations of *Gil Blas* and *Don Quixote* are of special interest. His *Gil Blas* in four volumes was reprinted three times in Ireland, in 1759, 1767, and 1785, and probably in 1795 as a part of Thomas Henshall's project, and twenty-six of the Irish library owners bought it, as did the Cork Library Society. As with most of the Irish editions, there was an American audience. The ever enterprising Patrick Byrne whether working in Dublin or Philadelphia, sent three sets of *Gil Blas* on 6 April 1795 to Mathew Carey to sell in his Philadelphia bookshop or to send to his many agents along the coast.[171] This late in the century the Dublin edition had to compete for American readers with American reprints of 1790 and 1795 by none other than William Spotswood in Philadelphia, Byrne's former colleague in the Dublin book trade.

Smollett's translation of *Don Quixote* was in forty-one Irish private libraries, second only to his *History of England*. The Dublin editions of 1766 and 1783 are of little significance, but John Chambers in 1796 printed an impressive four-volume large octavo edition for 338 subscribers to 647 sets which he advertised in the *Dublin Journal* for 27 February 1796 as "the most elegant Typographical Performance ever attempted and executed in Ireland." Chambers dedicated the edition to the Provost, Fellows and Scholars of Trinity College, Dublin, as "an Endeavor in the Art of Printing in Ireland," and in another notice as "an effort towards promoting a national taste for beautiful embellished typography." In addition to its typographical interest, the Chambers edition is important because its subscriber list provides the only concrete evidence of the size and nature of the audience for Irish reprints of Smollett's works. Of the total subscription of 647, 331 sets were purchased by twenty-one Irish and six English booksellers for their customers in Ireland, England, and the United States. The largest purchaser was the well-known Dublin bookseller John Archer, who subscribed for one hundred sets. John Archer also sold the competing London edition by C. Cooke of the same year as did several other Dublin booksellers as well as Thomas White in Cork, who subscribed for forty sets of the Chambers edition. But the six London booksellers, among them George Nicol, Bookseller to his Majesty, must have preferred the Chambers to the Cooke edition; by now there was no risk of confiscation in England of the Chambers edition since copyright had expired. This was true also of the five Londoners, the three landed proprietors of Counties Cumberland, Buckinghamshire, and Northumberland, the two gentlemen of Bath and Newcastle, and R. Bowyer, Miniature Painter to her Majesty.

Predictably, the Irish subscribers were mostly from the landed and professional classes like the 203 library owners and the subscribers to the other four subscription editions stressed in this study. Fourteen of the library owners had it, and six of the subscribers to *Don Quixote* also subscribed to the 1775 Dublin edition of Johnson's *Dictionary*, and six other subscribers to *Don Quixote* also subscribed to the 1777 Dublin edition of Goldsmith's *History of the Earth*. The Chambers edition at two guineas according to his first announcement in the *Dublin Evening Post* for 16 May 1795 was about the same price as the Johnson and the Goldsmith but far beyond the price range of most Irishmen. The largest group 189 subscribers have the title "Esquire"; a spot check of the thirty-eight who lack this designation or some other title suggests these were merchants. There were also twenty-one clergymen, twenty politicians including sixteen Members of Parliament, nineteen peers and baronets, and a scattering of military officers and physicians. Ten women subscribed in addition to Mrs. Harriet Colbert, a Dublin bookseller who subscribed for six sets. Chambers, who would transfer his book trade activities from Dublin to New York in 1805, on 26 March 1794 asked Mathew

Carey in Philadelphia to get some subscriptions to *Don Quixote*, and Carey replied on 19 June 1794 that he might be able to sell six sets. He was paying Chambers for books as late as 15 February 1803. One of the twenty-one subscribers to the edition Patrick Byrne sent a set to Carey to sell in 1796.[172] A subscriber for twelve sets, John Rice in 1803 would transfer to the Baltimore book trade; his kinsmen in Philadelphia Henry and Patrick Rice were selling the Chambers edition in 1796.[173] Ten sets of the Chambers edition are in institutional libraries in the United States today, far more than the two London editions of the 1790s and more than any London edition since the 1755 edition.

By 1771 all four major novelists were dead, and Dublin collected editions for Sterne, the most widely read novelist in the Irish reprints, began to appear and an expanded body of writing on the major novelists in the two leading magazines, both published by publishers of the major novels. First published in 1770 by Saunders, Chamberlaine, and Potts, Sterne's *Works* were purchased by fifty-four of the library owners, a number exceeded only by owners of Johnson's *Dictionary* and *Lives of the Poets*, and Gibbon's *Decline and Fall of the Roman Empire*. Other Dublin editions of the *Works* followed in 1774, 1775, 1779, 1780, and 1794. Edmond Malone in London owned the 1774 Dublin reprint, and nine sets of the 1794 edition are in institutional libraries of the United States today. Patrick Byrne published the 1794 edition, and he sold four sets on 21 July 1801 to Mathew Carey just a few months before his own transfer to the Philadelphia book trade; Timothy Brundige had two of these sets in his Dumfries, Virginia shop by 2 January 1796.[174] Not included in the *Works* were Sterne's letters in their various forms. *Letters from Yorick to Eliza* had been reprinted by Thomas Armitage before Sterne's death and printed again in 1775 at "a sixth part of the London price," twice in 1776, and then twice in 1776 as part of the collected *Letters of the late Rev. Mr. Laurence Sterne* in three volumes, once for Armitage, and again for twenty-three Dublin booksellers to meet the heavy demand in the English-speaking world; one of the twenty-three William Spotswood would sell sets later from his Philadelphia bookshop. Both trained in the Irish book trade, one Philadelphia bookseller John Dunlap reprinted *Letters from Yorick to Eliza* in 1773, and another Philadelphia bookseller Robert Bell reprinted *Letters of Sterne* in 1778. The English traveller Mark Elstob saw this latter edition being printed in Dublin and noted, contrary to his expectations, that the paper and type were good, and that a corrector attended the press. He also reported that *Tristram Shandy* was popular in Ireland but not *A Sentimental Journey* or his own favorite the *Sermons*, which he found "more instructing" and "more entertaining than Shandy." Had the *Sermons* been entitled "Uncle Toby's Plush Breeches, they, in all probability, would have been more universally known, and better accepted."[175] Several of the spurious collections of Sterne letters were also reprinted in Dublin, and Patrick Byrne sent copies of one of these the *Original Letters of the late Reverend Mr. Laurence Sterne* to Mathew Carey's bookshop in 1795.[176] Two of the publishers of this collection in 1788 would join the United States book trade, Byrne in 1801 and Bernard Dornin in 1803 after the collapse of the book reprinting industry in Ireland.

At the opposite pole from collected editions of Sterne's works was the popular distillation of Sterne the *Beauties of Sterne; Including all his Pathetic Tales, and most distinguished Observations on Life*, reprinted twice in Dublin in 1784. Samuel and Harriet Colbert, who reprinted the work, sold it, and lent it from their circulating library, made an extravagant claim for it in the *Hibernian Journal* for 26 March 1784: "A Selection of the Beauties of Sterne, is what has been looked for by a Number of his Admirers for some Time, well knowing they would form such a Volume, as this, nor any other Language could equal"; Harriet Colbert reprinted it again in 1788. The Trinity College, Dublin, copy of this exceedingly rare edition belonged to the large and distinguished Madden family, with several seats in County Monaghan and County Fermanagh. Notations by three members of the family are in the volume from three generations beginning with Catherine Madden's autograph of 3 November 1790. Catherine Madden was grandchild of the famous writer and philanthropist Samuel Madden (1686–1765), who had subscribed to the 1756 Dublin edition of Richardson's *Clarissa*. Another of the publishers of the 1784 *Beauties of Sterne* was William Spotswood, who also had it in his circulating library and then reprinted it in Philadelphia in 1789. A similar work *Beauties of Fielding* was reprinted by Dublin booksellers in 1783 and by one of their former colleagues Mathew Carey in Philadelphia in 1792.

Three of the leading publishers of novel reprints in Dublin were also publishers of the two principal Dublin magazines of the latter decades of the century, *Exshaw's* and the *Hibernian*. John Exshaw reprinted all four of the major English novelists, and James Potts, publisher of the *Hibernian Magazine* 1771–75, also all four, and Thomas Walker, publisher of the *Hibernian* 1775–1805, all but Fielding; presumbly all three used articles on the English writers in their magazines to publicize their reprints. Exshaw or one of his employees in the November 1782 issue finds Fielding and Richardson both masters of romance though quite different. Taking *Don Quixote* and *Gil Blas* as his models, Fielding excels in humor, in representing characters from common life, and in epic technique. But Richardson showed "the deepest penetration into the human heart, displayed a surprising power in describing it, and exhibited an instance of pathetic narration which has not been equalled"; he was "the Shakespeare of Romance." The September 1783 issue of *Exshaw's Magazine*, however, agrees with Jeoffry Wagstaffe of the *Dublin Mercury*, whose proprietor James Hoey reprinted Richardson and Fielding, that Richardson "is apt to be tedious, and to fall into a minuteness of detail, which is often unnecessary." The *Hibernian Magazine* for June 1787 picks up on an earlier article in November 1777 dubbing Fielding "the English Cervantes" and also the nature of his humor pursued in *Exshaw's Magazine*. The writer finds *Don Quixote* and Fielding's novels examples of serious humor rather than comic humor: "Fielding's grand talent was grave humour, and even his Partridge and Slip-Slop are more related to that class than to Comic." Though Fielding's novels are more humorous, Richardson's characters provide better models for the young according to the *Hibernian* for February 1789. No literary work displays morality and piety to greater advantage than *Clarissa*, whose heroine Richardson meant to hold up as a model of female virtue just as he meant to hold up Sir Charles Grandison as a model of male virtue. On the other hand, Fielding in making Tom Jones an attractive character also makes his lechery attractive to the young. Mathew Carey in Philadelphia reprinted this *Hibernian* article in his own magazine the *American Museum* for August 1791.

Exshaw's *Magazine* for March 1774, after reprinting without acknowledgement some of Burke's *Annual Register* article of 1760 on Sterne, comments on the popularity of Sterne's novels. Of *Tristram Shandy*, reprinted by Exshaw in 1767, the writer observes: "All people read, most applauded, but few understood it." *A Sentimental Journey* is "one of the most engaging compositions in any language, and the writer, presumably thinking of Exshaw's three editions, asks if there is any one who has not read it; Exshaw would reprint the novel a fourth time in 1780. James Potts and Thomas Walker of the *Hibernian Magazine* were more apt to include excerpts from Sterne's letters rather than commentary on the novels since both reprinted Sterne's *Letters* in 1776 and Potts also Sterne's *Works* in 1775 and 1789. Reprinting excerpts from Sterne without commentary was Walker's pattern in the *Hibernian* for the next decade, but the 1790s offer more criticism to the readers of the *Hibernian* and its proprietor's reprints. In a March 1791 article "On the Affectation of Sentiment and Sensibility," Walker or one of his writers shows Sterne's enormous influence on the emotions of the young. Young women in imitation of Sterne's character have become "forlorn Marias breathing their sympathetic sorrows at a ball," whose sentimentality has made them easy targets for romantic young men. Sterne's sensibility is a virtue, but young people misuse it or affect it. At least one *Hibernian* writer, however, defends Sterne against attacks on his originality. A certain M. H. in the issue for September 1798 claims that though Sterne got something of his whimsical sentiments and his style from Montaigne, this does not detract from his merit. Dublin readers should acknowledge Sterne's skill in using sources: "We ought not to withhold our admiration of his ingenuity in so nicely blending the sentiments of other writers, though differing in style and character, with his own. His phraseology and humour commonly struck his readers as equally original, peculiar, appropriate, and uniform: and though, in many stances, we can no longer insist on the first quality, we can hardly deny him the credit of preserving the others."

Beyond excerpts from Smollett's novels and his *Travels Through France and Italy*, reprinted by Exshaw in 1766, 1772, and 1792, Exshaw in his *Magazine* did little to publicize his reprints, but one article in March 1785 is worthy of notice because of its retrospective look at Smollett's novels. *Roderick Random* established Smollett's reputation so solidly that later works known or even suspected to proceed from his hand such as *Adventures of an Atom* reprinted by Exshaw in 1769 were guaranteed success, and Exshaw's and other Irish reprints of his works still have an extensive sale. Though *Peregrine Pickle* was well received by readers of the Irish reprints, it is now generally regarded as inferior to the first novel. *Ferdinand Count Fathom* and *Sir Launcelot Greaves* rank below the first two novels, but Exshaw or one of his writers sees them as "still in the list of what may be called reading novels." In *Humphry Clinker*, reprinted by Exshaw in 1771, 1774, and 1781, "an admirable knowledge of life and manners is displayed; and most useful lessons are given, applicable to interesting, but to very common situations." Two years later Thomas Walker in his *Hibernian Magazine* took up the theme of wit and humor in the novel. Smollett is one of the great masters of humor, but Sterne is not mentioned. The other great humorist among the novelists is Fielding, but Fielding represents serious humor and Smollett comic, although *Humphry Clinker*, reprinted by Walker in 1774, "affords exquisite examples of Serious Humour."

The most ambitious project by the Dublin book trade for reprinting and selling major English novels, however, was not by the proprietors of the leading magazines, Exshaw, Potts, and Walker, but by Thomas Henshall in the last decade of the century. Henshall's project to reprint twenty-eight "classic novels" began with *Tom Jones* published in nine separate numbers with engravings at 6d.h. each during the first five months of 1794 according to the *Hibernian Journal*. When he announced the third number on 17 February 1794 with its engraving of "the beautiful Sophia entreating her Father to desist from forcing her to marry Blifil," Henshall reported that he was "highly gratified having adopted a Publication so pleasing to all Ranks." The nine numbers were bound together and sold at the end of May for 6s.6d. with eleven copper plates. On Henshall's list Fielding's *Joseph Andrews* was third, Smollett's *Roderick Random* fourth, and Sterne's *Tristram Shandy* fifth. A development that augured ill for Henshall's project and the Irish reprint industry in general was the announcement in August 1794 by a leading Dublin bookseller John Archer that he was selling the series of classical novels published in London by C. Cooke at sixpence a number, slightly less than the charge by Henshall; this was the series that Henshall himself was reprinting. Archer sold a bound *Tom Jones* for two shillings less than Henshall. After reprinting *Tristram Shandy* Henshall urged prospective customers on 16 January 1795, in the *Hibernian Journal* to buy his reprints rather than London editions "to the discouragement of the Arts and Manufactures" of Ireland. Thomas M'Donnell of the *Hibernian Journal*, who had formerly employed Mathew Carey, and who continued to sell Irish reprints to Carey in Philadelphia, sold the sixty classic novels published by Harrison in London at Henshall's price. In Henshall's list Smollett's *Humphry Clinker* was seventh, Fielding's *Amelia* eighth, and Smollett's *Peregrine Pickle* eleventh, with Richardson's three at the very end. Since copies of few of these survive, and there is no newspaper evidence that the novels in the lower half of the list were published, the two London reprint series may have lead Henshall to drop his project. Unlike other publishers of magazines, Henshall did not use his new *Minerva Magazine* to review his new reprints of the English novelists.

Irish booksellers, then, successfully reprinted the major English novels of the time. They were able to acquire sheets from London printing offices or published copies fast enough to reprint them in Ireland within a month or two, sometimes in more than one edition, at much reduced prices, and demand was strong enough to make it profitable to reprint these novels with some regularity until the end of the century. Since many of the publishers of the four major English novelists also published magazines and newspapers, they had unusual opportunities for advertising and reviewing these novelists to enhance sales. Five of the publishers of Richardson, Fielding, Smollett, and Sterne in Ireland, Robert Bell, Patrick Byrne, John Chambers, Bernard Dornin, and William Spotswood, continued these reprinting activities in America, and other booksellers in America trained in the Irish reprint industry such as Mathew Carey, William Duane, John Dunlap, and Thomas Kirk issued their own reprints of these four giants of English letters. Irish booksellers, whether in Ireland itself or in America, thus augmented the audience for the major novelists in Ireland, Britain, and America. Although these booksellers usually reprinted the London editions without changes, they on occasion made modest contributions to bibliography and the book arts. Examples include the corrections in Fielding's *Tom Jones*, the abridgement of Richardson's *Clarissa*, the collected editions of Sterne's *Tristram Shandy* and his *Sermons*, Smollett's *Select Works*, and the typography of the 1796 John Chambers edition of Smollett's *Don Quixote*.

5

Repringting the great CHAM and his Satellite

As the British writer with the most impressive claim to be the literary giant of the age, or "that great CHAM of literature," in the words of Tobias Smollett, [177] Samuel Johnson is inextricably linked with his greatest biographer James Boswell. In Ireland itself Johnson's voluminous writings, usually in Dublin reprints, were in more private and community libraries than those of any other major writer of his time, and they were more often advertised and reviewed in Irish periodicals and in other forms of written communication. Dublin editions of Johnson's many works were also widely sold in both Britain and the Americas, and they survive in more institutional libraries than those of any major writer of this study. Irish booksellers probably made more money from their reprints of Johnson than from any other leading writer, but they also gave him more publicity than he would have gotten from the London editions. Boswell published much less, but the one Irish reprint of his *Life of Johnson* survives in more copies than any single Irish edition of a major writer. Johnson's attitude towards the Irish reprints is unknown, but his objections were probably not as great as those of such authors as Richardson and Goldsmith. Johnson did not share the belief of the London booksellers in perpetual copyright. He wrote to the well-known publisher William Strahan on 7 March 1774 after the London booksellers had lost their plea in the House of Lords for perpetual copyright that the Lords were right. Although "an Author should retain during his Life the sole right of printing and selling his work," and this right should continue for perhaps thirty years after his death, he or his heirs or publisher should not have perpetual copyright. Man as a social creature must give up after an appropriate time a natural right such as copyright to the common good.[178] Boswell shared his mentor's opposition to perpetual copyright, and his involvement in the question of literary property will be examined in detail.

Although Johnson's earlier works such as his poem *London* and his tragedy *Irene* were reprinted in Dublin in 1738 and 1749 respectively, the Dublin edition of the *Rambler* seems to have been his first work to create much stir in Ireland or elsewhere.[179] Individual *Rambler* essays appeared in Faulkner's *Dublin Journal* and the *Dublin Gazette* from time to time during the years 1750–51. Faulkner first announced them on 19 June 1750 with considerable fanfare: "As there is a general and just complaint by all Strangers who come to this Kingdom, as well as from the Natives who have travelled abroad, that polite Amusements are much wanting in this great City, especially Papers of Entertainment, which are carried on weekly in most great Towns of Europe: It is proposed by George Faulkner, Printer hereof, to publish one every Thursday (or oftener, if required), under the Title of The *Rambler*, which Paper is now carrying on in London with the greatest Success, being wrote by a Sett of Gentlemen of the greatest Learning, Wit, and Abilities; and is allowed to be equal to those excellent Writings of the Spectators, Tatlers, and Guardians, which have improved the Minds and Morals of most People who have read them." Although Faulkner did not adhere to his ambitious plan of printing an essay each week, interest was sufficiently keen that he reprinted the London collected edition of July 1752 on 12 December 1752 in a six-pocket-volume set and in a three-volume set. Though the London edition of 1752 had taken over the translations of mottoes and other quotations from the authorized Edinburgh edition of 1750–51, Faulkner was the first to incorporate translations into the text, and the 1756 London edition preserved Faulkner's innovation.[180] Charles O'Conor wrote to Faulkner of his edition on 4 May 1757 that the *Rambler* and Johnson's other works had "set him (as Mr. Pope expresses it) 'at the Top of the Sublime Character.'"[181] Since Faulkner's nephew and successor was advertising the same edition of the *Rambler* at the same price as late as 1 July 1780, it must not have sold well. Nevertheless, there was sufficient demand from Ireland and elsewhere to warrant reprintings in 1785 and 1793, and Timothy Brundige in Dumfries, Virginia, sold the latter edition for Mathew Carey;[182] Thomas Kirk, formerly of the Cork book trade, issued a New York reprint in 1812. Among the 203 private libraries in Ireland the *Rambler* was fifth in popularity. Four readers, all landed gentry, put down deposits to take the Dublin *Rambler* from the Armagh Public Library during the years 1796–1800.

The *Idler*, Johnson's second group of periodical essays, appeared first as individual essays in Sleater's *Public Gazetteer* during the period 1759–60 and then were collected in two volumes and published by Peter Wilson on 12 December 1761. Samuel Richardson had made Peter Wilson's name especially abhorrent to the London book trade because of his pirating of Richardson's *Sir Charles Grandison* in 1753. Wilson's reprint of the *Idler* essays were originally published in the *Univeral Chronicle* of London, but when they were collected in 1761 for the London edition, *Idler* 22, the powerful beast-fable on the horrors of war usually called "The Vulture" was not included. Wilson must have reprinted from the newspaper rather than from the London collected edition since *Idler* 22 is in his edition; thus the Dublin reprint is the first complete collected edition. In his advertisement in the *Dublin Journal* Wilson does not mention his addition of "The Vulture" but simply quotes from the *Monthly Review* for November 1761: "As these Papers have been so long before the Public, all we shall add and concerning them, is that the Rambler was no Idler, neither is the Idler a Rambler, However it must be allowed that the hand of Mr. Johnson is conspicuous enough in this Work to recommend it to a Place in the Library of every Man of Taste." The *Idler* had a limited appeal, and no further Dublin edition was needed in the eighteenth century.

Johnson won his greatest fame among readers of the Dublin editions as lexicographer. Of the 203 private libraries in Ireland, 113 had Johnson's *Dictionary*, the only work by the eight major authors in most libraries, usually in one of the several Dublin editions. The great London folio edition of 1755 printed in two thousand copies selling for £4.105.0d. was never reprinted in Dublin, but in 1758 the shorter 1756 London octavo edition was reprinted by G. and A. Ewing of Dublin at seven shillings for a one-volume octavo edition. The Ewings included the preface to the London octavo edition and Johnson's own preface but then added their own statement: "The Editors of this Dublin Edition have endeavoured to render it more worthy of the public attention, by adding at full length, the Author's curious preface to the Folio Edition, his History of the English language, and by inserting in their proper places, about 500 Words from the Folio Edition, none of which are contained in the London Octavo: As to Paper, Print and Correction, they will be found, on comparison, much superior, although the Book is given for near one half of the price of the London Edition." The editors of this rare Dublin reprint are not identified, but one of them was probably John Morris, noted in the newspapers as the corrector of the Ewing edition of the *Dictionary* in 1775. During the years 1756–89 Morris edited three Roman Catholic works published by subscription in Dublin, and he subscribed to at least four more subscription works including the 1756 *Clarissa* cited in chapter four. A second edition was published by Thomas Ewing in 1764, and his advertisements in Sleater's *Gazetteer* for 9 August 1763 and 2 December 1766 assure the buyer: "To this Edition are added the English Grammar, all omitted by the Author in the London edition of this Abridgement." Thomas Ewing's third edition of 1768 adds to the London preface the same note used above in the 1758 edition. Norborne Berkeley, Lord Botetourt, Governor of Virginia 1768–70, owned this edition,[183] and the *National Union Catalog* lists twelve copies in the United States without including the Yale copy that I have examined but only seven of the 1766 London edition that it reprinted. One of the Trinity College, Dublin, copies has several autographs and the dates 1790 and 1848, with ownership changing from William Colles, Esquire, to the Trinity College Historical Society to the Trinity College Lending Library. The Cashel Diocesan Library, County Tipperary, founded c.1744, had it,[184] and James Rivington in New York offered it for sale to Henry Knox for his bookshop in Boston on 15 March 1773.[185]

On 16 April 1772 Thomas Ewing first announced in the *Dublin Journal* his plan to publish a fourth edition by subscription in two volumes quarto, and the progress of this impressive edition corrected by John Morris may be followed through this newspaper and the *Hibernian Journal* until its publication on 24 December 1774, with the date 1775 in the imprint. The subscription list in the edition shows that 280 subscribers signed up for 401 sets, though Ewing originally called for only two hundred subscriptions. Fifteen booksellers, including ten in Dublin and others in Belfast,

Cork, and Limerick, purchased 115 sets, and eight individuals bought twenty-four sets; John Morris the editor took six sets himself. Since many of the subscribers can be found in standard directories, the list provides a third opportunity, after the 1756 *Clarissa* and the 1796 *Don Quixote*, to study the clientele for a Dublin reprint of a major author. Fifty-eight clergymen make up the largest group among the subscribers, followed by fifty-seven landed gentry, perhaps twenty-eight lawyers, perhaps twenty-one civil servants, ten physicians, ten members of the nobility, and six soldiers. Forty-eight subscribers are identified simply as "Mr."; a spot check turns up a number of merchants in this group, but one of the forty-eight was an apothecary named Stephen Reynolds, who also subscribed to the expensive eight-volume edition of Oliver Goldsmith's *History of the Earth and Animated Nature* in 1777. Seven of the subscribers were women, five of the landed class and two booksellers, Mrs. Mary Hay, who subscribed for six sets for her customers in Belfast, and Miss Frances Smith, who subscribed for six sets for her customers in Dublin; Lady Elizabeth Ponsonby had also subscribed to *Clarissa* in 1756, as had several members of her family, and the book had been dedicated to her. Of the twelve subscribers living in England, the famous critic and editor Edmond Malone was one, and John Holroyd, later Lord Sheffield, was another; one London bookseller named Robert Rayment subscribed for six sets, even though these were subject to confiscation in England. Two subscribers are listed as residents of Portugal. Three sets survive in the British Library, and the *National Union Catalog* lists four but not the set I have examined at the University of North Carolina at Chapel Hill. Thomas Jefferson owned one,[186] as did Robert Jones III (1733–93), of Fonmon Castle, Glamorgan, Wales.[187] In an effort to encourage subscriptions Ewing announced on 31 January 1774 that subscribers would pay a guinea less than non-subscribers. In the *Hibernian Journal* for 31 May 1775 he reminded prospective buyers that he had spent two thousand pounds on the edition and that in comparison with the London edition it was "more commodious in Size, more satisfactory in the Distribution of the Matter, *less faulty* by many Degrees, *in the Printing*, and inferior in Price by nearly one Half." Johnson himself may have commended the 1775 Dublin edition; Charles Sharpe, the prominent Dublin auctioneer whose catalogues were discussed in chapter two, wrote of this edition in his catalogue of the books of the Dublin Institution sold on 20 May 1833, that "the printer (Ewing) received from Dr. Johnson a highly complimentary letter, on the extreme accuracy of the present edition." Johnson's letter does not survive, but there is confirmation from another source; John Warburton and his fellow Dublin historians reported in their definitive history of 1818 that Johnson found this Dublin edition "was more correct than the folio edition completed under his own inspection."[188]

The 1775 Dublin edition was Ewing's valedictory, and he shortly retired from business and sold his edition to Samuel Watson, who announced on 29 February 1776 that he was selling the work at the subscription price of two guineas but would soon raise the price. That the edition was larger than 401 is suggested by the fact that forty-four of the library owners had sets, though only fifteen had subscribed for it. One of the most interesting owners, though not an original subscriber, was Conolly McCausland (1713–94), who bought the set now at Yale. A member of a landed family of Walworth, County Londonderry, McCausland was also a ship captain. He is mentioned in the *Pennsylvania Gazette* for 1 December 1773 as the captain of the ship *Walworth*, presumably named after his estate, and as the captain of the ship *Faithful Steward* on 15 September 1784 and 14 September 1785. In all three instances and undoubtedly others he was transporting goods and Irish emigrants from Londonderry to Philadelphia. McCausland was one of sixty-eight who escaped from the sinking of the *Faithful Steward* on 2 September 1785 when 181 lives were lost.

The Ewing edition met the demand for a Dublin edition for the next twenty years until Robert Marchbank of Dublin in 1798 published another two-volume quarto edition. As with the Ewing edition the Marchbank edition was a lengthy undertaking which may be traced in the *Hibernian Journal* and other Dublin papers from August 1794 until publication. Marchbank reported in the *Hibernian Journal* for 22 August 1794 that the venture would cost £2,500 and that he would need at least eight hundred subscriptions. He also said that although his edition would be essentially a reprint of the last London edition, he was adding a pronunciation key not to be found in any other edition. In the preface, rare for Dublin reprints, Marchbank complains of lack of support for his edition, even though there are fewer errors in it than in the London edition. He also quotes Johnson to describe his own labors amidst

"Want and Distraction, in Sickness and in Sorrow." He is grateful to William Gilbert, Jeremiah Sullivan, and especially to the Dublin schoolmaster, scholar, and poet Samuel Whyte, "who, in adjusting the Pronunciation, took the Trouble through the course of the work of revising the Sheets in that Particular, previous to their being printed; so, in that difficult and important Article ... it may be presumed unexceptionally correct." Marchbank did not get his eight hundred subscriptions but only 601, of which 308 sets were taken by twenty Irish booksellers, fifteen in Dublin and others in Cork, where John Cronin subscribed for forty-two sets, Carrick-in-Suir, Coleraine, Belfast, where William Magee took twenty-one sets, and Newry. The edition was aimed especially at users in Ireland, Scotland, and Wales, since Whyte's pronunciation section was addressed to them. The majority of the subscribers were clerics, landed gentry, and lawyers, as usual, but there were no peers, as contrasted with the ten peers who subscribed to the 1775 edition, and most of the clerics were Roman Catholic rather than Church of Ireland, a new development. Though most subscribers were Irish, there were also residents of England, France, New York, and Bartholomew Casey of Oporto, Portugal; the *National Union Catalog* identifies three sets in the United States. Whyte and John Lees, the head of the Postoffice in Ireland, were the only subscribers to both the 1775 and the 1798 Dublin editions. American graduates of the Irish reprint industry did not issue a reprint of the *Dictionary* until Mathew Carey's of 1817.

After the *Dictionary* Johnson's next important work was *Rasselas*, always printed in Ireland as in London as *The Prince of Abissinia, A Tale*, which appeared on 12 May 1759 at 2s.8d.h., less than a month after the London edition at five shillings. Demand was not great, and another Dublin edition was not needed until 1777, but then interest increased, and new printings were issued in 1787 and 1795. This latter reprint was presumably the one Mathew Carey received on 6 April 1795 from Patrick Byrne; Carey forwarded three copies to Timothy Brundige to sell in his Dumfries, Virginia shop.[189]

The year 1765 saw the publication in London of Johnson's massive edition of Shakespeare, but the Dublin reprint did not come out until November 1766. One of the Dublin publishers was a woman Anne Leathley, who advertised the ten-volume sets at

£1.12s.6d. in Sleater's *Gazetteer* for 13 December 1766: "The Publishers have not omitted an Opportunity of making this Edition as complete as possible. They have carefully corrected a large Errata [sic] in that printed in London; and with great Pains and Trouble have distributed into their proper places a Number of interesting Notes, sent to Mr. Johnson by some of his learned Friends, and inserted by him in an Appendix. They have also made some valuable Additions from the Twenty Plays of Shakespeare lately published by that ingenious Critic George Stevens, Esq; by which Means they hope to give this Edition a Preference to any hitherto published." David Hay sent two sets of this Dublin edition on 13 April 1770 to William and Thomas Bradford to sell in their Philadelphia bookshop.[190] Although there seems to have been no response in Irish periodicals, sales must have been brisk since Thomas Ewing brought out two editions in 1771, one in six volumes and one in twelve; Robert Addison bought the latter in England and took it with him to Canada in 1791.[191] Thirty-four library owners had Johnson's *Shakespeare*, usually in a Dublin edition, and the set was available to readers in St. Canice's Library of Kilkenny Cathedral, the Armagh Public Library after 1774, the Marsh Library of Dublin after 1793, and the Dublin Library Society after 1793. Although John Bell by 1785 was selling individual Shakespeare plays with Johnson's notes at sixpence both in London and Dublin, some demand for Irish editions continued. Massive editions were published in 1791 and 1794, and William Jones's subscription edition of 1791 cited in chapters one and three had a number of American and British subscribers and was sold in 1794 by Samuel Campbell in his New York bookshop and by Patrick Byrne in his Philadelphia bookshop in 1802 a few months after his arrival from Dublin; Byrne had also been involved in the sixteen-volume edition of 1791.

Three years after Johnson's edition of Shakespeare Johnson's disciple of five years James Boswell published his tribute not to Johnson but to another of his tutors Pascal Paoli. Boswell's *Account of Corsica the Journal of a Tour to that Island; and Memoirs of Pascal Paoli* went through three London editions in a little over a year, but the Dublin booksellers delayed reprinting it until the publication of the second London edition of 1 April 1768, which made corrections in the first London edition of 13 February 1768; these two London editions accounted for seven thousand copies. The first Dublin reprint was not announced until 24 May 1768 in William Sleater's *Public Gazetteer* at a price of 2s.8d.h. bound, a price significantly below the London price of six shillings.[192] This reprint of the second London edition was sold out by August when another printing was issued. These first two printings were also sold in Belfast, Newry, Kilkenny, and Cork, the provincial newspapers show. The third Dublin reprint called the "fifth edition" in the imprint and in the newspapers, was advertised in March 1769, with one of its six Dublin booksellers William Sleater noting that the new edition was "ornamented with a striking likeness of that Great General [Paoli]," that had been taken from the London third edition. The collapse of the Corsican rebellion in June 1769 and the flight of Paoli hurt the sale of Boswell's book since Sleater was still trying to sell the last edition as late as March 1774. Sleater used his *Public Gazetteer* to advertise and excerpt his editions of Boswell's *Corsica*, and these excerpts were often copied by other Dublin newspapers and those in Belfast and Cork.[193]

These reports in Irish periodicals undoubtedly encouraged sales of the three Dublin editions of Boswell's book. Even more helpful to the sale, however, were Boswell's travels in Ireland during May and June 1769 after the three Dublin editions of his book had come out. Boswell was the only one of the eight major authors to visit Ireland during the course of his literary career; though Goldsmith and Sterne were born in Ireland, they left Ireland before their careers began, and they never returned to their native place. Five Irish periodicals during the period 11–16 May 1769 reported the arrival in Ireland of "James Boswell, Esq., author of the account of Corsica, and the memoirs of Paschal Paoli," and two of these periodicals the *Dublin Journal* and the *Freeman's Journal* throughout June and July carried Boswell's lengthy appeal for funds for Paoli and the Corsicans in their war against the French; all these periodicals had advertised and excerpted Dublin editions of Boswell's *Corsica*. Boswell's appeal is similar to the earlier ones that he made in England and Scotland except that it is naturally aimed at an Irish audience: "Having had the pleasure to find that a generous Zeal for the Corsicans prevails in Ireland, I have been encouraged to hope that a Contribution may be raised here in Support of the Cause of Liberty, in which this Country has on many Occasions so gloriously distinguished herself." The fourth paragraph of Boswell's appeal suggests an organized campaign for funds for Paoli: "Contributions for the brave Corsicans are received by Messrs. Latouche, Bankers in Dublin, to whom the Gentlemen who make Collections in their several Counties and Boroughs, will please to remit what is raised. Messrs. Latouche will in due Time, be ready to satisfy Contributors, that their Bounty is properly conveyed to Corsica."

Probably encouraged by his Dublin publishers, Boswell also called on another technique that he had used repeatedly in London and Edinburgh periodicals, writing under a pseudonym. A letter on the Corsican cause by "A Free Hibernian" in the *Freeman's Journal* of Dublin in June 1769 is almost certainly Boswell's.[194] The pseudonym allowed him to "speak the Sentiments of every Irishman" on the cause of Corsican freedom and to urge his "Countrymen to contribute towards a scheme, which will be attended with so many good Consequences." The letter also gave him an opportunity to mention "Mr. Boswell's Advertisement" and to affirm that he was writing to the newspaper "solely from Motives of Compassion to the Distressed." The Latouche Bank in Dublin did receive contributions for Paoli, though the Corsican rebellion had collapsed before many had been made. Three Dublin newspapers announced the founding of the Corsican Club in early June "to support the Cause of Liberty and Paoli"; the announcement, probably by Boswell, concludes with the hope "that Irishmen will distinguish themselves, and do Honour to their Country, by associating to support a Nation of Heroes, and their illustrious Chief, who dignify human Nature by their Patriotism and Virtue."

These many accounts in the Irish periodicals and the three Dublin editions of *An Account of Corsica* show that Boswell was not exaggerating when he wrote to his friend Sir Alexander Dick in Edinburgh on 29 May 1769 about his reception in Ireland: "I found myself treated with a distinction that has been very flattering to the blood of Auchinleck. Though my book has told almost everything that I know, there is still a great curiosity to hear many little particulars, which different minds are eager to ask."[195] Public figures welcoming Boswell to Dublin included the Lord Lieutenant of Ireland, the Duke of Leinster, the Lord Mayor of Dublin, Lord Charlemont, the historian Thomas Leland, the orator and stateman Henry Flood, the physician and scientist David Macbride, and George Faulkner, though Faulkner was not one of the six Dublin booksellers reprinting Boswell's book. This kind of publicity the six Dublin booksellers presumably translated into sales of their third edition of Boswell's *Account of Corsica*.

Appraisals of Boswell's book in its Dublin dress are less common in Irish periodicals than excerpts from it or news items about Boswell himself. One response was by Jeoffry Wagstaffe in the *Dublin Mercury* of 27 December 1768: "The public is undoubtedly much indebted to Mr. Boswell for his sensible and spirited account of Corsica. He has made us acquainted with Pascal Paoli, a man whose sayings and actions may convince us, that Plutarch's heroes are not fabulous." Wagstaffe, however had reservations about Boswell's use of French sources for his history of Corsica. One of the six Dublin booksellers reprinting Boswell's book John Exshaw published in *Exshaw's Magazine* for May 1769 notice of Boswell's arrival in Dublin and Lord Lyttelton's tribute to Boswell used in the preface to *An Account of Corsica* and then added his own comments on Boswell the traveller and libertarian: "This gentleman whom Lord Lyttelton expresses so much esteem for, and to whom He and the Public are indebted for the Account of Corsica, and the Memoirs of its Chief, lately made a visit to this kingdom, that Ireland might be taken in his view, as well as the other parts of Europe: we hear he has communicated a design of promoting a free-gift here, for the support of oppressed Freedom in Corsica, as he hath done both in Scotland and England; and in this his expectations are not a little raised, from the general character of this kingdom. How far the public are interested in the manner this gentleman has employed his time, and the observations he has made while abroad, must appear from what he has obliged them with, in the piece just mentioned." Clearly, Exshaw was promoting the sale of a book reprinted and sold by himself. How many copies Exshaw, Sleater, and their colleagues sold is unknown, but it is unlikely to have exceeded two thousand copies for the three Dublin editions. Thirty-one of the Library owners had it, usually in a Dublin edition, more than had any of Smollett's five novels, for example, and it was also in the Dublin Library Society in one of the 1768 Dublin editions. Such luminaries as Lords Avonmore, Charlemont, and Clonmell bought a Dublin reprint.

For the copyright of *An Account of Corsica* Boswell received a hundred pounds from his London publisher Edward and Charles Dilly,[196] but neither he nor his London publishers were paid by the

Dublin booksellers, two of whom, John Exshaw and Henry Saunders, had been involved in the most notorious of all the Dublin piracies, Richardson's *Sir Charles Grandison*. Nevertheless, Boswell probably did not object to the three Dublin reprints of *An Account of Corsica* or his later *Tour to the Hebrides with Samuel Johnson*. His letter to William Johnson Temple on 24 August 1768 says of the enthusiastic reception of the Dublin editions, "That is no bad circumstance."[197] Boswell's memoirs in the *European Magazine* for June 1791 show that he was proud of the several translations of *An Account of Corsica*, even though he had received no payment from the French, German, and Italian publishers. Boswell was strongly opposed to the perpetual copyright that the London publishers took as an article of faith in spite of the 1709 law providing for limited copyright, and as a lawyer, the only one of the eight major authors with such a calling, he was able to defend in the courts his views on limited copyright. He was one of the three lawyers for Alexander Donaldson in Hinton *vs* Donaldson in 1773, in which Donaldson won the right to reprint Stackhouse's *History of the Bible* and thus strike a blow against the London bookseller's claim of perpetual copyright. The following year Boswell published his summary of the trial and the speeches of the Scots judges in the *Decision of the Court of Session upon the Question of Literary Property*. The pamphlet consists of thirty-seven pages reporting the speeches of the thirteen judges present, all of whom were opposed to Hinton's claim of perpetual copyright except Lord Monboddo.[198] The *Belfast News-Letter* in late July 1773 reported Boswell's participation in the trial, but the Irish booksellers must not have seen Boswell's pamphlet as an attack on their own enemies the London booksellers, though certainly not a defense of the unauthorized reprints that their publishing industry depended upon; at least they did not reprint the work or give it publicity in the periodicals that many of them published.

Although Boswell's Dublin bookseller John Exshaw did not mention Boswell's pamphlet on copyright in his *Magazine*, he did include in the August 1773 issue Anne Laetitia Aikin's tribute to "generous BOSWELL" in her "Corsica: a Poem," and Exshaw also recalled Boswell's book that he had published and that Boswell had "promoted the subscription in England and Ireland, for the assistance of the brave Corsicans." Even so, it was not from Exshaw's reprint of *An Account of Corsica* that Boswell took presentation copies for the Lord Lieutenant and other friends in Ireland. One of the Yale copies is the London edition that Boswell presented in 1771 to the young heiress he had courted in Ireland in 1769 Mary Ann Boyd. Married three times in later years, never to Boswell, Mary Ann after her third marriage gave the book to a physician and civic leader in Belfast Dr. James McDonnell on 12 August 1818 and wrote on the title page that Boswell had made her paint the arms of Corsica on a sash for Pasquale Paoli, the hero of *An Account of Corsica*. The Dublin bookseller's portrait of Boswell as a libertarian and the champion of General Paoli outlasted his travels in Ireland and the three Dublin editions of his book. In 1770 J. S. Dodd of Cork in his *Essays and Poems*, published for 289 subscribers in Ireland, paid tribute to Boswell as "that ornament to letters and friend of liberty, to whom we owe that elegant account of Corsica." Even in his later years after his two books on Samuel Johnson, Boswell was still known in Ireland primarily as Paoli's public relations man. As late as 4 February 1793 Patrick Duigenan spoke in the Irish Parliament of Boswell as the "illustrious biographer," but he meant, as his further remarks on Paoli make clear, the biographer of Paoli rather than the biographer of Johnson, even though Boswell's *Life of Johnson* had been reprinted in Dublin the previous year.[199]

In addition to his involvement during his early career with Paoli and the Corsican rebellion, Boswell was active both as lawyer and as writer in another great controversy with international ramifications, the Douglas Cause.[200] In defense of Archibald Douglas's claims to the estates and honors of the Duke of Douglas Boswell published three works in 1767, *Dorando*, *The Essence of the Douglas Cause*, and *Letters of Lady Jane Douglas*, and dozens of anonymous articles in the newspapers. Many of the latter were reprinted in the Irish newspapers as were excerpts from all three pamphlets. John Exshaw had reprinted Boswell's *Letters of Lady Jane Douglas* three months before he reprinted Boswell's *Corsica* and included several letters by Boswell writing as Lady Jane in *Exshaw's Magazine*. He was still advertising the work in June 1769 during Boswell's stay in Dublin, and he presented more letters in his *Magazine* "as models well worth imitating, for sentiment, diction, and polite respect." Exshaw's edition was also sold in Dublin by Luke White and in Kilkenny by Edmund Finn in 1768. Among the library owners Lord Clonmell and Thomas Fox had Exshaw's edition as did

Francis Houstoun, a Trinity College, Dublin, graduate of 1727, whose autograph with the date 1769 appears in the Yale copy. As late as 1794 Samuel Campbell was selling the Exshaw reprint in his New York bookshop, probably ordered from the *Dublin Catalogue*, which listed it both in 1786 and 1791. I have found no printed evidence of Dublin editions of Boswell's other works on the Douglas Cause, but Boswell's steward at Auchinleck James Bruce wrote to Boswell on 18 July 1767 that an Irish edition of *Dorando*, Boswell's allegory of the Douglas Cause, had arrived at the neighboring town of Cumnock.[201]

For the remainder of the century Dublin reprints of the works of Johnson and Boswell are intertwined, and the first of many is Johnson' *Journey to the Western Islands of Scotland*. This was immediately preceded by Dublin reprints of Johnson's four political pamphlets of 1770–75 followed by a collected edition in 1777. One of the publishers of the latter was Christopher Talbot, soon to continue the Irish reprinting tradition in Philadelphia, and one of the buyers of the Dublin edition in London was Edmond Malone, the eminent critic and scholar. Trained in the Belfast reprint trade, Hugh Gaine reprinted one of the political pamphlets in New York in 1771. One political pamphlet often attributed to Johnson at the time, *Hypocrisy Unmasked*, should be mentioned because the imprint notes it was printed in London by G. Nicol and reprinted in Dublin by Wogan and Bean in 1776; presumably this was an authorized reprint. The most interesting Johnson work of this decade, however, is his record of his tour with Boswell preserved in not fewer than four separate Dublin reprints in the same year. James Williams announced his reprint in the *Hibernian Journal* for 1 February in 1775, only twelve days after the London edition and at half the price. The copy in the Liebert collection has autographs of four owners and three dates, 1794, 1822, and 1890; the 1822 owner Elizabeth Dobson lived at Trésorières on the Loire. A reprint by ten Dublin booksellers was announced five days later at the same price but in two volumes bound in one. Nine days later Thomas Walker announced his edition at the same price; the Trinity College, Dublin, copy was originally owned by Arthur James Plunkett (1759–1836), 8th Earl of Fingall, who also owned the 1785 Dublin edition of Johnson's *Rambler*. The editions by Williams and Walker have the same pagination but different type, and the page is smaller in the Williams edition, though both editions are 12mo. There was a fourth Dublin reprint in 1775, though it seems not to have been advertised in the papers. According to its imprint it was printed for J. Pope of London, but the Trinity College and the Liebert copies appear to be the Williams edition with a false imprint.[202] A rival Dublin bookseller probably was trying to capitalize on the more prestigious London imprint. This latter device was sometimes used by Dublin booksellers as in Churchill's *Poems* published in Dublin in 1767 by one group who warned in the *Dublin Gazette* of 2 June 1767 of a "piratical Edition of these Poems printed in Dublin under a London Imprint." Most of the twenty-nine library owners had a Dublin edition, as did Edmond Malone in London, and Timothy Brundige had one of them in his Dumfries, Virginia, shop on 2 January 1796.[203] Another owner the antiquarian Charles O'Conor, who received two letters from Johnson that Boswell published in his *Life of Johnson*, wrote to his son Denis in Belanagare, County Roscommon, on 11 April 1775 that the *Journey* would afford him "useful knowledge" and was being sent in its Dublin edition to him along with other books.[204]

The tour of Scotland by Johnson and Boswell was widely reported in Irish newspapers during the fall and winter of 1773–74, but Boswell delayed the publication of his *Journal of a Tour to the Hebrides with Samuel Johnson, LL.D.* until after Johnson's death in 1784. The *Dublin Evening Post* on 17 November 1785 gave the first advertisement of the Dublin reprint by Patrick Byrne, John Cash, and Luke White of the London edition published only a month before. The Dublin bound edition sold for 6s.6d. and the edition in pasteboard covers for 5s.11d.h, only a halfpence less than the London edition in boards. Since the London newspapers advertise only copies in boards, this is a rare example of a Dublin edition selling for more than the London edition it reprinted. Probably this is why the Dublin edition, though it corrected errata in the London edition, was unable to compete with the London edition, whose 1,500 copies according to Edmond Malone were almost all sold by 17 October 1785.[205] A second London edition at six shillings again was announced by 22 December 1785, but a second Dublin edition was not required. Boswell hoped for a second Dublin edition, even though there was no financial benefit to him because he wrote to J. C. Walker in Dublin on 20 December 1785: "If ... the Irish booksellers should have occasion to reprint my book, it will be obliging if you will suggest that the reprint should be made from my second and more perfect edition.[206] Twenty-five of the library owners had it, most of them the Dublin reprint, and the Dublin Library Society. Patrick Byrne was probably selling it after 1801 in Philadelphia from his Dublin warehouse as he sold so many of the works he had reprinted in Dublin. The copy of the Byrne edition at Yale may have been purchased in the eighteenth century by a noted French family; the copy was sold after the death in 1888 of its most eminent nineteenth-century representative Paul Edouard Didier, comte Riant, the historian.

Excerpts from the Dublin edition were frequenty published in Dublin periodicals and also in the *Belfast News-Letter* 1785–86, and there was a variety of response from the periodicals and individual readers, some favorable and some hostile. Charles O'Conor referred favorably to the Dublin edition twice in his letters of 1786,[207] and Joseph Cooper Walker bought the Dublin edition even before the newspaper announcement and conveyed his reaction to Boswell himself on 13 November 1785: "It is exquisitely entertaining. I have hardly ate, drank or slept since I got it. It was with pain I laid it down to take up my Pen." Walker further urges Boswell to return to Ireland and publish a tour of Ireland like his tour of Corsica, though he warns him not to expect a Paoli.[208] Although Patrick Byrne, the Dublin–Philadelphia bookseller who figures so largely in this study, had reprinted Boswell's *Tour*, he apparently envisaged more sales for parodies of the Tour than the *Tour* itself and reprinted the two most famous verse satires on the *Tour, Bozzy and Piozzi*, by John Wolcot, better known as Peter Pindar, and the same author's *Poetical Epistle to James Boswell*. Large portions of the first were reprinted, to cite one of many examples, in the *Hibernian Magazine* for June 1786, that ridiculed both Boswell and Johnson's female biographer Hester Lynch Thrale Piozzi, with such choice lines for Boswell as these: "For thee, James Boswell, may the hand of fate/Arrest thy goose quill, and confine thy prate;/ Or be in solitude to live thy luck,/A chattering magpye on the ISLE of MUCK." The *Hibernian* writer commented, however, that he was "not disposed to join in the censure of Mr. Boswell" because he "read the book through with great avidity," and that "it had a charm to rivet the attention." Other periodicals excerpted Byrne's reprint of Pindar's *Poetical Epistle to James Boswell*, which found Boswell "like a watchful Cat before a hole,/ Full twenty years (inflamed with letter'd pride)/ Didst mousing sit before Sam's mouth so wide,/ To catch as many scraps as thou wert able,/ A very Lazarus at the Rich Man's table." Booksellers in America trained in the Irish book trade such as William Spotswood, Henry and Patrick Rice, and James Rice also reprinted Pindar's parodies of the *Tour* rather than the *Tour* itself.

In between the two books on the Scottish tour, Johnson's in 1775 and Boswell's in 1785, Johnson published his monumental *Lives of the Poets*. Among the Irish library owners the *Lives of the English Poets* was second in popularity only to the *Dictionary* — seventy-four had the set, more than for any work of the eight major authors. The first twenty-two *Lives* were reprinted in October 1779 from the London edition of June; thirteen Dublin booksellers are in the imprint, but omitted from the imprint are two Dublin–Philadelphia booksellers Patrick Byrne and John Parker, both of whom announced in the newspapers that they were publishing the work. The copy in the Liebert Collection belonged to Sir John Freke(1765–1845), of Castle Freke, County Cork, who succeeded as 6th Lord Carberry in 1807. The thirteen booksellers added volumes two and three in July 1781. Some owners had their copies beautifully bound by William McKenzie of Dublin in green morocco with red strips at the top and bottom of the spine and red lettering pieces and brown medallions for volume numbers.[209] The Trinity College set formerly belonging to Viscount Gormanston is bound in calf, and the spine has gold lettering on a red background. In the same year the thirteen Dublin booksellers reprinted all three volumes under the dates 1779 for the first and 1781 for the second and third at least once with minor variants and perhaps twice.[210] The University of North Carolina (Chapel Hill) set was owned by Susanna Johnston Barton, wife of General Charles Barton (1760–1819), who was a younger son from an old landed family of County Fermanagh. William Wilson, one of the thirteen Dublin booksellers, brought out under his name alone a collected edition during 1780–81, but it is a reprint of a reprint. The *Dublin Evening Post* for 2 December 1789 shows that Wilson also published Johnson's poets in sixty volumes for ten guineas, and Timothy Brundige had one of these editions of Johnson's *Lives* from Mathew Carey to sell in his Dumfries, Virginia, shop in 1796.[211] These Dublin editions met the need until 1793 when James Moore, publisher of the *Dublin*

Magazine and one of Mathew Carey's suppliers, began to issue an eight-volume edition of British poets with Johnson's prefaces, which was not complete until 1801. In the first volume dated 1795 Moore included sixty-six lives of poets, the fifty-two that Johnson had written and fourteen of more recent poets, all minor except for Goldsmith and Johnson himself. To publicize his massive edition Moore included many excerpts in his *Dublin Magazine* 1798–1801. A 1795 one-volume edition of the first twenty-two *Lives* attributed to R. Dodsley of London appears to be a reprint of the 1779 Dublin edition. Not only are the pagination and type identical, but the printer's ornaments on pp. 131 and 247 are identical.[212] One Philadelphia bookseller trained in the Dublin book trade Augustine Fagan issued his own reprint of Johnson's *Lives* both in 1811 and 1819. The original purchasers of the Dublin editions of the *Lives of the Poets* valued and preserved their copies; twenty-three copies survive in the United States alone according to the *National Union Catalog*.

Thomas Walker publicized the Dublin edition, for which he was one of the publishers, in his *Hibernian Magazine*. In response to the first volume the *Hibernian Magazine* printed in different issues much of Johnson's essays on Dryden and Milton. When the complete Dublin edition came out in 1781, the *Hibernian* excerpted several of the *Lives* and in the October issue appraised Johnson's treatment of Thomas Gray: "Our biographical legislator, in another part of his work, has again boldly steered against the tide of popular opinion, by calling into question that transcendant excellence of our modern Pindar, Mr. Gray, whom he has dethroned and degraded ... Gray has been placed by his sanguine admirers by the side of Dryden and Pope. Dr. Johnson seems to have levelled him with the minor bards of a much inferior rank: half a century hence he may, perhaps, be fixed in his right and proper station." A more comprehensive review is in the issues of January and February 1782 in which Walker or one of his writers acknowledges Johnson's *Lives* as the work of a "great master, neither obscured by dogmatism, nor sullied by private prejudices." The most concrete testimony to the actual readership of the *Lives of the Poets* in its 1779–81 Dublin edition is provided by the deposit books of the Armagh Public Library. Eight readers during the years 1796–1802 deposited large sums for the privilege of borrowing Johnson's *Lives*. One reader named George Pepper, for example, deposited

£3.8s.3d. in August 1799 to take out Johnson's *Lives*, and he did so again in August 1801 and in September 1802. Young Daniel O'Connell, the future "Liberator," was reading the Dublin edition in the Dublin Library Society in 1797.

Johnson's death in 1784 was followed by collected editions and by an expanded body of writing in many forms. Newspapers during the period 1784–1800, the two major magazines *Exshaw's* and the *Hibernian*, both published by major publishers of Johnson, and the eight new magazines of the last decade of the century, are full of Johnsoniana, often reprinted from Dublin editions by Exshaw and Thomas Walker of the *Hibernian Magazine*. These new magazines in some measure were called into being by the Dublin editions. An important posthumous event in Ireland was the Dublin reprint by Luke White, Patrick Byrne, and Robert Marchbank of the London collected edition of Johnson's *Poems*. Just six weeks after the London edition the three announced their edition in the *Dublin Evening Post* for 10 May 1785 at 3s.3d. This is a rare example of the Dublin reprint selling for more than the London edition, which, according to the *St. James's Chronicle* for 24 March 1785 sold for only 2s.6d. Patrick Byrne was still trying to sell his edition ten years later when he shipped copies to Mathew Carey in Philadelphia.[213] In the same year and also in 1795 the Dublin booksellers, again including Patrick Byrne for both editions, reprinted Johnson's *Prayers and Meditations* and an anonymous *Life of Johnson* usually assigned to the Irish writer William Cook[e], now of London but originally from Cork. Cook knew Johnson and had formerly published an anthology in London entitled the *Beauties of Johnson*, which was reprinted by twelve Dublin booksellers in 1782 and frequently quoted from in Irish periodicals and lent by the circulating libraries. Three of these booksellers Patrick Byrne, John Parker and William Spotswood joined the Philadelphia book trade, and Spotswood issued his own American reprint in Philadelphia in 1787.

The many biographies of Johnson published shortly after his death were quickly reprinted in Dublin. Patrick Byrne helped to reprint four popular works about Johnson, Mrs. Piozzi's *Anecdotes of the late Samuel Johnson*, her *Letters to and from the late Samuel Johnson*, John Courtenay's *Poetical review of the literary and moral character of the late Samuel Johnson* and Sir John Hawkins's *Life of Johnson*. Twenty-two of the Irish library owners bought the *Letters* in two volumes, and Byrne sent Mathew Carey four sets in February 1795, one of which was sent on to Timothy Brundige in Dumfries, Virginia.[214] The Trinity College, Dublin, set of the *Letters* has three inscriptions. It originally belonged to a Trinity graduate John Jebb, later Bishop of Limerick, who in turn presented this edition to the Historical Society at Trinity on 14 January 1794, and at a later date it became part of the lending Library at Trinity. The printer of Hawkins's *Johnson* was John Chambers, who would emigrate to the United States four years after Byrne. In February 1795 Byrne sent eight copies of his reprint of Hawkin's *Johnson* to Mathew Carey in Philadelphia.

These books on Johnson were all eclipsed several years later by Boswell's masterwork the *Life of Samuel Johnson, LL.D.* The London edition in three volumes appeared on 16 May 1791, but received little advertisement in the London newspapers probably because Boswell had it published at his own expense without selling the copyright to London publishers, who would presumably have advertised the work more extensively. To make the price more attractive and to anticipate the cheaper Dublin reprint, Boswell had the three volumes published in pasteboard covers at two guineas. He may also have believed that lack of publicity would delay the inevitable Dublin reprint. The work sold well, and Boswell had earned £550 more by the end of the year than the thousand pounds he had been offered for the copyright.[215] He asked his friend and mentor Edmond Malone on 12 March 1791 whether the Irish booksellers would take some of the 1750 sets from the London edition.[216] Whether they did or not is unknown, but contrary to their normal practice of reprinting a London edition within a month or two after its publication in London, they did not reprint the *Life of Johnson* until 21 August 1792, fifteen months after the London edition. The usual customers for the Dublin reprints in Ireland, Britain, and America may have been reading the London edition for these fifteen months, or after February 1792 the Dublin reprint selling for only 3s.3d. of the London abridged edition. The London edition in boards still could not match the price of the three-volume Dublin reprint; the thirteen booksellers whose names appear in the imprint plus at least three more advertising the work in the Dublin newspapers sold a bound edition for 22s.9d. The Dublin edition in boards sold in Dublin, Belfast, and Cork, according to the Irish newspapers, sold for even less, 19s.6d. Four of the Dublin publishers, P. Byrne, J. Jones, W. Jones, and J. Rice, were all active suppliers of Dublin editions for the American market; these four were also in the group of eleven Dublin booksellers who reprinted the abridged *Life of Johnson* in 1792, and Byrne had reprinted Boswell's *Tour to the Hebrides* and the two satires on it by Peter Pindar. Byrne, Rice, and John Chambers, the printer of the first volume of the Dublin *Life of Johnson*, would transfer to the American book trade after the Union, Byrne to Philadelphia, Rice to Baltimore, and Chambers to New York. Two of the sellers of the *Life of Johnson* whose names do not appear in the imprint also would leave the Dublin book trade; George Folingsby would be one of the rare examples of a transfer to the London book trade,[217] and Bernard Dornin, cited in chapter two for his circulating library and in chapter five for his reprint of Sterne's *Letters*, would become part of the large Irish contingent in the Baltimore book trade.

Purchased by forty-five of the Irish library owners, mostly in the Dublin reprint of 1792, the *Life of Johnson* is tied with Smollett's *History of England* as the seventh most widely purchased work by the eight major authors. The Apollo Circulating Library of Dublin lent the Dublin reprint by 18 October 1792, and it could also be read by members of the Dublin Library Society along with Boswell's other major works, by members of two provincial library societies, the Belfast Society for Promoting the Knowledge and the Cork Library Society, and by students, faculty, and graduates of Trinity College, Dublin. Exceeded only by Gibbon's *Decline and Fall of the Roman Empire*, the Dublin *Life of Johnson* was borrowed from the Armagh Public Library by fifteen persons 1797–1802; a particular admirer of the work was Rev. Dr. Hugh Hamilton, Dean of the Armagh Cathedral, who checked it out three times. By the end of the century it was in at least two institutional libraries in the United States, the Redwood Library, Newport Rhode Island, and the Library Company of Philadelphia; its presence in nineteen institutional libraries in the United States today, more than for any single Dublin edition of a work by the major authors, suggests that its original purchasers valued and preserved it. One of the Yale sets of the Dublin edition was purchased for 22s.9d. in 1802 by Jonas Stawell, of Old Court, County Cork, a graduate of Trinity College, Dublin, in 1790, and father of the Australian jurist Sir William Foster Stawell (1815–89). Though cheaply and poorly printed, this set is in its original calf binding with gold tooling. The second of the Yale sets of the Dublin edition is in the original blue pasteboard covers.

In spite of these indications that the Dublin edition of the *Life of Johnson* sold well, specific responses to the Dublin edition were mixed. The Rev. Dr. William Maxwell of Tynan, County Armagh, wrote to Boswell himself on 15 November 1792 that the Dublin edition, though "not very accurately printed," had been "very generally demanded, and Universally Esteemed, as it well deserves, for a Work more replete with Instruction and Amusement has seldom appeared." Maxwell hopes that Boswell will "continue to Amuse and Instruct Mankind by Compositions of that Nature."[218] Excerpts were printed in the *Hibernian Magazine* and the new *Universal Magazine and Review, or Repository of Literature*, and Patrick Byrne, who published the latter periodical 1789–93, did not miss his opportunity to extol the work that he had helped to reprint. Byrne had reprinted two verse satires on Boswell's *Tour to the Hebrides with Samuel Johnson*, but his attitude towards Boswell is quite different in the February 1792 issue of his magazine which notes that Boswell's *Life of Johnson* "is now printing in Dublin"; "Among the literati of the present age, and particularly those who were intimately conversant with Dr. Johnson, we know of none better qualified, from a personal acquaintance with the hero of the story, than is Mr. B. for the complete execution of the task which he had imposed on himself, in writing the life of this extraordinary man." Boswell "was happy in the kind regard and unreserved confidence of his venerable friend; who, it unquestionably appears, was fully apprized of his biographical intention, and manifested no disapprobation of it."

John Exshaw, the printer of the second volume of the Dublin *Life of Johnson*, was not encouraged by his involvement with the Dublin edition to promote its sale by an enthusiastic review in *Exshaw's Magazine*, as he had done with the novelists reprinted by him. More than any member of the book trade, John Exshaw had been linked with Boswell through the years. He had published all three of the Dublin editions of *An Account of Corsica* 1768–69 and the *Letters of Lady Jane Douglas* in 1768, and his comments in *Exshaw's Magazine* in 1769 suggest that he had probably met Boswell. Nevertheless, his review in *Exshaw's Magazine* for August 1794 gives both Boswell and Johnson short shrift: "Mr. Boswell seems to be one of those good natured people whose praises are of no more value than the smiles of the courtesan, or the ribbons of a king. In the ardor of an imagination for whatever is good and great, he forgets the more faulty parts of a character, which are often a balance to its merits, and are sometimes found to predominate. Classing Dr. Johnson with those 'illustrious characters which humanity produces but a few times in the revolution of many ages,' if not ironical, is certainly a hyperbole—Johnson was no phoenix. Although such characters do not swarm like sparrows, they are surely at least as common as the eagle."

Daniel O'Connell, the future "Liberator" of the Roman Catholics in Ireland, apparently never bought the work, or at least it was not in his library, but as a twenty-year-old law student he read the set of the Dublin edition in the Dublin Library Society with some attention. His journal records that after having read with approval Arthur Murphy's biography of Johnson in January 1796, he began Boswell's *Johnson* on 13 December 1796, read 122 pages on December 16th and another hundred pages the next day, and then jotted down a succinct reaction: "I do not admire this work. Yet I will read it through." By December 23rd he had finished the first two volumes of the Dublin edition and was well into the third volume without having altered his opinion much: "I dislike Boswell very much. Yet why should I? He was not a man of genius. He ought not to have obtruded himself on the public notice." O'Connell seems to contradict himself in his next statement that Boswell's *Johnson* "will long be read with pleasure." He also noted on this day his strong disapproval of the Tory conservatism reflected in Boswell and Johnson, and he recorded Margaret Boswell's quip about the bearish Johnson's influence on her husband: "I have seen many a bear led by a man; but I never before saw a man led by a bear." By the end of the year he had concluded the work and recorded his final estimate: "On the whole I am better satisfied with this work of Boswell than I expected I should have been. Indeed, I entered upon it with a very unfavourable impression of the merit of the performance. For a long time ... I considered it through the clouded medium of prejudice. But the candid criticism of the reviewers has made me regard it in a new point of view. Boswell was certainly a well-disposed man. Johnson I admire and pity. I love him one moment, and almost hate him the next. He must indeed have been a great man, and his minutest actions and expressions are very well worth the relation. His mind was powerfully strong. His intellectual view was most acute and distinct. Yet his mind was clouded with many prejudices. He was intolerant of any opposition to his own orthodox opinions on Church and State."[219]

An owner of the Dublin edition and a future Lord Chief Justice of the King's Bench in Ireland Charles Kendal Bushe was more enthusiastic than O'Connell as he told William Henry Curran that Boswell's *Johnson* was "the most delightful of books, first because he found everything in it so charming in itself, and next, because he no sooner finished it, than he forgot it all, and so could return to it, *toties quoties*, and be sure to find it all so charming as before, and almost as new.[220] Arthur Browne, a prominent lawyer and one of the 203 library owners, agreed more with the young O'Connell than with Bushe. Browne, whose library contained the Dublin edition, found that Boswell, rather than revealing the giant that Johnson was, showed him "in religion a bigot, in politics a tyrant, and in manners a barbarian." In Boswell's pages Johnson emerges as "alternately insolent and servile, according as his commerce was with the great or with the humble: his opinions never free from the most inveterate and narrow prejudices: his consistency ready at any time to submit to his love of contradiction and affectation of superiority: unfair and uncandid in controversy, ridiculously partial to his friends and absurdly detracting from his enemies." Boswell "has brought to light the hidden dross of his friend, and mistaken it for ore.[221]

Vying with Boswell's *Life of Johnson* as the most significant posthumous work on Johnson is Arthur Murphy's edition of Johnson's collected *Works*, which was reprinted in 1793 by Luke White, probably the wealthiest and best known of the Dublin booksellers. Murphy was born in Ireland and spent some of his early years there, but he had done all his writing in London. The Dublin periodicals often quote from Murphy's life of Johnson included in the six-volume Dublin edition; one admirer of Murphy's portrait of Johnson was the young Daniel O'Connell, who read it in the Dublin Library Society in 1796 along with several of Johnson's works.[222] Murphy's judgment that the *Lives of the Poets* is "the most brilliant, and certainly the most popular of all our Author's writings" reflects the sales to the Irish library owners. Similarly, Murphy's judgment that the *Rambler* essays are

Johnson's great work and the "basis of that high reputation which went on increasing to the end of his days" reflect the high priority assigned the *Rambler* by the library owners. The absence of comment on the Dublin edition of Johnson's *Works* in the two principal magazines probably reflects the fact that neither John Exshaw nor Thomas Walker, their proprietors, had joined Luke White in reprinting the work. A reprint by Irish booksellers in America did not come out until the Philadelphia reprint by Mathew Carey in 1825.

Thomas Walker's many reprints of Johnson, *Shakespeare* in 1766, *Journey to the Western Islands of Scotland* in 1775, *Johnsoniana* in 1776, four editions of the *Lives of the Poets* 1779–81, and *Beauties of Johnson* in 1782, are reflected in the considerable Johnson material in his *Hibernian Magazine* during the years following Johnson's death in 1784. Much of this material is not significant but combined with several longer articles by Walker or his employees undoubtedly helped to keep buyers for Walker's reprints of Johnson. In October 1788 Walker responded to strictures on Johnson's Latinate style by Archdeacon Robert Burrowes in the *Transactions of the Royal Irish Academy* for 1787. Walker finds Burrowes's remarks just on the whole but wonders if he has been "more astute in hunting out the errors than displaying the beauties of his great subject." Walker finds Burrowes's conclusion an elegant one, however, and one "such as even Johnson might be pleased to hear," and he quotes it: "I [Burrowes] have singled him out from the whole body of English writers, because his universally acknowledged beauties would be most apt to induce imitation; and I have treated rather on his faults than his perfections, because an essay might comprize all the observations I could make upon his faults, while volumes would not be sufficient for a treatise on his perfections." Patrick Byrne, who also reprinted much of Johnson and Boswell, essentially agreed in his *Universal Magazine and Review* for August 1789 with Walker's judgment though in briefer form. Charles O'Conor, who owned Dublin reprints of Johnson and Boswell, in an undated letter to Joseph Cooper Walker finds some of Burrowes's points sound but wonders with Thomas Walker and Patrick Byrne if Byrne sees "that the spots which the Telescopical Eye of Criticism discovers ... are lost in the blaze of his [Johnson's] perfections, as a Phraseologist, and a Philosopher."[223]

Thomas Walker in his *Hibernian Magazine* for March 1795 offered another criticism of Johnson's prose style in the form of a dialogue between Addison and Johnson reminiscent of Lord Lyttelton's *Dialogues of the Dead*. Addison is grateful for the *Dictionary* but has doubts about the style of the *Rambler*, though the matter is excellent. Addison speaks at length about Johnson's style in general: "It has too unwieldy and too uniform a dignity. In composition even excellence itself will tire, if continued without variety. And your very best performances, from too free a use of uncommon words, and from a constant endeavour at quaintness, antithesis, and wit, are destitute of that simplicity, without which there can be no true elegance. ... And my greatest objection to it is, that you have laboured it too much; or, at least, that its elaborateness is too apparent. It savours more of art than of nature, more of the midnight lamp than of the pure radiance of noon; and in your readers either produces inattention to the sense, while they are occupied in considering the words by which it is expressed; or makes them doubt the sincerity of one, who seems less concerned about what he shall say than how he shall say it." Johnson is made to agree that his style should have been simpler.

A final commentary on Johnson's prose style is provided by the Peter Burrowes papers in the Royal Irish Academy which contain interesting exchanges by letter between two lawyers and politicians in Dublin Peter Burrowes and George Knox.[224] In a missing letter Burrowes who as a charter member of the Dublin Library Society read Johnson in Dublin editions, apparently praised Johnson's prose style for its harmony. In his response of 21 April 1800 Knox agrees with Burrowes that individual sentences are harmonious but that after a succession of these sentences the reader grows as tired of them as if he heard "churchbells ringing on one unvaried repetition of notes." For Knox, Johnson's style is especially suitable for public speaking, and he agrees with Burrowes that it is very similar to the speaking style of the great Irish orator Henry Grattan. In the missing letter Burrowes seems to have quoted several examples of Johnson's oratorical style, and Knox reports that a mutual friend David Plunket had quoted even better examples. Knox then adds to his letter examples from Johnson's *Rambler* which have the same oratorical qualities of Grattan's speeches. The well-known lawyer and Fellow of Trinity College, Dublin, Arthur Browne, who owned Dublin reprints of five of Johnson's works, agreed essentially with his fellow lawyers on the merits of Johnson's prose style but had doubts about his literary criticism. Johnson's demands for precision are excessive and render him insensitive to beauties in poems of Addison, Pope, Waller, and Milton. Johnson is wrong in thinking that every image must be distinct, "preferably contoured like a sensible object," and capable of representation in painting. Many poetic images are indistinct but effective to readers who have the poetic sensibility that Johnson lacks. Johnson as a literary critic also "wants a heart."[225]

The Irish booksellers through their cheap reprints were as successful in circulating the works of Samuel Johnson and James Boswell throughout the English-speaking world as in making the four great English novelists known. The audience in Ireland itself was small and elite as for the novelists, but there is considerably more evidence of an American audience. Irish booksellers, as in their reprints of the novelists, made some modest contributions to bibliography in their reprints of Johnson's works. Examples are the 1752 Dublin *Rambler*, the 1761 Dublin *Idler*, and the 1775 and 1798 Dublin subscription editions of the *Dictionary*. The two Dublin editions of the *Dictionary* also offer the most accurate picture of the patronage for any writer published in Ireland. As with the novelists, reprints of Johnson and Boswell reflect strong links between Irish booksellers in Ireland and Irish booksellers in America. Patrick Byrne in Dublin reprinted fifteen works by or about the great CHAM and his satellite and then continued his reprinting in Philadelphia. Other booksellers in America trained in the Irish book trade reprinted works by or about Boswell and Johnson — Robert Bell, Mathew Carey, Augustine Fagan, John Parker, Henry and Patrick Rice, all in Philadelphia; Thomas Kirk in New York; James and John Rice in Baltimore; and William Spotswood in Philadelphia and Boston.

6
Irish Booksellers and Goldsmith

Of the eight major British writers used in this study of Irish reprints, only Oliver Goldsmith was Irish born and bred. After graduation from Trinity College, Dublin, he left his native Ireland in 1752 never to return. Like his compatriots Edmund Burke, Edmond Malone, Arthur Murphy, Richard Sheridan, and many lesser lights, Goldsmith had to leave Ireland to make a living as a writer, since Irish booksellers reprinted London editions instead of paying Irish writers for original works. Goldsmith spent his short but exceedingly productive literary career in London, where he won considerable recognition and financial reward. His success in London made certain that his many works published in London would be quickly reprinted by Irish booksellers without regard for his Irish origins or his many ties with Ireland. An examination of the 203 Irish private libraries shows that Goldsmith was second only to Samuel Johnson in popularity among the landed and professional classes. To the Irish library owners and to Irish schoolchildren Goldsmith was probably best known as an historian, and this aspect of his literary achievement will be considered in chapter seven on Irish editions of the historians. Goldsmith's essays, poems, and plays in their Irish editions also sold well, however, both at home and abroad. The most popular of all his works was undoubtedly the *Vicar of Wakefield*, which was reprinted in Ireland at least ten times before the Union and its Irish dress found a larger audience than any work by a major author.

Although Goldsmith's *Enquiry into the Present State of Polite*

Learning in Europe is of interest today primarily to the literary historian, the circumstances of its publication shed more light on Goldsmith's attitude towards the Dublin reprints than any other work. On 7 August 1758 Goldsmith asked his friend Edward Mills to get subscriptions in Ireland to the London edition of the *Enquiry* because "Every work publish'd here the Printers in Ireland republish there, without giving the Author the least consideration for his Coppy"; he added: "I would in this respect disappoint their avarice, and have all the additional advantages that may result from the sale of my performance there to my self."[226] Goldsmith said Hulton Bradley would collect the money in Dublin and transmit the subscriptions to Goldsmith in London. A week later he wrote to Jane Lawder for her husband's aid in circulating the subscriptions in order to prevent the Dublin booksellers from reprinting his book, and he asked Daniel Hodson for the same help. Mills and Lawder seem not to have obtained many subscriptions, and Goldsmith told his brother in January 1759 that he was sending 250 copies of the London edition to Ireland for Hulton Bradley to sell. Bradley's announcement in the *Dublin Journal* in May 1759 sounds like his own subscription edition, but the price of 5s.5d. was so high that it must have been the London edition, which sold in London for only 2s.6d., plus a generous cut for Bradley and perhaps for Goldsmith. No institutional library today appears to have a Dublin edition of the work.[227]

Goldsmith's first significant work was the *Citizen of the World*, announced in *Sleater's Gazetteer* on 30 November 1762 at 5s.5d., a shilling less than the London edition published in May 1762.[228] Separate letters by the Chinese philosopher had been printed in the *Gazetteer* and *Exshaw's Magazine* 1760–61, both of whose publishers issued reprints of various Goldsmith's works, but there was no significant response until Jeoffry Wagstaffe's in the *Dublin Mercury*, whose proprietor James Hoey issued six reprints of Goldsmith's works. Wagstaffe wrote on 13 June 1767: "I cannot here omit to mention an author who is now living, who inherits a large portion of the spirit of the three great geniuses I have mentioned [Swift, Cervantes, Butler]. He, with the most settled composure, treats the gravest subjects in so pleasing a manner, as to make me laugh, whilst he conveys the most interesting lessons for our conduct in life. He has hit on the true method of Horace, of *ridentem dicere verum*; that is, he sets forth truth in a laughing manner. The reader need hardly be informed, that I mean the author of some essays lately published, and of the VICAR OF WAKEFIELD. I defy a reader of taste to read his Description of Epidemic Terror, or of Beau Tibbs, without laughing very heartily; and yet he seems to have written them with the most composed gravity." Demand was great enough to warrant reprintings in 1769 and 1775, but only twenty-one Irish library owners had it, and only seventeen the sequel the collected *Essays* of 1767. James Williams reprinted the second London edition of 1766 rather than the first and was thus able to include one of the two new essays in the second London edition, though he rejected the other. The Trinity College, Dublin, copy of Williams's 1772 edition was purchased by Thomas Fitzgerald of Lisheen, County Tipperary, created a baronet in 1801, and the copy also has the autograph of his sister Clotilda dated 1775 and a twelve-line original poem by her beginning "Tis said tis woman prone to changing/Through all the rounds of folly ranging." John Stockdale, one of many Irish bookmen who would join the Philadelphia book trade after the Union, reprinted the *Essays* in 1793 after copyright had expired. The only published response to an Irish edition of the *Essays* seems to have been *Exshaw's Magazine*, whose publisher had reprinted seven works by Goldsmith; Exshaw in March 1773 commended the essays as the work of a poet rather than a philosopher, but there were still "many good precepts blended with much anecdote."

During the period between Goldsmith's two achievements in the essay genre the Irish booksellers reprinted the *Vicar of Wakefield*, the most often reprinted work by the major writers of this study. Published on 27 March 1766, the London edition was followed exactly two months later by the cheaper Dublin reprint. A second Dublin edition was out two weeks later at a slightly higher price; if James Hoey's *Dublin Mercury* was not indulging in "puffing," the second edition was "nearly all sold off" by 22 July 1766. There was also a Cork edition in 1766 by Eugene Swiney, who publicized it well in his *Corke Journal* and his *Cork Evening Post*. The 1767 Dublin edition had an unusual fate in the American colonies. Apparently the Dublin imprint was sufficiently prestigious even before the American Revolution when the export of Irish books to the colonies was prohibited that at least one American bookseller wanted to pass off an American edition as a Dublin edition. In

1767 John Mein, a bookseller in Boston and proprietor of a circulating library mentioned in chapter three, had William M'Alpine reprint either a London or Dublin edition of Goldsmith's novel but use a Dublin rather than a Boston imprint. John Eliot Alden in 1942 reported that no copy had survived,[229] but Yale has the copy owned by Philip Wentworth in 1801, who wrote on the flyleaf that he had received the book as a gift. Wentworth presented it the next year to John Franck, Junior, of Boston, who four times autographed the second volume, the only one that survives. Mein's bibliographer identifies several books that Mein published in Boston with a London imprint but no other books with a Dublin imprint.

The heavy demand for Irish editions of the work in the English-speaking world required a total of ten editions before the Union. The 1793 edition was printed for James Moore by John Stockdale, who would transfer from the Dublin to the Philadelphia trade after the Union. The next year the *Vicar of Wakefield* was reprinted by Thomas Henshall in his series of twenty-eight classic novels reprinted from the Cooke series in London. Goldsmith's novel was published in June 1794 according to the *Hibernian Journal*, second only to Fielding's *Tom Jones* in Henshall's list. The Henshall edition was probably the one that Timothy Brundige had in his Dumfries, Virginia, bookshop on 2 January 1796 from Mathew Carey.[230] Of special interest is W. Gilbert's 1797 reprint of the 1796 London translation by M. J. B. Biset, *Le curé de Wakefield*. Whether this Dublin reprint was aimed at the large French Huguenot community in Ireland or at an audience in France is unknown, but the Yale copy was owned by Emma Anne Jameson of the landed family of Winfield, County Galway, headed by John Jameson (1740–1824). Using the book as a means to improve her French, Miss Jameson made numerous marginal notes such as English translations of French words or alternative French forms, and she was apparently struck by the last clause in the novel, which she copied out, "Je n'avois eu de resignation dans l'adversité." Three Dublin booksellers were known in international book trade circles in 1781 for handling French books, and Gilbert may have been a later one.[231]

John Exshaw and James Hoey, two of the publishers of the three Dublin reprints of the *Vicar of Wakefield* 1766–67, also published *Exshaw's Magazine* and the *Dublin Mercury* respectively. Both used their periodicals to sell their reprints by including such excerpts in their periodicals as the Vicar's sermon to his fellow prisoners and the ballad "The Hermit." Other Irish periodicals excerpted the novel, too, but only Hoey offered a review. Hoey's columnist in the *Dublin Mercury* Jeoffry Wagstaffe contrasted on 16 December 1766 the *Vicar of Wakefield*'s "fine sense, the pleasing strokes of humour, and the true picture of real life" with the vapidity of most other modern novels. Again trying to promote his employer's publication Wagstaffe two months later castigated recent fiction with a few exceptions such as Goldsmith's novel: "The *Vicar of Wakefield* will enjoy the bloom of youth, whilst our language lives. But the list of deaths of other performances would swell a volume." Though the ten editions suggest a large audience, the audience did not come from Irish landed and professional classes; only twenty-four of the 203 Irish library owners had the novel, usually in an Irish reprint. Whoever the readers were, however, they valued and preserved the Irish reprints of the novel, and thirty copies survive in institutional libraries in the United States alone. Some of the readers were Americans since Patrick Byrne, the quintessential Dublin–Philadelphia bookseller, sent copies to Mathew Carey's bookshop in Philadelphia on 26 February 1795.[232]

Irish reprints of Goldsmith's two comedies were more successful than their possession by only one of the 203 Irish library owners would indicate. The London edition of the *Good Natur'd Man* had been reprinted for twelve Dublin booksellers by 14 April 1768, and the same group, which included Exshaw and Hoey again, and William Sleater of the *Public Gazetteer*, had it reprinted twice in 1770 and produced on the Dublin stage. The success of these 1770 Dublin reprints encouraged James Rivington in New York to order copies, four of which were on sale in Henry Knox's bookshop in Boston by 15 June 1774 when Rivington sent his invoice.[233] Demand fell off until 1784 when twenty-five Dublin booksellers, including Exshaw, Hoey, and James Potts of the *Hibernian Magazine*, issued a new edition that satisfied readers in the English-speaking world for the rest of the century. The play was infrequently given in the Dublin and provincial theaters,[234] and Exshaw, Hoey, Potts, and Sleater gave it little notice in their four periodicals. These four Dublin booksellers and publishers of newspapers and magazines, even though they were publishing Goldsmith's comedy, may have agreed with the vogue for sentimentalism attacked by Goldsmith and by the reviewer of the play in the *Sentimental and Masonic Magazine* for September 1793: "Nothing but morality and sententious writing lifted upon stilts, could meet the vitiated taste of the audience; in vain did the fine writing and yet finer acting of Croaker ... engage the applause of the judicious few — in vain did the bailiff scene mark with true comic discrimination the manner of that tribe, with the elegant and embarrassed feelings of the benevolent man. The predominate cry of the prejudiced and illiterate part of the pit was, 'it was low — it was d-mn'd vulgar, etc.,' and this barbarous judgment had very nearly damned this comedy the very first night."

The demand for cheap editions of *She Stoops to Conquer* in 1773 by readers was great. James Magee in Belfast anticipated the Dublin announcement by one day with his advertisement in the *Belfast News-Letter* of his reprint selling for less than half the London price. The Trinity College, Dublin, copy of the Belfast edition was purchased by an English landowner, George Birch (1739–1807), of Hamstead Hall, Staffordshire. The first of two 1773 Dublin reprints was issued by seventeen Dublin booksellers on 17 April 1773 less than a month after the London edition of 26 March 1773. The Trinity College copy of this first Dublin edition is of exceptional interest because of its use in the famous amateur theatricals at Kilkenny. The play is bound with four other Dublin reprints of comedies in a volume entitled "Kilkenny Theatre 1810, 1812." The volume was owned by James Corry, a graduate of Trinity College in 1793 and an intimate of the poet Thomas Moore, who acted periodically in the Kilkenny theatricals 1808–1810, as did many others who would win fame as lawyers and politicians in Ireland and Britain. Goldsmith's play is annotated in the margins for the actor playing Hardcastle, probably James Corry himself, who like Moore was most apt to play comic roles.[235] The play's five acts are divided up into nine entrances for Hardcastle, with his lines counted up in each entrance for a total of 426 lines. In the hilarious three-way exchange of Act II among Hardcastle, Marlowe, and Hastings, which ends with Hardcastle's famous lines, "This may be modern modesty, but I never saw any thing look so much like old-fashioned impudence," some lines are either crossed out or slightly altered. The most significant alteration of Hardcastle's part comes at the end of his final speech to Marlowe about Kate is crossed out and another substituted for it that does not appear to represent an improvement on Goldsmith.

The second Dublin printing of 1773 is the same as the first except that the name of Colles is dropped from the list of seventeen Dublin booksellers in the imprint. The Trinity College copy belonged to the Dublin playwright and one of Goldsmith's rivals Kane O'Hara. Kane O'Hara's copy is bound with three other popular comedies of the time, all in Dublin reprints, but these four comedies are not annotated by O'Hara, who apparently did not object to Dublin reprints. James Rivington in New York also did not object to the Dublin reprints and sent twelve copies of the 1773 *She Stoops to Conquer* to Henry Knox's bookshop in Boston according to his invoice of 15 June 1774.[236] In Philadelphia John Dunlap, formerly of the Belfast book trade, reprinted the comedy the same year. The 1774 Dublin printing by Bartholomew Corcoran is the same as the two Dublin reprints of 1773 except that to the subtitle of the 1773 editions "a Comedy as acted at the Theatre Royal" Corcoran added "in London And Dublin." The Trinity College copy is annotated for acting but presumably for a Victorian company since the copy was owned by Hamilton Sharp of Dublin in 1873, and there are other nineteenth-century autographs. Essentially the same alterations are made in Act II as noted above in the Kilkenny Theatre copy.

These four early Irish reprints of the London edition of 1773 got mixed reviews even from their publishers. An essay on Goldsmith's work as a whole entitled "A Short Character of Dr. Goldsmith" in *Exshaw's Magazine* for March 1773 does not reflect the fact that John Exshaw was publishing and selling the two 1773 Dublin reprints of *She Stoops to Conquer*; Exshaw or one of his writers commends Goldsmith's essays and poems but in the last few paragraphs condemns the plays: "Were a profound theologist to write lectures upon practical commerce, or the professed merchant give the world a new system of metaphysics, we should probably regard them in the same point of view in which we see Dr. Goldsmith writing comedy .... We are not doing an injury to the poets of our time, when we assert that Dr. Goldsmith's verses are at least as pleasing as the best of theirs: we are not treating Dr. Goldsmith with injustice when we believe his drama to be very indifferent. Those writings of Dr. Goldsmith which have been most successful have been evidently the produce of a speculative study;

but the path of a comic writer lies in the opposite extreme The doctor's genius is happiest when in the closet; now, a comic writer ought to be in his closet but seldom. Dr. G. ought therefore to have avoided comedy. Dr. Goldsmith's poems are full of delicate thinking, elegant painting, and harmony: his comedy is destitute of character, of spirit, of business. His poems open our hearts; his comedies shut our eyes." Hoey of the *Dublin Mercury*, Potts of the *Hibernian Magazine*, and Sleater of the *Public Gazetteer* were no more positive in their comments about the comedy they were themselves publishing.

A less obtuse response to *She Stoops to Conquer* appeared on 29 March 1773 in the *Hibernian Chronicle* of Cork where Dublin reprints of the comedy were sold by Thomas White. The writer approves of Goldsmith's attack on sentimental comedy and extolls his "infinite matter for risibility." The essay concludes: "What the critics may think of this piece must be left to time; and while we are constrained to acknowledge, that some of the characters and incidents are too farcical, yet we confess, that, in the present lamentable dearth of good Comic Writers, the piece before us, with respect to its originality and attempt at humour, claims great indulgence from the public." The same newspaper for 12 April 1773 prints the same scene from Act II noted above in the two Dublin editions annotated by their owners. These were original responses to the comedy, but a favorable critique accompanying a long summary in the April 1773 issue of *Exshaw's Magazine* and James Pott's *Hibernian Magazine* comes without acknowledgment from the *Westminster Magazine* of London for March 1773. Just as Exshaw and Potts reprinted the play, so they reprinted a critique of it, as Dublin booksellers were apt to do. They were apparently hoping that mention in their magazines of "a great deal of laugh" and "humour strewn through the scenes very plentifully" would help to sell their reprints of the play.

Readers called for the cheap Irish editions of *She Stoops to Conquer* until nearly the end of the century. A Dublin edition for 1784 reprinted for not fewer than twenty-five Dublin booksellers, again including Exshaw, Hoey, Potts, and Sleater, and the new proprietor of the *Hibernian Magazine* Thomas Walker, has seventy-five pages rather than the sixty-six of the four previous editions, and the 1785 edition has the same twenty-five booksellers and the same pagination. The two editions of 1784 and 1785 by the twenty-five Dublin booksellers and the "puffs" from the leading periodicals helped to create the audience that demanded that the comedy be staged in January 1787 after an absence of several years. The *Dublin Journal* for 25 January 1787 finds that "the great variety of character it possesses, the wit and humour diffused throughout by the pen of the immortal Goldsmith renders encomium unnecessary." A Dublin edition printed by Graisberry and Campbell for William Jones, one of the several Dublin booksellers who exported heavily to America, came out in 1792 with two full-page engravings preceding the title page, but there was no reprint by an Irish bookseller in America until Carey's in 1824. That readers held on to their copies is suggested by the presence of twenty-one copies of Dublin reprints in institutional libraries in the United States alone.

In addition to enlarging the audience for Goldsmith the essayist, novelist, and dramatist, the Irish booksellers through their inexpensive reprints made their countryman better known as a poet. Whoever the new readers were, they were apparently not members of the Irish landed and professional classes, or at least not the 203 Irish library owners; Goldsmith's collected poems were in only fourteen libraries and individual editions of the *Traveller* and the *Deserted Village* in but one library each. Although no copy seems to survive, George Faulkner announced his reprint of the *Traveller* on 2 February 1765, just six weeks after the London edition. Faulkner's 1767 edition in an attractive octavo met the demand for a cheap edition until Faulkner's third edition in November 1770. That at least one copy of Faulkner's 1770 edition made its way across the water to the American colonies is shown by one of the two copies of this edition at Yale. One Yale copy was owned by Oliver Wolcott, eventually to become Secretary of the Treasury and Governor of Connecticut, who as a schoolboy bought the 1770 Dublin edition of the *Traveller* on 13 December 1783 in Litchfield, Connecticut. For neither of his editions did Faulkner use the 1765 London edition with its several alterations of lines in the first London edition of 1764. In both his surviving editions and presumably his first of 1765 Faulkner uses these lines (37–40) from the first London edition:

When thus Creation's charms around combine,
Amidst the store, 'twere thankless to repine.

'Twere affectation all, and school-taught pride,
To spurn the splendid things by heaven supply'd.

In 1765 Faulkner could not afford to wait for alterations in the second London edition, and for his later editions he did not want to waste time and money incorporating these altered lines, among others, from the second London edition of 1765:

When thus Creation's charms around combine,
Amidst the store, should thankless pride repine?
Say, should the philosophic mind disdain
That good, which makes each humble bosom vain?

The second Yale copy of the 1770 Dublin edition belonged to Charles Tottenham (d. 1795), a Trinity College, Dublin, graduate and an Irish M.P., whose care in reading the poem, or perhaps doubts about the accuracy of his Dublin edition, is shown by such alterations in his own hand as *breaths* for *Breasts* in lines 185–86: "Cheerful at morn he wakes from short repose,/Breasts the keen air, and carrols as he goes." Faulkner, however, had transcribed the word *Breasts* accurately from the London edition. In Philadelphia Robert Bell did his own reprint in 1768, only a year after his transfer from the Dublin book trade.

There was more demand for a cheap edition of the *Deserted Village* and booksellers responded in 1770 with two editions. The first was announced by eleven Dublin booksellers in the *Dublin Journal* for 9 June 1770 at 6d.h., a price considerably lower than the London edition of December 1769 at two shillings. A Belfast edition of the poem appeared in 1775, taken from the Belfast edition of Goldsmith's collected *Poems* of the same year,[237] and another Dublin edition printed in 1784 for not fewer than twenty-five Dublin booksellers from the tenth London edition of 1783. The only published response to the 1770 Dublin edition seems to have been in *Exshaw's Magazine* for June 1770; Exshaw was one of the eleven Dublin booksellers listed in the imprint of the 1770 editions of the *Deserted Village*. Working harder this time to sell the poem, Exshaw or one of his writers stresses the poem's universality and concludes: "Our author shews himself to be no less a patriot than a poet, and deplores the continued decay of population, and the daily distress occasioned to thousands by over-growing pride and luxury, in the scandalous enclosure of commons, etc. with a nervousness, which, however it may fail to touch the hearts of the great, is sensibly felt by every good man — The Doctor's picture of a Village-Parson and a Village-Alehouse afford no less pleasure, than we are moved to compassion by his description of a Colony driven from home to seek for shelter in America, here his strokes are truly pathetic. His description of a county Schoolmaster is picturesque, and highly filled with fine humour." Readers of the Irish reprints were apt to seize on these portraits; Charles O'Conor, for example, who knew Goldsmith's uncle the Reverend Thomas Contarine, regarded Contarine as the model for the parson, and in his unpublished notes for his memoirs quoted from his Dublin reprint of the poem the eulogy of the parson: "More bent [sic] to raise the wretches [sic] than to rise."[238] Hoey, Potts, Sleater, and Walker, who reprinted the poem along with Exshaw and others, also described the parson and the schoolmaster in their periodicals.

After Goldsmith's death John Exshaw reprinted the obituary by the Irish writer Samuel Glover in the June 1774 issue of his *Magazine*, stressing the poems as had Exshaw himself earlier in his *Magazine* after reprinting the *Deserted Village*: "Though his embarrassed situation prevented him from putting the last hand to many of his productions, his *Hermit*, his *Traveller*, and his *Deserted Village*, bid fair to claim a place among the most finished pieces in the English language." James Potts, who had reprinted the *Deserted Village* in 1770 with John Exshaw, also reprinted Glover's judgment in his *Hibernian Magazine* in 1774. Thomas Walker, Potts's successor at the *Hibernian Magazine*, continued to reprint Goldsmith's works, the *Deserted Village* in 1784, the *Poems and Plays* in 1785, the *Good Natur'd Man* and *She Stoops to Conquer* in 1784, and the *Beauties of Goldsmith* in 1783, but except for scattered excerpts seems not to have promoted his Goldsmith editions in his *Magazine* until the end of the century. In November 1800, for example, Walker or one of his writers found the *Deserted Village* "abounding in more beautiful descriptions, more lively and justly drawn pictures of rural life, than any poem in our language." Goldsmith's *Traveller* is almost as successful. Thomas Walker in 1783 added a reprint of the popular *Beauties of Goldsmith* to his list of Goldsmith reprints. He was joined by his chief rival John Exshaw, as he had been so often in reprinting Goldsmith, and also, among others, by Patrick Byrne, the quintessential Dublin–Philadelphia bookseller.

and also, among others, by Patrick Byrne, the quintessential Dublin–Philadelphia bookseller.

Glover's biographical sketch appears again as a preface to James Magee's 1775 Belfast edition of *Poems by the late Dr. Oliver Goldsmith. Viz. The Traveller, The Hermit, The Deserted Village, Retaliation.* Magee's edition is not a simple reprint of the London edition of 1775 because the selection of poems is different. The English traveller Richard Twiss saw Magee's edition in 1775 and commended it and Magee's other editions as executed "in a much neater manner than in any other part of Ireland, both as to the beauty of the types, and the fineness of the paper."[239] Two years later an even more significant Irish edition was published, the Dublin edition of *Poems and Plays. By Oliver Goldsmith, M.B.*, which anticipates by three years the London edition of *Poems and Plays*. There were two issues of the 1777 Dublin edition, both in a small paper and a large paper format. Thirty-two Dublin booksellers, the largest number for any work by the eight major authors of this study, announced their edition in the *Hibernian Journal* for 4 August 1777. Although William Wilson was one of the thirty-two Dublin booksellers listed in the imprint, he must have believed the demand at home and abroad was great enough to warrant his own printing both in a small paper and a large paper edition, although the collation is the same as the rival edition. Wilson's imprint is engraved, however, and he does not claim, as do the thirty-two booksellers, that his edition makes "several Additions and Corrections never before printed, being the only perfect one ever published of this celebrated Author's Poems." Both 1777 editions add to the four poems of the 1775 Belfast edition all the short poems and the two plays at the end. Nevertheless, W. B. Todd has shown that all texts are from earlier printed editions of the separate poems and plays.[240] The anonymous preface and biographical sketch is usually attributed to Edmond Malone, an Irish expatriate like his fellow Trinity College, Dublin graduates Goldsmith and Burke, but Malone's is essentially a revision of the Glover sketch cited above and a correction of such key facts as the date and place of birth and date of admission to Trinity College; much of the Glover sketch Malone takes over word for word. Malone may have supervised the printing of the edition since he reported to Bishop Percy of Dromore, County Down, on 18 September 1786 that he had gotten the Dublin edition printed, "taking care to make them print from the best editions."[241] At least one copy of the Wilson edition crossed the Irish Sea to Beaumaris, Wales, where it was bought by Thomas James Bulkeley (1752–1822), Viscount Bulkeley, in 1785. The Yale copy of the Wilson large paper edition is impressively bound in green morocco with gold tooling and formerly belonged to John Dawson (1744–98), first Earl of Portarlington. The rival large paper edition is handsomely bound in calf with gold tooling in the Yale copy but with no indication of the original purchaser, clearly a person of means. The 1777 edition was reprinted in 1785 for twenty-five of the original thirty-two Dublin booksellers. Two of the seven booksellers dropped from the original group were Christopher Talbot and William Spotswood, both of whom had transferred their book reprinting activities from Dublin to Philadelphia in 1784. Readers preserved their copies and fourteen copies of the two Dublin editions of Goldsmith's *Poems and Plays* survive in the United States alone.

The *Poems and Plays* was a step towards an Irish collected edition of Goldsmith's works. Although no such edition appears to survive and may not have been published, there is evidence that such a collected edition was planned before the London collected edition of 1801.[242] The Irish cleric Thomas Campbell did the major part of the writing of the memoirs of Goldsmith by Bishop Percy published in London in 1801 as the preface to the four-volume collected edition of Goldsmith's *Works*, the poems, plays, essays, and fiction for which he is best known today.[243] The Bishop's plans to publish the work in Ireland failed, and the London publishers planned an edition of 250 copies, half to be sold in Ireland for the benefit of Goldsmith's niece. Bishop Percy's friends doubted that many copies could be sold in Ireland, and Andrew Caldwell, one of the 203 Irish library owners, wrote to the Bishop twice in 1803 from Dublin that John Archer, the largest bookseller in Dublin, could not sell his sets in Dublin or elsewhere in Ireland. Caldwell was surprised: "The book is not dear as prices now prevail, it is a publication of great variety and entertainment." The Irish copies were not sold as late as 1808.[244] Why the demand was so weak is unknown; Goldsmith, in Irish editions at least, had always sold well. By this date, however, the Union had taken place, and many of the landed and professional classes, the primary buyers of books as the 203 private libraries suggest, had fled to London. There may also have been some resistance to a London edition; the 203 library owners bought Irish editions for the most part.

The Campbell–Percy life of Goldsmith is a lengthy one of 118 pages, with biographical and critical materials collected over twenty-five years by several Irish writers. Though published in London, it should probably be considered a composite response to Irish reprints of Goldsmith and a kind of valedictory since the Union had put an end to the Irish reprint industry. This final word after forty years of Irish reprints of Goldsmith stresses Goldsmith's achievement in prose even more than the verse emphasized by most of the earlier evaluations. Goldsmith's "elegant and enchanting" prose style flowed from him without need of revision, but in his two great poems, "Nothing could exceed the patient and incessant revisal which he bestowed upon them." The writers conclude with the great CHAM's tribute: "As a writer he was of the most distinguished abilities. Whatever he composed, he did it better than any other man could. And whether we consider him as a Poet, as a Comic Writer, or as a Historian, (so far as regards his powers of composition,) he was one of the first writers of his time, and will ever stand in the foremost class."

Significant responses to the Irish editions of Goldsmith's work were also made by Archdeacon Robert Burrowes, previously cited for his views on Johnson. A lifelong reader of Goldsmith, Burrowes as a student at Trinity College, Dublin, had subscribed to Goldsmith's massive *History of the Earth and Animated Nature* in the 1777 Dublin edition. In a paper about style read before the Royal Irish Academy in 1793 and published in their *Transactions* of 1794, Goldsmith is one of Burrowes's examples of how authors reveal themselves in their writings, specifically in the *Vicar of Wakefield* and the *Good Natur'd Man*. "Goldsmith has drawn all his principal personages awkwardly ignorant of the world, as if he had wished to insinuate that this quality is generally an associate of virtue, and a necessary component part of an amiable character. His Good-Natur'd Man, Young Marlowe, and the Vicar of Wakefield agree in this particular with each other, because in this particular they all agree with the author himself." Because Goldsmith was naive about the world, incidents in his works frequently defy credulity, but "It is a sure criterion of merit in a very high degree that, utterly incredible as his incidents are, his plays and his novels are such favorites with the public." Although Goldsmith was artless, he was also vain and did every type of writing because he thought he did all types well; vanity prevented him from recognizing his limitations.[245]

In a later paper for the Royal Irish Academy Archdeacon Burrowes dealt with Goldsmith's skills as a poet. Though Goldsmith wrote only 1800 lines of verse, "Such is the transcendent merit of his two principal poems, that as a poet Goldsmith is more generally known and celebrated than many of those who have composed whole volumes." He had all the qualities needed to be a popular poet: "His language is simple, his versification flowing and familiar, his sentiments natural and pathetic." Nevertheless, his ideas were not always sound. His thesis in the *Traveller* that happiness is essentially the same everywhere is dubious, and Johnson's lines written for Goldsmith at the end of the poem that happiness is in the mind make more sense. The *Deserted Village* is wrong, too, in its analysis of depopulation. Readers are not interested in Goldsmith's thoughts or his lessons but in his word portraits such as those of the clergyman, the schoolmaster, and "the sad historian of the pensive plain" in the *Deserted Village*. Goldsmith's peculiar excellence is "natural and affecting simplicity," but "Those who think his excellence is of that common nature which any person might reach have only to make the attempt and thus convince themselves of his merit."[246]

Although Goldsmith was one of the few professional writers who saw the Irish reprints as a threat to his career, he may have benefited more from these productions of his countrymen than any other major writer. Readers in Ireland and abroad not only purchased the Irish reprints of Goldsmith's many works in significant numbers but valued and preserved them; the best evidence is the presence of 153 copies in institutional libraries of the United States alone. Because six of the main publishers of Goldsmith in Dublin, John Exshaw, George Faulkner, James Hoey, James Potts, William Sleater, and Thomas Walker, were also publishers of important newspapers and magazines, they were able to give their reprints ample publicity through excerpts and reviews and hence increase their sales. Though Goldsmith may not have benefited financially in a direct way from the Irish reprints, the additional publicity must have strengthened his hand in negotiating for ever-increasing copyright payments from his London publishers, and Irish booksellers, whether in Ireland or in

America, certainly enhanced his posthumous reputation. Reprints of Goldsmith's works show many links between the Irish book trade and the American book trade, both of them largely reprint industries and the latter dependent to some extent on the former. As members of the Dublin book trade, Patrick Byrne, John Rice, William Spotswood, John Stockdale, and Christopher Talbot reprinted various works by Goldsmith before continuing Irish reprinting practices in the American book trade. Rice and others from the Dublin book trade such as Bernard Dornin, Augustine Fagan, and Thomas Murphy, reprinted Goldsmith's histories, to be discussed in chapter seven, as members of the American book trade. Still other American booksellers trained in the Irish book trade such as Robert Bell, Mathew Carey, William Duane and John Dunlap, reprinted various Goldsmith works in Philadelphia, though Carey also imported Irish reprints extensively. Though John Mein was not trained in the Irish reprint industry, his Boston edition of the *Vicar of Wakefield* with its Dublin imprint attests to the prestige which the Dublin reprints enjoyed in America. Just as they had with certain reprints of the novelists and of Samuel Johnson, so did the Irish booksellers make modest bibliographical contributions with their 1775 Belfast edition of Goldsmith's *Poems* and their 1777 Dublin edition of the *Poems and Plays*.

7

Irish Booksellers and the Historians

The late twentieth-century reader in the English-speaking world may read little history, but his eighteenth-century counterpart found this genre especially attractive, and he often satisfied his taste for history with an Irish edition selling for much less than the London edition it reprinted. Certainly most owners of libraries in late eighteenth-century Ireland bought and probably read the major historical works of their time, usually in an Irish reprint. As noted in chapter two, table two, Gibbon's *Decline and Fall of the Roman Empire*, Gibbon's *Miscellaneous Works*, Smollett's *History of England*, and Goldsmith's *History of the Earth and Animated Nature* were in the top ten, and Goldsmith's *Roman History, History of England*, and *Grecian History* were not far behind.

The Irish reprints contributed much to Smollett's reputation as a writer of prose fiction, but readers from the landed and professional classes in Ireland regarded Smollett as a historian rather than as a novelist. Not many of the library owners had his novels, but forty-five of them had his *History of England* in one of its three forms. The London edition of Smollett's *Complete History of England*, from the descent of Julius Caesar, to the treaty of Aix-la-Chapelle, 1748 had been extraordinarily successful. From ten to twenty thousand readers had bought the weekly numbers 1757–58 for sixpence each, and the profit of ten thousand pounds had been the largest ever made on any one book.[247] Its success in London led George Faulkner in a move unusual for Irish booksellers to pay James Rivington, the London publisher of Smollett's *History*, forty guineas for publishing rights in Ireland.

Faulkner's announcement in his *Dublin Journal* for 8 April 1758 represents the common apologia for Dublin reprints in general:

> All the Money of the Dublin edition will be laid out here among the Letterfounders, Paper Makers, Printers, Rag-gatherers, and other Poor People depending on those Branches of Business; whereas any Money that is subscribed to any foreign Edition will drain this poor Country of so much Cash, and be a means of destroying the above Manufactures, and enrich one London bookseller. The Dublin Edition will not only be better printed and much sooner published than the English one, but be almost as cheap again; and may not only be a Means of supporting the above Manufactures in Ireland, but also to frustrate the evil Designs that have been made to destroy Printing in this nation, many attempts having been made for that Purpose.

By September, however, Faulkner had cancelled his plans for a Dublin edition because, according to Faulkner's accusation at least, Rivington had flooded Ireland with his own London edition. The only evidence for London editions seems to be James Williams's announcement of 3 December 1763 in the *Public Gazetteer* and William Flyn's query in his *Hibernian Chronicle* (Cork) in April 1770 whether Thucydides could be compared to Dr. Smollett as a historian. Faulkner's hopes that Smollett would come to Ireland to write a history of that country also came to naught.[248]

Smollett's second *History of England* was his *Continuation* of 1760–65, which was not reprinted in Ireland, and his third the *History of England from the Revolution to the death of George II*, published in London in 1785. Luke White, one of Dublin's most successful booksellers, saw a market for a Dublin reprint of this work and announced in the *Dublin Evening Post* for 5 December 1786 that he would print a five-volume edition from a copy in his possession, presumably the 1785 London edition, "with the Author's last corrections." White published the work in April 1787 at £1.12s.6d. This is a rare example up to this time of a Dublin edition selling for more than the London edition it reprinted and an augury of what would happen regularly by the end of the century with the new London reprint series; the London edition sold for £1.5s.0d. according to the *Morning Herald* (London) for 28 February 1785. Unable to compete with the London edition in price the Dublin edition was still advertised as late as November 1793. Luke White added his five-volume Smollett to his eight-volume Hume in 1788 to make one massive *History of England.* Irish library owners seem to have bought the Irish reprints rather than the London editions of the major authors whether out of patriotism or parsimony or both. Smollett's *History of England*, however, represents a striking exception, and the purchase of the 1785 London edition by most of the library owners rather than the 1787 Dublin reprint suggests that the "Buy Irish" policy lost out to the lower price of the London edition. The 1787 Dublin reprint was in the Dublin Library Society, which required the purchase of Dublin editions, and the Cork Library Society. The only Smollett work in the Library of Trinity College, Dublin, before 1800 was the *History of England* but in the London edition of 1760–65 rather than the Dublin reprint of 1787. The only surviving set of the Dublin edition that I am aware of is the Trinity College, Dublin, one obtained from Arthur James Plunkett (1759–1836), eighth Earl of Fingall. Though demand in Ireland was weak, Patrick Byrne dispatched six sets of the Dublin edition of 6 April 1795 to Mathew Carey, and by 2 January 1796 three of these had made their way south from Philadelphia to Timothy Brundige's bookshop in Dumfries, Virginia.[249]

A certain "C. Sh." in an article for James Moore's *Dublin Magazine* in August 1799 recommended a reading program for the periodical's readers that would include for the historians Smollett, Goldsmith, and Gibbon; James Moore published histories of both Gibbon and Goldsmith. Like Smollett, Goldsmith was very successful as a historian. His London publishers paid him eight hundred guineas for the copyright of his *History of the Earth and Animated Nature*, five hundred pounds for his *History of England*, 250 guineas for his *Roman History*, and £250 for his *Grecian History*.[250] Though posterity has tended to regard these compilations as hack work or "well-written potboilers,"[251] they were the most popular of Goldsmith's many works in their Irish editions. Readers of the Irish editions seem to have agreed with Samuel Johnson's statement to Boswell in April 1773 that Goldsmith stood in "the first class" of historians.[252]

The best received of the many Irish reprints of Goldsmith's histories was the *History of the Earth and Animated Nature*.[253] James Williams on 3 March 1775 in the *Hibernian Journal* said that he was taking subscriptions for an eight-volume edition of the *History of the Earth* that would sell for two guineas as compared with the price of

£3.12s.0d. for the 1774 London edition. Similar advertisements by Williams appeared in the newspapers of Belfast, Cork, Kilkenny, and Limerick. The work was ready by 16 September 1776, and some sets must have been sold with a 1776 imprint and without the subscription list, as suggested by the Yale set of 1776. The *Dublin Journal* announcement of 21 January 1777 gives the publication date as March 1st, and the three sets I have seen all have a first volume imprint of 1777 with a subscription list and the other seven volumes dated 1776. The *Dublin Journal* also includes a puff by Williams "We had long been in want of a Work of this Kind, executed in a masterly Manner; and which united the *utile et dulci*. We had scarce any Book on this Subject in our Language except Nature displayed; but this being in the form of a Dialogue, and the Cartesian and Ramistic Systems of Philosophy being their retained, (though now exploded) it was neither an entertaining nor sufficiently instructive Book. These Defects, and many others, are rectified by Dr. Goldsmith. … this Production, of so celebrated an Author, may therefore be impartially pronounced a valuable acquisition to English Literature." Irish reprints of London editions rarely include a preface by the publisher, but Williams in his preface claims to have excelled London editions in this and other works and hopes to have his name enrolled with such famous British publishers as Tonson, Millar, and Foulis: "The celerity of putting a work of merit, beautifully printed, into every one's hands, (which is my principal desire) must always draw the applause of the learned and curious, since we see as many fond of a new book to read, as to be the first night at a new play. The Animated World is the object of every rational being: Dr. GOLDSMITH'S History of it is the first work of its kind in point of merit. He has made the study of it easy and familiar. My boast is to have represented the Doctor in an handsome garb, such as He deserves to appear in; I have made more room for him to exhibit in, and I am happy, that thro' me, my Countrymen will be gratified with this charming repast." Williams dedicates his edition to Edmund Sexton Pery, Speaker of the Irish House of Commons: "Dr. Goldsmith's *History of Animated Nature*, is a composition of the first merit, and I offer it to Your perusal in an Irish dress, as I am persuaded You will be pleased to see an attempt, to remove the reproaches which Ireland has laboured under for bad Printing." The eight-volume set makes an impressive appearance, and the four sets I have seen are all beautifully bound in either green morocco or calf with gold tooling and lettering.

The subscription list for the edition tells us much about the clientele for Irish editions of Goldsmith and other major authors, for the subscribers to Goldsmith's *History* fall into the same categories as those to the two subscription editions of Johnson's *Dictionary*, Richardson's *Clarissa*, and Smollett's *Don Quixote*; the Goldsmith subscribers also represent the same groups as the 203 library owners and the owners of copies that survive today in institutional libraries. The subscription list to Goldsmith's *History* especially invites comparison with the 1775 Dublin edition of Johnson's *Dictionary* since the two works were separated by only two years. Although the price of two guineas was the same for both works, there were a hundred more subscriptions to Goldsmith than to Johnson, and far more booksellers subscribed for their customers. The 501 sets of Goldsmith were bought by 297 persons, but after the thirty-two booksellers, one of whom was William Spotswood, the Dublin–Philadelphia bookseller who appears so often in this study, are deducted, 265 individuals remain, all Irish except for a Canadian merchant and a London lawyer. Where clergymen and landed proprietors are about equal in numbers among the library owners and the Johnson subscribers, the thirty-three clergymen were less than half the number of landed gentry who subscribed to Goldsmith. The merchants appear to be the next largest group followed by at least twenty-three lawyers, thirteen civil servants, and thirteen medical practitioners, including two apothecaries, one of whom also subscribed to Johnson's *Dictionary*. Thirteen women subscribed to Goldsmith, mostly from the landed class but also three booksellers and an actress; one of the booksellers Mrs. Mary Hay also subscribed to Johnson's *Dictionary*. Forty-eight subscribed to both Johnson and Goldsmith, but Goldsmith did not attract the English subscribers that Johnson did. Anglo-Irish subscribers were in the majority for both works, but nearly forty percent of the Goldsmith subscribers had old Irish names. Most of the booksellers subscribing to Goldsmith for their customers were from Dublin, but booksellers are also listed from Belfast, Clonmell, Cork, Drogheda, Kilkenny, and Waterford. The set now at Yale has the Trinity College, Dublin, seal in gold on green morocco and was awarded in 1785 as a prize for academic excellence at Trinity to Simon Purdon of the landed family of Tinerana, County Clare; its next owner was another Trinity College graduate Archdeacon John O'Regan of County Kildare.

The 501 sets or more in the 1777 edition seem to have met the demand for an Irish edition until 1782 when Williams reissued the work in a smaller format and at a lower price, and this printing was still being advertised as late as 31 December 1791 by John Rice in Dublin, who would join the Baltimore book trade in 1803. This was probably the edition that Mathew Carey got from Patrick Byrne on 14 March 1795, even though Carey the same year published his own extraordinarily popular edition of the work; Timothy Brundige had the Dublin edition in his Dumfries, Virginia, shop on 2 January 1796.[254] A wider audience for the work in Ireland is shown by its use in the schools of Kildare and Leighlin Dioceses at the end of the century.[255] Whether Goldsmith's subscribers or other readers of the Irish editions agreed with a modern scholar that the work is Goldsmith's "most substantial literary legacy"[256] is unknown, but Bishop Percy of County Down, who did not subscribe to the Dublin edition of 1777 praised the work as a literary composition if not as a scientific treatise: "The elegance and purity of the style, the interesting and striking reflections with which it abounds, and the powers of description which so frequently appear must atone for the want of original information on the subjects introduced, and for the occasional mistakes, which were impossible to be avoided by a writer who took all his materials on trust."[257]

Goldsmith's *History of England* in its two forms went through nine Irish reprints by my count, eight in Dublin, and one in Belfast, though few of these survive. One buyer of the 1765 *History of England in a Series of Letters from a Nobleman to his Son*, the first of four Irish editions, was Edmond Power (fl. 1739–75), of Gurteen, County Waterford, who claimed the outlawed barony of Power and Curraghmore. Power's bookplate apears in both volumes of the set now at the National Library of Ireland and also a Latin inscription in his own hand: *Ex Libris Edmundi, Domini Power et Curraghmore, Gurteen.* The Yale set of the same Dublin reprint has eighteenth-century autographs of four persons, two of them daughters of the Irish statesman and one of the 203 library owners John Beresford. The reprint by fifteen Dublin booksellers of the *History of England, from the Earliest Times to the Death of George II* came out in 1771 in four volumes, and there was a Belfast edition the same year, followed by Dublin editions in 1789 and 1796 after copyright had expired. A Philadelphia bookseller trained in the

Dublin book trade Mathew Carey issued his own reprints in 1806, 1808, and 1810. Twenty-seven of the library owners had either *History of England* usually in Dublin reprints, and both Thomas Jefferson and Edmond Malone in London owned Dublin reprints. The Trinity College, Dublin set of the 1771 edition was owned in 1779 by Catherine Spring of the landed family of County Kerry, one of whose members was Lord Monteagle, a friend of the poet Thomas Moore. That the response to the work was from a wide spectrum of readers is shown by two reports on the texts used by schoolchildren. Parish priests in Ireland reported to the Commission on Education set up by Parliament in 1825 that Goldsmith's *England* had been widely used as a text in parish schools for many years.[258] A more specific report on school texts notes that Goldsmith's *England* c. 1800 was used in twenty-one schools in Kildare and Leighlin Dioceses.[259]

Goldsmith's second *History of England* appears to have served as a text also at Trinity College, Dublin. The Trinity College set of the 1796 edition first belonged to James Gibbons of Cabragh, County Dublin, and Ballynegall, County Westmeath, and later to Gibbons's cousin and successor at his Ballynegall estate J. W. Middleton Berry, whose bookplate bears the motto *Nihil sine Labore*. A holder of two degrees from Trinity, Gibbons in 1806–07 made notes in all four volumes that show a close study of the work presumably at Trinity. He marked important dates at the tops of many pages, and at the end of each of the four volumes he made a list of monarchs whose reigns were described in that volume. Scattered throughout the first volume are numerous autographs besides Gibbons's own, that of his father, who was High Sheriff of Westmeath, and those of six contempories. One of the six was Bartholomew Lloyd (1772–1837), who wrote that he hoped to become Professor of Natural Philosophy at Trinity, an honor that he would achieve in 1822 along with the many other honors that won him a place in the *Dictionary of National Biography*. Gibbons also noted that he was writing an essay in French for one of his tutors. This Dublin edition of 1796 like the edition of 1789 was published by John Rice, who sent sets of the 1789 edition to Mathew Carey on 31 December 1791 and in 1803 joined the Baltimore book trade; Timothy Brundige also sold it in Dumfries, Virginia.[260] Thomas Walker probably included Thomas Davies's comments in his *Hibernian Magazine* of June 1780 that the work was "one of the pleasantest and most instructive books in our language" and one "in everybody's hands" to "puff" a work that he and fourteen other Dublin booksellers had published.

Goldsmith's *Roman History* had the same large audience as his *History of England* in its two forms. By my count there were eight Irish editions before the extension of copyright law to Ireland in 1801, all from Dublin except for one in Cork. Four of these are interesting because of evidence about their readers in Ireland and America. The Trinity College, Dublin, copy of the 1769 reprint originally belonged to William Thomas Monsell of Tervoe, County Limerick, a Dublin civil servant who also subscribed to the 1775 edition of Johnson's *Dictionary*. The 1771 edition now at Trinity was originally owned by Samuel Waring of Waringstown, County Down, who also owned the 1748 *Roderick Random* now at Yale. The 1792 edition was in Timothy Brundige's shop in Dumfries, Virginia, in 1796.[261] Brundige's supplier had presumably been Mathew Carey, whose Dublin supplier was probably John Rice, one of the five Dublin booksellers handling the work, and a frequent supplier to Carey. In 1806 Miss C. Moore, daughter of the Hon. Ponsonby Moore (1730–1819) of Ballyhale, County Kilkenny, bought the copy of the 1801 Cork edition now at Trinity. The work was in thirty-four of the private libraries, though a few of these were London editions, and again there was a large audience of schoolchildren. Parish priests listed it as a popular text for the Commissioners of Education, and eleven of the schools of Kildare and Leighlin used it as a text as did the new Roman Catholic theological seminary at Maynooth.[262] In the United States two former members of the Irish book trade Bernard Dornin and Thomas Murphy reprinted Goldsmith's *Roman History* in 1804 and 1818 respectively.

Goldsmith's *Grecian History* was somewhat less popular than the other histories though still bought by twenty-four library owners, more than bought Goldsmith's plays and poems. The three Dublin editions 1774–1801 maintained the price advantage that Dublin editions usually had over the London editions they reprinted, 5s.5d. *vs.* 10s.6d. for the London editions according to the *General Evening Post* (London) in March 1785. Like Goldsmith's other histories the *Grecian History* was a school text according to the parish priests's report for the Commissioners of Education, and it was specifically used in three schools in Kildare and Leighlin.

Knowledge of this kind of response may have led Mathew Carey in 1800 to issue his own reprint of three thousand copies for sale in America, and he published other editions in 1805, 1808, and 1809; another former member of the Dublin book trade in Philadelphia Augustine Fagan issued a reprint in 1811. Although Exshaw, Hoey, Potts, Sleater, and Walker issued many reprints of Goldsmith's histories, they did not use the periodicals that all of them published to enhance sales of these works as they had often done for their reprints of Goldsmith's poems, plays, and fiction. In spite of his eleven reprints of Goldsmith's histories, Exshaw saw Goldsmith as a poet and fiction writer rather than as an historian, as he wrote in his *Magazine* for March 1773: "The province of Dr. Goldsmith's genius may be said to be speculation. In his prose as well as in his poetical works, fancy is predominant, Hence, perhaps, his taste is superior to his judgment. He is not equal to the labour of grave researches and deep disquisitions; and for this reason he ought not to have attempted to write history." In January 1775, moreover, Exshaw or one of his writers lamented that Goldsmith the "good poet" became a "compiler of historical epitomes."

Exshaw's verdict on Goldsmith's histories was certainly not true for the master historical work of the century and also the most controversial, Edward Gibbon's *History of the Decline and Fall of the Roman Empire*, which was purchased by sixty-seven of the library owners as compared with forty-five who bought Smollett's *History of England* and thirty-seven who bought Goldsmith's *History of the Earth*. Moreover, Gibbon's *Rome* was exceeded in popularity among the library owners only by Johnson's *Dictionary* and the same author's *Lives of the Poets*. Unlike many of the Irish editions, however, few copies of the early editions of Gibbon's *Rome* have survived.[263] William Hallhead first advertised his edition on 18 July 1776, five months after the London edition it reprinted, at a price of 10s.10d. bound or 9s.9d. in boards, as compared with the London price of one guinea. His announcement in the *Freeman's Journal* quoted from the *Monthly Review* for March: "We have now before us one of those Productions, which will do honour to the Literature of our Country, and give the Author a just Title to a distinguished Rank among the most celebrated Historians of the present Age." As an additional "puff" for his edition Hallhead told prospective buyers that the London edition had sold off in three days though selling for twice the Dublin price. John Hay announced the Hallhead edition in the *Belfast News-Letter* for 9 August 1776 and continued the notice from the *Monthly Review*: "The Subject he hath chosen is highly interesting to every Class of Readers, and must afford both Instruction and Entertainment. It naturally leads to Points equally curious and important, the Discussion of which requires an uncommon Share of Learning, Judgment and Sagacity. Mr. Gibbon in every Respect appears equal to the Task; his Stile is well suited to the Dignity of his Subject — elegant, perspicuous and manly." The Trinity College, Dublin, set, the only one that appears to survive in public libraries, originally belonged to its Historical Society founded in 1770.[264] Gibbon himself owned the Dublin reprint, and he commented to his mother on 25 September 1776: "The natives have printed it very well, and the notes at the bottom take up much less space than I could have imagined."[265] The Dublin edition encouraged Gibbon to drop his opposition to footnotes, and the next London edition used footnotes instead of endnotes.

To meet the demand Hallhead had to reprint in 1777 the two volumes octavo he had done the year before, and he capitalized on the heavy sale by reprinting Gibbon's early work *Essai sur L'Étude de la Littèrature*. To meet the need for a smaller format Luke White in the same year reprinted the work in six volumes duodecimo. The most striking response generated by the Dublin reprints was from a Dublin cleric the Rev. Smyth Loftus, whose *Reply to the Reasonings of Mr. Gibbon in his History of the Roman Empire, which seem to affect the Truth of Christianity* was published in Dublin in 1777 and reprinted in London the following year.[266] The work is a pamphlet of eighty-seven pages which Loftus says he intended to be bound with Bishop Watson's *Apology for Christianity* reprinted in Dublin in 1777. Loftus makes specific references to the Dublin edition of Gibbon's *Rome* but is primarily concerned with a defense of the Christian faith. He finds some validity in Gibbon's identification of five secondary causes for the rise of Christianity but objects to Gibbon's subtle undermining of the Christian faith; in Loftus's unhappy metaphor Gibbon's "Jaundiced eye" ... turns everything to its own blackness and horror." Gibbon was right in attributing the growth of the Christian Church in part to the belief in its miracles but wrong in suggesting that these miracles did not happen; for Loftus the apostles who witnessed the miracles could not be deceived. Gibbon was also selective in his evidence; instead of concentrating on the great early days of the Church in the first century, he stressed abuses that developed in later centuries. To Loftus, Gibbon's analysis encourages scepticism and infidelity, and in the interests of truth, his country, and the welfare of mankind he should strike out the anti-Christian passages primarily in chapters fifteen and sixteen. Stung by the many attacks on his analysis of Christianity, Gibbon published his *Vindication of some passages in the fifteenth and sixteenth chapters of the history and decline and fall of the Roman Empire*, and this work was reprinted by thirteen Dublin booksellers in 1779, including John Exshaw of *Exshaw's Magazine* and Thomas Walker of the *Hibernian Magazine*. Now that he was trying to sell Gibbon, Walker may have regretted his comments in his *Hibernian Magazine* in 1776 about Gibbon's "disgusting gallicisms" and other French aspects of his style which contributed "an air of pertness and flippancy." The Irish library owners were more impressed with Gibbon's *Vindication* than with his many assailants since thirteen of them bought the *Vindication* and almost none bought published attacks on Gibbon. The survival rate of the *Vindication* has been far better than the *Decline and Fall* itself since ten copies of the Dublin edition are to be found in public libraries in the United States alone.

Gibbon added two volumes to his *Decline and Fall of the Roman Empire* in 1781, and the London three-volume quarto edition was announced on 4 April 1781 at three guineas; Hallhead's reprint was out by 4 August 1781 at £1.19s.0d. bound or £1.16s.0d. in boards. Maurice Craig cites the binding of one six-volume octavo set in green morocco as an outstanding example of eighteenth-century Irish bookbinding.[267] William Wilson, among the most active of the Dublin publishers and a frequent supplier of Dublin editions to Mathew Carey and other Philadelphia booksellers, issued further Dublin editions in 1782 and 1784. Gibbon completed the last three volumes in 1788, and the Dublin edition for Luke White in 1788 in six volumes octavo reprinted the fourth, fifth, and sixth volumes of the London quarto edition, and the following year White reprinted the first six volumes to make a twelve-volume set. Maurice Craig again cites the beautiful green morocco bindings of two sets from the 1784 Wilson edition and the 1788 White edition as examples of the Irish bookbinder's art. The White edition of twelve volumes priced at £3.18s.0d. was still well below the London quarto edition at £6.6s.0d. but above the London twelve-volume octavo set at three pounds. Although Gibbon and his publishers Strahan and Cadell were getting no money from these Dublin reprints, they were getting the publicity that stimulated sales, and their earnings from the *Decline and Fall* by the end of the century amounted to nine thousand pounds for Gibbon and twelve to fourteen thousand for his publishers.[268] The Dublin reprint was able to compete successfully with the London edition in the United States, as seen by the three sets that Patrick Byrne sent from Dublin on 6 April 1795 to Mathew Carey in Philadelphia, and Timothy Brundige had them in Dumfries, Virginia, eight months later.[269] When Thomas Dobson reprinted Gibbon's *Rome* in Philadelphia, he reported in the *Pennsylvania Gazette* for 18 June 1788 that prospective buyers could match up his set with either the London or the Dublin editions. For those readers daunted by the twelve volumes and their price William Porter in March 1790 reprinted the London two-volume abridgement of 1789 for nine Dublin booksellers including Patrick Byrne at thirteen shillings.[270] The Trinity College, Dublin, set was originally received as a prize by Robert Harrison at Mr. Sutton's academy in Dublin and then became the property of General Robert Taylor (1760–1839), Colonel of the 6th Dragoon Guards and second son of the first Earl of Bective; the initials RT are in gold on the spine. Seven of the library owners also had this Dublin abridgement.

Although excerpts from the several Dublin editions of the *Decline and Fall of the Roman Empire* appeared sporadically in the popular press, there was little comment. Publisher of Gibbon's *Vindication*, John Exshaw in *Exshaw's Magazine* printed excerpts in four monthly issues in 1781 and in the April issue reported Samuel Johnson's comments in the *Rambler* 122 that England had excelled in every type of writing except history. Johnson's statement is obsolete: "To authors of the present day we are indebted for historical performances, which may dispute the palm with any living foreign writers, and almost with the greatest historians of antiquity. Hume, Robertson, and Gibbon, have redeemed the credit of this country." Also publishing Gibbon's *Vindication*, Thomas Walker in a May 1791 article in his *Hibernian Magazine* agreed that Gibbon and the others refuted the charge that the present age was characterized by literary decline, but had some reservations about Gibbon's style, as he had had in 1776. Though Gibbon is responsible for "one of the noblest monuments of modern literature," he sometimes sacrifices clarity to an Italianate ornamentation, "and the attempt to reconcile the redundancy of a picturesque imagination with the appearance of energy and compression, produce, not infrequently, a confusion and incoherency in his sentences, which, in despite of their musical cadences, cannot fail to displease the attentive reader." By assuming too many facts at the command of the reader, Gibbon often fails in his duty as a historian to instruct and inform. His love of irony also detracts from the "utmost simplicity," which should be the historian's goal. Walker or another *Hibernian* writer in September 1795 made some of the same points about Gibbon's obscurity and artificiality of style but still found the style elegant.

After Gibbon's death in 1794 his Irish friend John Baker Holroyd, since 1781 Lord Sheffield in the Irish peerage, published Gibbon's autobiography, his letters, and his minor works in London on 31 March 1796 as *Miscellaneous Works of Edward Gibbon, Esquire* at a price of £2.10s.0d. in boards. Thirteen Dublin booksellers, three of whom were Patrick Byrne, John Chambers, and John Rice, all to transfer soon to the American book trade, announced their reprint as early as 23 April 1796 but did not actually publish the work until 7 July 1796 at £1.2s.9d. in boards. The autobiographical portion of the Dublin edition had been anticipated as early as 13 May 1794 in the *Dublin Journal*: "Those who know the acuteness and brilliancy of his remarks, will be able to estimate what a valuable present this Life will be to the Republic of Letters." Though a reprint as usual, the Dublin edition includes a long note on Mme. de Sévery that is not in the London edition; the note was probably written by Daniel Levade, professor of theology at Lausanne, and sent to booksellers of his native land by Lord Sheffield.[271] At least one Dublin bookseller John Archer said he would bind the set to match any set of the *Decline and Fall*, including the London editions of both the *Decline and Fall* and the *Miscellaneous Works*, both of which he sold. Some sets of the Dublin edition crossed the Irish Sea where in London both Samuel Rogers (1763–1855), the poet and anecdotalist, and his friend Richard Porson (1759–1808), the Greek scholar, purchased them because they were cheaper than the London quarto edition. Whether Porson, who according to Rogers regarded the *Decline and Fall* as "beyond all comparison the greatest literary production of the eighteenth century, and was in the habit of repeating long passages from it," had also purchased a Dublin edition of the *Decline and Fall* is unknown. Porson and Rogers "eagerly devoured" the autobiography and letters, though Porson objected to Gibbon's characterization of the republican John Wilkes and told Rogers that "Gibbon must have been drunk when he wrote that passage."[272] Seventeen sets eventually crossed the Atlantic, and the forty-eight library owners in Ireland who had it make it the sixth most popular work.

Although Thomas Walker was not one of the publishers of Gibbon's *Miscellaneous Works*, a highly laudatory review in his *Hibernian Magazine* for July 1796 immediately after the publication of the Dublin edition was followed by excerpts from the work throughout the year. The July review echoes the historian William Robertson's comment about the *Decline and Fall* that he knew "no example, in any age or nation, of such a vast body of valuable and elegant information communicated by an individual." The article notes of the *Miscellaneous Works*: "Precision and elegance mark even the least studied productions of his pen, his letters, and his diurnal minutes. His more elaborate writings are uniformly stamped with the characters of strength, energy, richness, and harmony, and, as Sir William Jones has said, abound in elegance of all kinds." Walker or one of his writers, as in the review of the *Decline and Fall* in May 1791, had some reservations, however, about stylistic excesses, and he also had doubts about Gibbon's political and religious views. "Highly amused" by Gibbon's memoirs and hoping Lord Sheffield would publish more of Gibbon's papers soon, Joseph Cooper Walker, an owner of many Dublin reprints, a month later found considerable vanity reflected but also Gibbon's essential greatness and goodness.[273] Walker exclaimed further over Gibbon's beauty of diction which revealed "the splendid treasures of his opulent mind."

As the century neared its end and Gibbon's works had all been published in their Irish editions, more systematic appraisals of his canon began to emerge. The most extensive appraisal of Gibbon's work in its Irish editions comes from Arthur Browne's *Miscellaneous Sketches* of 1798, previously cited for evaluations of Johnson and Goldsmith; Browne owned both the 1781 Dublin reprint of Gibbon's *Rome* and the 1796 Dublin reprint of his *Miscellaneous*

Works. In "On the Stile of Gibbon" Browne asserts that because Gibbon's style "dazzles the world," it is a bad example to young writers, and "glaring deformities" need to be identified. He contrasts the uniformity of Gibbon's sentences with Addison's variety: "Addison's Periods with easy air embrace infinite variety, Gibbon's with uniform disposition and monotonous cadence, offend the ear of every lover of true harmony in composition." Browne finds most of Gibbon's sentences following a formula: "Let the sentence be formed of two great members, and no more, nearly of the same dimensions, and of corresponding sound, sometimes copulated by means of the particle *and*, sometimes contrasted by means of the particles *but* or *yet*." In his own rich style Browne echoes some of the same points about Gibbon's obscurity in the *Decline and Fall* made by earlier readers of the Irish editions:

> His history is a perpetual enigma, with the grandeur and the darkness of an oracle. Each sentence is a riddle, which by obscure allusions to events scarcely if at all mentioned before, by circuitous and obscuring descriptions of well known personages, or on the contrary, by mentioning others never before introduced as if perfectly known to the reader, opens an occasion for conjecture, and presupposes a previous knowledge, which would make his history unnecessary.

After assembling considerable documentation for Gibbon's obscurity, Browne concludes his critique with a personal confession: "With heavy and tedious splendor, like a garment of glittering brocade stiffened with gold and silver, its style oppresses me with its weight, and offends me with its violation of taste, and never was I able to labour through the work or read more than detached passages, until my present object made it a duty." In an essay from the second volume of his *Miscellaneous Sketches* Browne finds Gibbon, like many great writers, presenting a more attractive portrait of himself in his personal letters than in his formal writings: "Gibbon in his laboured writings has to me a stiff, pedantic odious dress, and I dislike him; in his letters he is the easy, pleasant, amiable gentleman, and I love him."[274]

James Roche (1770–1853), an Irish merchant and banker of Cork and London, did not share Browne's distaste for Gibbon's style. Though Roche's essay primarily reviews early nineteenth-century reactions to Gibbon, Roche compares these responses with his own when he first read a Dublin edition of Gibbon's *Rome* in eighteenth-century Cork. Although Gibbon is "a protagonist of unChristian belief" and a disciple of "the soul-depressing earthbound Voltairian school," Roche's fervent Catholicism does not prevent him from paying this extravagant tribute to Gibbon's style: "No English writer abounds with more pregnant evidence of the splendour, power, and copiousness of our tongue — none more eloquent, more energetic in its expression. He is peculiarly felicitous in his translations, for there … his imagination is coerced, without impairing the riches or command of the language …. It may be asserted of him, as Johnson did of Pope's Homer, and encomium could scarcely proceed further, that there exists not a happy combination of words in the English language, not one of which it is susceptible, that is not exemplified in the *Decline and Fall*."[275]

Two other Catholic readers more actively involved in the struggle for Catholic emancipation than Roche found Gibbon interesting for different reasons. Young Daniel O'Connell was not only reading Johnson and Boswell in the Dublin Library Society but also Gibbon's *Decline and Fall of the Roman Empire* regularly during the years 1796–99 and the *Miscellaneous Works* intermittently, all in the Dublin editions. Late in 1798 he had nearly completed six volumes of Gibbon's *Rome* and observed: "It is an extraordinary, it is an admirable work. The genius, the critical acumen, the laborious research, of the author were unrivalled. He has mended my style. He has improved my thoughts. He has enriched my memory."[276] Another Catholic apologist and a loyal buyer of Dublin reprints Charles O'Conor was not troubled by Gibson's anti-clerical remarks because he thought of them as a challenge, and the ridicule of Irish antiquities did not bother him because Dr. Johnson had praised them, Johnson, who was not only a better scholar but "much a better man." O'Conor's nephew reported that his uncle applied Prudentius's comment as translated by his uncle to the *Decline and Fall*: "A golden statue such a wit might claim/ Had Gold and virtue raised the noble flame/ But oh! what shameful subjects has he sung,/ What vile obscenity disgraced his tongue." Although O'Conor, whose grandson Thomas would be in the third wave of sixty-two Irish bookmen to join the American book trade after the Union, had doubts about

Gibbon's piety, he still recognized his genius as a historian and found him in 1786 "equal to Tacitus in Talents, and perhaps Superior in Composition."[277]

By the end of the century Gibbon's *Decline and Fall of the Roman Empire* had achieved the status of a classic and was as widely found in private and institutional libraries in Ireland as any work by a major writer except for Johnson's *Dictionary*. In its Dublin editions it was in both public libraries, the Marsh in Dublin and the Armagh Public Library, and in such institutional libraries as that of Trinity College Historical Society, the King's Inns, which also had the *Miscellaneous Works* in its Dublin edition, the library of St. Canice's Cathedral in Kilkenny, which also had the *Miscellaneous Works*, the Royal Dublin Society, and the Royal Irish Academy. I have found no record of it in the commercial circulating libraries, but it was in all three of the non-profit subscription library societies in Belfast, Dublin, and Cork in its Dublin editions. The work could be borrowed from these latter three libraries and also from the Armagh Public Library where it was checked out eighteen times 1796–1802, more than any work by a leading contemporary author. Three readers of Gibbon's *Rome* were especially persistent. George Pepper deposited £5.2s.4d. on 4 September 1798 for the privilege of checking out the first two volumes of the 1781 Dublin edition; he got the next two volumes on September 20th after returning the first two and the fifth and sixth volumes on October 9th after returning the third and fourth. Lieutenant Sandy checked out all six volumes from 27 November 1799 to 30 January 1800, and Surgeon Caldwell all six from 9 July to 6 August 1800.

The demand for history books by readers in the English-speaking world during the eighteenth century was heavy, and Irish booksellers cashed in on it. They issued their reprints of the historical works of Smollett, Goldsmith, and Gibbon, among others, in significant numbers and sold them at home and abroad at greatly reduced prices. In serving themselves the Irish booksellers also served readers in Ireland, Britain, and America who either could not or would not pay for the expensive London editions. The subscribers to Goldsmith's *History of the Earth and Animated Nature* show that the audience in Ireland itself for the Irish reprints of the histories was the same small, elite audience that read the fiction of Richardson and Smollett, studied the two Dublin editions of Johnson's *Dictionary*, and compiled sizable private libraries. Reports on the reading of Irish schoolchildren, however, point to a wider audience at least for Goldsmith's several historical works. As with the other literary genres scattered evidence exists for sales of the Dublin histories in Britain and solid evidence for sales in the United States. Irish reprints of the histories show other links with the American book trade. As members of the Dublin book trade Patrick Byrne, John Chambers, and John Rice reprinted histories of Gibbon and Goldsmith before continuing the Dublin reprint tradition in America. Other members of the Dublin book trade such as Mathew Carey, Bernard Dornin, and Thomas Murphy reprinted histories of Goldsmith in America, Carey issuing eight editions while at the same time importing Dublin editions from Patrick Byrne, John Rice and others. Smollett, Goldsmith, and Gibbon were all well paid for the copyrights to their historical works by their London publishers, and what dents in the sales of the London editions were made by the Irish reprints were absorbed by the London publishers rather than by the authors. The Irish reprints in affording greater publicity and sales for the three historians in the English-speaking world may well have effected more generous copyright payments for their later works.

8
Irish Booksellers in America
The third wave, 1795–1820

The reprint industry in Ireland flourished until the end of the eighteenth century when three developments dealt it a crippling blow. Its success had been artificial since, unlike the book trade in most countries, it was based not on printing and selling original works by native authors but on reprinting works written by foreign authors and published in a foreign country. Most of these reprints were unauthorized, though some were issued jointly with the London publisher, and others were simple reprints of London editions for which copyright had expired. The three developments that brought the reprint industry to an end in Ireland itself occurred sequentially. The first was the development of a reprint industry in Britain and then in the United States. The second was the greatly increased duty on paper imported into Ireland. The third and most catastrophic was the Union with Britain in 1800, which extended British Copyright Law to Ireland.

The earliest of these, the British reprint industry, developed because of significant legal actions concerned with copyright that took place in Scotland and England during the second half of the eighteenth century. Although the 1709 Copyright Act specified a copyright of only twenty-one years for an old work and fourteen years for a work not yet published and another fourteen years if the author were still alive, London publishers believed that by common law an author or his bookseller-assignee had a perpetual copyright that survived the passage of the 1709 Act.[278] Their view was upheld in 1769 when the Court of the King's Bench in the case of Millar *vs* Taylor found for Millar, the publisher of James

Thomson's *Seasons*, even though by the terms of the 1709 Act the copyright had expired in 1758; the reprint of the *Seasons* by Taylor was not allowed. The London booksellers, however, lost in Scotland where the Court of Session in 1773 allowed Alexander Donaldson to reprint Stackhouse's *History of the Bible*, whose copyright had expired in 1760. James Boswell was one of the lawyers defending Donaldson against John Hinton, Stackhouse's publisher, who claimed perpetual copyright. As noted in chapter five, Boswell thought the case so important that he published a book on it. Agreeing with the Court of Session ruling against perpetual copyright in Scotland and applying it to England, the British House of Lords in 1774 overruled the lower court in Millar *vs* Taylor in 1769 and in Donaldson *vs*. Beckett allowed Alexander Donaldson to reprint Thomson's *Seasons* and repudiated Beckett's claim to perpetual copyright.

This 1774 ruling by the House of Lords opened the way to cheap reprints in England for books whose copyright had expired under the 1709 Act. As copyrights on the works of the eight major authors expired, the London reprints entered the market and gradually replaced the Irish reprints. John Bell's famous series of *Poets of Great Britain Complete from Chaucer to Churchill* began in 1775 at 1s.6d. a volume for 109 volumes, and his British Theatre series started the same year; he added to his poets and playwrights as copyrights expired. By 1785 Bell was a threat to the Irish reprint industry, and some Dublin booksellers decided that since they couldn't beat Bell, they had better join him. John Magee, publisher of the *Dublin Evening Post* and also a bookseller and stationer, agreed to be Bell's agent in Ireland for both Bell's *Poets* and Bell's *Shakespeare*. Magee's newspaper shows that in the spring of 1785 he was selling individual plays of Bell's *Shakespeare* for as low as eight-pence and a twelve-volume set in cheap paper for twelve shillings. The latter may be compared with the Dublin edition of Johnson's *Shakespeare* in ten volumes at £1.12s.6d. Two years later Henry Whitestone, another Dublin bookseller, was Bell's agent, and by 6 November 1788 it was the always enterprising Patrick Byrne, whether in Dublin or Philadelphia. C. Cooke's *Pocket Editions of British Poets* at sixpence a volume as advertised in the *General Evening Post* (London) in June 1795 also undermined the Irish reprints of older books.

The two series of cheap reprints of novels developed in London by C. Cooke and the Harrison brothers in the last decade of the century have already been discussed in chapter four on the leading novelists. Thomas Henshall's series of "classic novels" beginning in 1794 in Dublin may never have been completed because these twenty-eight novels could not compete in price with the reprints of Cooke and Harrison. Other threats to the Irish reprints came from London booksellers like Lackington, Allen, and Company, whose shop is described in the *General Evening Post* (London) in November 1794 and August 1796 as the "most Elegant and Cheapest Shop in the World." They will ship anywhere and their catalogue has "Half a Million Volumes." Richard Altick has recorded the delight that many impecunious but intellectually curious readers in England at the turn of the century had in reading the Bell, Cooke, and Harrison classics.[279] Up to this time readers like these may have read the Irish reprints in England. Readers in Ireland itself presumably reacted in the same way as they replaced their Irish reprints with the cheaper London reprints. In this way booksellers in Ireland who had pioneered with the cheap editions of contemporary writing were hoist with their own petard. By 1795 all eight major authors were dead and the copyrights on most of their works expired, and the new London reprints were rapidly taking over the market in Britain and Ireland and to some extent the United States, but the American reprint industry, small up to this point, was ready to boom. A leading Dublin bookseller John Archer advertised in his massive catalogue for 1793 more London than Dublin reprints, and he announced in the *Dublin Evening Post* for 11 August 1795 that he was off to London to buy books for his customers. One of these customers in 1801 was Lord Clonbrock, for whom Archer obtained London editions worth £166.5s.3d. rather than the Irish editions he had formerly sold him.[280]

Although the new London reprints hurt the Irish reprints of old books, they did not affect the mainstay of the Irish book trade, the reprinting of new books by English writers, but two developments at the end of the century dealt the reprint trade in Ireland a mortal blow. The first of these was a large increase in the duty on paper imported into Ireland from England, which the Irish Parliament imposed in 1795 to raise revenue and to encourage Irish papermaking. Since most Irish books were printed on imported paper, the increased duty deprived Irish editions of their price advantage.[281] Dublin printers and booksellers had warned Parliament before the increase was passed that their flourishing export trade especially to America, which was "greater in amount than the home Consumption," would be destroyed by the increased duty. There were fifty-three paper mills in Pennsylvania alone they reported in the *Dublin Evening Post* for 24 February 1795, and they predicted even more accurately than they probably supposed that many of their colleagues would be obliged to emigrate to America to practise their bookmaking crafts. Eight prominent Dublin printers and booksellers reported to Parliament a year later that their predictions had been accurate. Irish papermakers were unable to provide enough paper to keep the Irish book trade going, and the increased duty on British paper made it too expensive for them to use even if they could get it. Many of their colleagues had already left for America.[282] Several years later one of the most prominent of these Irish bookmen who had left for America stressed the importance of cheap paper for a prosperous book trade. Writing in the *Aurora* of Philadelphia for 23 April 1802, Patrick Byrne, now operating his own printing and bookselling firm in Philadelphia, claimed that cheap paper in America helped to make it possible for him to sell his American reprints of British law books for one-fourth the London price. In the debate in Parliament about whether to drop the increased duty on paper Henry Grattan agreed with the Dublin book trade that the increased revenue did not make up for the harm done especially to book exports to America. Cited frequently in this study for his library and his responses to Johnson, Boswell, and Gibbon, Arthur Browne stressed that the duty hurt education for the poor who were dependent on cheap reprints. Browne also observed that several important printing projects such as William Robertson's *History of America* could not be completed because of lack of paper; one printer needed sixty reams of paper but got only sixteen. Nevertheless, most members defended the increased duty, and it was allowed to remain.[283]

Several months later William Preston in his influential paper on Irish manufacturing noted in chapter one identified some of the dire consequences of the increased duty on imported paper. Although Preston was much interested in encouraging the Irish paper industry, it would be some years before this industry could supply enough paper for the Irish book trade. Dependence on

English paper made more expensive by the increased duty ran the booksellers's costs up twenty percent and the cost to book buyers up thirty percent. Preston may have exaggerated the dire results of this one development, but his statement, revised as it was for publication in 1803, should be quoted at length because it probably is an accurate picture of the depressed Irish book trade after being hit by the combination of the British reprints, the paper duty, and the Union:

> No sooner was the tax imposed, than violent combinations, for increase of wages, took place among the workmen, employed in the paper manufacture. The printing business in Ireland was immediately extinguished; a lucrative and promising trade was annihilated, a meritorious and industrious set of manufacturers were thrown out of employment. Nor was the calamitous effect confined to mere printers; it extended to a variety of manufacturers, connected with the art of printing, either immediately or indirectly; as bookbinders; leather-dressers; makers of pasteboard, glue and parchment; dealers in colours, thread and silk, and gold-beaters.

The book trade was put to work printing the parliamentary journals, but this was only a stop-gap measure.[284] It is clear, however, that removing the increased duty would have helped the Irish booksellers little because the competition provided by the British reprints and a little later the American reprints would remain, and the final disaster for Irish booksellers was in the offing.

The Act of Union of 1800 that made Ireland an integral part of the United Kingdom gave the *coup de grâce* to the dying Irish reprint industry and with it the Irish book trade in general. The Act of Union extended the 1709 Copyright Act to Ireland as of 2 July 1801. The new London reprints had already taken from booksellers in Ireland much of the reprint business for works whose copyright had expired; the market was gone, for example, for Irish reprints of the works of all the authors of this study except Boswell and Gibbon. For the new works of the Romantic Age by Sir Walter Scott, Robert Burns, William Wordsworth, and Lord Byron, the Union meant that the Irish booksellers could not issue cheap reprints but would be obliged to pay the London publishers for publication rights. The Union also deprived the Irish book trade of large numbers of its audience. Under the Union Dublin was no longer a capital of the site of a parliament; symbolically, Parliament House designed by the great James Gandon in College Green facing Trinity College became the Bank of Ireland, as the commercial classes took over from the governing classes. There was a flight of nobility, gentry, members of Parliament, and people of wealth and culture in general to London. Three Dublin historians wrote in 1818 that before the Union there were 249 temporal peers, twenty-two spiritual peers, and three hundred Members of Parliament living in Dublin, but after the Union these numbers were reduced to twenty-nine, six, and five respectively.[285] By 1861 Sir John Gilbert, Dublin's most distinguished historian, could write that the number of works published in Dublin had decreased by about eighty percent since the Union.[286] Gilbert's view tends to confirm the judgment of his three predecessors that the Union and its extension of copyright to Ireland was "nearly to extinguish printing and literature in Dublin." The three also claimed that "great numbers who formerly were in the habit of reading are by this act interdicted from doing so." Dublin was a backwater with the loss of the Parliamentary debates and intellectual exchange in general: "Now, the lively tumult is at rest, and all is secret or silent, as in a Turkish Divan."[287]

These observations do not represent simply the nostalgia of upper-class intellectuals. They were echoed by members of the book trade themselves in the Dublin newspapers and through their trade union the Guild of St. Luke the Evangelist, to which cutlers, painters, paper-stainers, and stationers also belonged. Even before the Union they realized what the Union would do to their business. On 7 January 1799 they had resolved unanimously to oppose the Union, to publish their opposition in all the newspapers, and through a committee of five, four of them booksellers, to instruct the Irish Parliament to vote against the Union. Ireland needed its own Parliament, which had caused "Commerce, Agriculture, and Manufacturing to prosper in a manner unexampled in the Annals of any other Country." After Parliament voted for Union, the booksellers voted thanks on 23 January 1800 to those in Parliament who had voted against the Union. The opposition to the Union by members of the Guild of St. Luke and their belief that the Union had ruined their business did not moderate through time. On 30 August 1810 they remarked considerable corruption brought by the Union and called for its repeal. It is not possible under the Union to protect Ireland's "infant manufactures" or "to increase the consumption of her home productions" such as books printed in Ireland.[288]

Testimony by the Dublin book trade to the disastrous impact of the Union on their business continued through the early years of the new century and reached its culmination in the interviews with Irish booksellers and educators conducted in 1821 by the British Commissioners of Inquiry into the Collection of the Revenue arising in Ireland. One Dublin bookseller told the Commissioners the Union had "almost annihilated" the book trade, another that "scarcely any thing was sent over from Dublin to London," unlike the old days before the Union. A prominent educator who had conducted interviews with five leading Dublin booksellers blamed the Copyright Act for the destruction of the Irish book trade and also for poor schools in Ireland since books had to be imported from England at prices Irish schools could not afford. Convinced by what they had seen and heard, the Commissioners concluded their report to the British Parliament: "At the time of the Union the Copyright Act was extended to Ireland, and the Irish publisher was then deprived of the power of re-printing British publications for the supply of the home market. The extension of the law, however just in principle, has had the effect of nearly destroying the trade of publication in Ireland; and the Press at this time affords no supply beyond that of a few tracts of local interest, and some school books used exclusively in that country."[289]

These reports by the four Dublin historians, the Irish booksellers themselves, and the Revenue Commissioners are impressively confirmed by the Irish Customs House Books. The average annual value for books bound and unbound imported into Ireland for the five-year period 1782–86 immediately following Irish legislative independence was only £655. The average annual value for books imported into Ireland for the five-year period 1807–11 after the Union was £6,123 or over nine times as much. The Customs House Books on Exports are less reliable because they record only legal exports and not the large volume of clandestine export of books before the Union. But it is certainly clear the export trade which by the end of the century was an absolute necessity for the Irish book reprinting industry dropped to almost nothing after the Union.

The average annual value for books bound and unbound exported from Ireland for the five-year period 1807–11 was only £428 or two percent of the value of the imports for the same period.

The Irish reprint industry might have been able to survive to some extent in spite of the damage wrought by the London reprints, the paper duty, and the Union if the American market had continued. By 1800, however, the American reprint industry was no longer a fledgling. American booksellers, many of them trained in the Irish book trade, would no longer need reprints from Ireland because they were reprinting the London editions themselves. The leading reprinter in America was the ex-Dublin bookman in Philadelphia Mathew Carey, who in turn had bought the press of his older Dublin colleague in Philadelphia Robert Bell. In addition to the Bibles for which he was probably best known in the United States, Carey reprinted many works by the eight major authors of this study, and one of the most successful was Goldsmith's *History of the Earth and Animated Nature*. As noted in chapter seven, Patrick Byrne, soon to join the Philadelphia book trade himself, sent sets of the Dublin edition of Goldsmith's work to Carey in 1795, but the very same year Carey issued his own reprint of the work, and its three thousand sets at ten dollars each were quickly sold by Parson Weems and others along the Atlantic seaboard. Carey's reprint of Goldsmith and at about the same time his reprint of William Guthrie's *Geography* earned him sixty thousand dollars;[290] Carey had formerly imported the Dublin reprint of Guthrie's *Geography* from John Chambers, who was soon to join the New York book trade, and Carey had printed excerpts from the Chambers edition in his *American Museum* for January 1790. Carey's reprint of Goldsmith's *Grecian History* in three thousand copies was also a big seller.[291] His most famous reprints were probably the Douai Bible in 1790 and the King James Bible in 1805, for which Carey, unlike his Dublin mentors, took great pains to print a correct text. In 1801 he collated eighteen editions of the King James Bible "and found a most extraordinary number of discrepancies, some of which are incredible."[292] Contrary to his usual practice of importing Irish editions, Carey on 6 January 1803 exported his Douai Bible to one of his many Dublin suppliers Bernard Dornin, who the same year was to emigrate to New York.[293]

The American reprints of Carey and many others helped to throw Irish printers, booksellers, bookbinders, and engravers, out of work. The response of many of them was the same as the response described earlier of John Magee, John Archer, Thomas M'Donnell, Patrick Byrne, and others in Dublin to the London reprint series of Bell, Cooke, and Harrison, 1785–95: "If you can't beat them join them." The report by the Dublin book trade to the Irish Parliament in 1796 cited above mentioned emigration of many of its members to America, and it is clear that at least sixty-two Irish bookmen left Ireland at about the time of the Union to join the thirty-nine Irish bookmen already working in the American book trade. The story of these sixty-two Irish bookmen making up the third wave of emigration to the United States is an extraordinary one and one that remains untold. Though political motivation had always been an important supplement to economic motivation in the two earlier phases of emigration of Irish bookmen to America, it was especially important for the third wave. A number of those in the third wave were United Irishmen, who had taken part in one way or another in the Rebellion of 1798 and a number were Roman Catholics. This third wave is the culmination of the transfer of the book reprinting industry from Ireland to the United States, the new home of "the world's most prolific book pirates," as the United States in the nineteenth century is called by one distinguished historian of the American book trade David Kaser.[294] In another publication Kaser observes that "the impact of this great influx of experienced, competent, hot-blooded Irish printers, editors, and booksellers upon the American scene has never been properly assessed."[295] The British Copyright Acts of 1709 and 1739 extended to Ireland in 1801 eliminated reprints of new books at home, but the American Copyright Act of 1790 protected only American writers while British writers would not be protected until the Chace Act of 1891. American publishers with their large Irish contingent reprinted the eighteenth-century classics for which copyright had expired, and most had no qualms about reprinting without authorization the new works of Robert Burns, Thomas Moore, Lord Byron, and above all Sir Walter Scott. Phoenix-like, unauthorized reprinting of new books was reborn in the United States from its Dublin ashes; the "great Age of Piracy," as John Tebbel terms it, was about to begin.[296]

As the heart of American publishing and the center of a flourishing Irish-American book trade community headed by Mathew Carey, Philadelphia naturally attracted large numbers of Irish bookmen thrown out of work by the combination of the British and American reprints, the paper duty, and the Union. Undoubtedly, Carey, now the leading publisher in the United States and the founder of a great publishing dynasty that would produce seven members recognized in the *Dictionary of American Biography*,[297] was a magnet, and as early as 1792 he had set up the Hibernian Society to help Irish emigrants. Carey and the survivors from the original twenty-seven Irish bookmen in Philadelphia attracted at least twenty-four more about the turn of the century. Although his publishing activities in St.Louis earned him his place in the *Dictionary of American Biography*, Joseph Charless first came from Dublin where he had worked as a printer to Lewiston, Pennsylvania, to print a newspaper and to sell books for Mathew Carey. In 1796 he returned briefly to Dublin "to print Books for the American Market," as he told Carey, but he presumably realized that the Dublin book trade was declining and returned to Philadelphia the next year. As one of Carey's printers he printed such works as Carey's best-selling King James Bible during the years 1799–1802. He also printed works for other fellow refugees from the Dublin book trade Henry and Patrick Rice and Patrick Byrne; Byrne's long career in the book trades of Dublin and Philadelphia will be discussed at length in chapter nine. Charless was printing books and two newspapers in Lexington, Kentucky, by 1803 and in St. Louis, Missouri, by 1808 where he set up the first press and the first newspaper and printed the first book west of the Mississippi.[298]

A year after Charless the Binns brothers, Benjamin and John, fled Dublin to Philadelphia primarily because of their involvement in the 1798 Rebellion. They had a rural newspaper in Pennsylvania 1802–7 and then in Philadelphia John Binns published another republican newspaper the *Democratic Press*, pamphlets on local politics, some reprints, and such well-known works as the first facsimile edition of the Declaration of Independence.[299] John Binn's eminence as a publisher and civic leader in Philadelphia 1807–29 secured him recognition in the *Dictionary of American Biography*. The latter distinction was also won by Bernard McMahon for his achievements in horticulture, but McMahon, who came from Ireland to Philadelphia in 1796, also sold and published books usually concerned with botany, gardening, or natural history. He sold seeds and other garden supplies to Thomas Jefferson, among others, but the *Aurora* especially in 1806 calls McMahon's shop the Botanical Bookstore, and the advertisement of 2 February 1804, for example, lists thirty titles for sale.

The *Dictionary of American Biography* also honored the two William Duanes, who in 1796 emigrated from Clonmell, County Tipperary, where they had worked as printers, to Philadelphia. The Duanes first worked with their fellow Irishmen Andrew Brown and John Henry on the *Philadelphia Gazette*, but the senior Duane in 1798 succeeded Benjamin Franklin's grandson Benjamin Franklin Bache as the editor and publisher of the *General Advertiser*, better known as the *Aurora*, the leading journal of republican opinion in the United States, and in Duane's hands the main voice for the large Irish community in Philadelphia. Like his fellow Irish publishers of newspapers Mathew Lyon and John Daly Burk, the senior Duane was a fiery republican who antagonized the Federalists and ran afoul of the Alien and Sedition Acts of 1798, though unlike Lyon and Burk he was not forced to leave for another part of the country. Even so, Duane by 1806 had sixty court actions brought against him.[300] Duane's *Aurora* 1800–11 regularly includes long lists of books published or sold by Duane. Though Duane published many government pamphlets, much of his publishing consisted of reprinting London editions; his advertisement of 13 August 1811 is typical as he announced his edition of *Plutarch's Lives* in eight volumes "literally copied from the London edition published in the last year." Duane reprinted London editions of such significant authors as Cicero, George Colman, Maria Edgeworth, Fielding, Goldsmith, Mary Wortley Montagu, and Sterne, among many lesser writers. Presumably he purchased the copyrights of the American works he published, and his advertisement of 23 December 1811 mentions his ownership of the copyrights of four works. Duane gave up bookselling in 1812 to devote himself to his newspaper and to the publishing of at least 370 books and pamphlets. His stock sold early in 1812 was valued at fifty thousand dollars, and among his larger holdings were 5,100 copies of the *Pleader's Guide*, 1,100 of the *Republican Harmonist*, a thousand copies of *Arts and Sciences*, and 732 copies of Goldsmith's *Vicar of Wakefield*, most of which were almost certainly his own reprints of 1801 and 1809.

An enthusiastic backer of Thomas Jefferson, Duane also provided a number of books for Jefferson's library, some of them of his own authorship. Jefferson mentioned his gratitude to Duane many times and on 30 March 1811 wrote that the *Aurora*, a complete file of which was in Jefferson's library, "unquestionably rendered incalculable services to republicanism thro' all it's struggles with the federalists, and has been the rallying point for the orthodox of the whole Union." Jefferson himself did much of the editing and translating of Destutt de Tracy's *Commentary and Review of Montesquieu's Spirit of the Laws* published by Duane in 1811.[301] William John Duane left employment in his father's newspaper and bookshop in 1810 for a distinguished career in the law and in political life culminating in his appointment as Secretary of the Treasury in 1833 by Andrew Jackson. One of the Duane employees was a young Irish printer Samuel Cuming.[302]

Other Irish bookmen in Philadelphia did not qualify for the *Dictionary of American Biography* but still helped to perpetuate the Irish reprint tradition in America. William Mitchell from the Irish book trade was an assistant to the colorful British journalist and Parliamentary reporter William Cobbett during the latter's brief career 1796–98 as a publisher, printer, and bookseller in Philadelphia. Cobbett described Mitchell as "a man of talents ... expert, honest, and faithful" at the time of Mitchell's death in 1798. Exceedingly popular for a short period during Cobbett's brief but tumultuous career in America, Cobbett's *Porcupine's Gazette* achieved a circulation of three thousand a day because of Cobbett's constant battles with the Republicans. Mitchell worked on the paper and also sold books for Cobbett.[303] Second only to Mathew Carey as a printer and seller of Catholic Bibles and devotional works, Eugene Cummiskey had emigrated from Ireland by 1810, though he did not issue the first of his many reprints until 1819; following the common Irish practice, Cummiskey's firm was continued by his son.[304] Augustus Fagan learned the printing business in Ireland and was in Philadelphia from 1803 until 1823 mainly as a printer and seller of Catholic reprints,[305] but he also reprinted Goldsmith's *Grecian History*, Johnson's *Lives of the Poets* three times, and three works by the distinguished historian William Robertson.

John Stockdale has appeared in this study as the printer of the 1793 Dublin reprints of Goldsmith's *Essays* and his *Vicar of Wakefield*, and the *Bradshaw Collection* credits him with nine original pamphlets and reprints. He is also listed in the *National Union Catalog* for an additional twenty Dublin editions 1797–1813, including reprints of important works by Tom Paine, Ann Radcliffe, Monk Lewis, William Robertson, and the extremely popular *New Universal Gazetteer* by Clement Cruttwell. Stockdale also printed Arthur O'Connor's radical newspaper the *Press*, and he printed a number of original pamphlets on Irish controversies. As a United Irishman and the printer of the *Press*, Stockdale was imprisoned in 1798 like his colleagues in the Dublin book trade Patrick Byrne and John Chambers, and like them he switched to the American book trade; he was in Philadelphia by 1820 as a printer and as a teacher.[306]

Four book illustrators from Dublin were also active in the Philadelphia book trade. John James Barralet, after engraving plates for a number of books in Dublin 1783–93, emigrated to Philadelphia in 1795 where he continued illustrating books and engraving portraits until 1814.[307] H. H. Houston was a book illustrator and engraver of portraits in Philadelphia 1796–98 after engraving in Dublin for the *Hibernian Magazine*. William Humphrys emigrated from Ireland as a youth to engrave plates in Philadelphia for an encyclopedia during the years 1805–18 and was doing various kinds of engraving there as late as 1825.[308] James Neagle came to the Philadelphia book trade from Dublin by a circuitous route. Trained as an engraver in the Dublin Society's Drawing School, he joined the London book trade as an engraver like fourteen other engravers from Dublin, and the engravings that he executed 1789–1816 were of sufficient quality to earn him a place in the *Dictionary of National Biography*. He was engraving for the Philadelphia book trade by 1819, and his son John Neagle followed the same career with the same attainment that brought him recognition in the *Dictionary of American Biography*.[309]

Six more Irish bookmen in Philadelphia are linked together by their participation in the Hibernian Society. From the Armagh book trade came John Campbell to work in Philadelphia as a bookseller in 1814. Following a common pattern for Irish book trade families in the United States, Campbell's son worked in editing and publishing and compiled the massive history of the Hibernian Society.[310] Probably a United Irishman, Robert Poalk began work in Philadelphia as a book auctioneer in the fateful year 1798 and continued until 1818, issuing three catalogues in 1800 and advertising frequently in the *Aurora*;[311] he joined the Hibernian Society in 1802. James Wilson from either County Donegal or County Londonderry where he had taken his printing apprenticeship was a printer in Philadelphia 1806–14 before leaving for Ohio;[312] he also worked on the *Aurora* with his countrymen the Duanes. John Wilson was a printer from 1811 until 1822 when he joined the Hibernian Society.[313] A number of the Dublin booksellers sold tickets to the state lottery, and this was an activity of Thomas Hope's in Philadelphia as it had been in Dublin where he had also published with John Magee *Magee's Weekly Packet or Hope's Lottery Journal of News, Politics, and Literature.* In Philadelphia Hope was a publisher of books and a newspaper *Hope's Philadelphia Price-Current* 1804–13, a bookseller and stationer, and shipbroker 1804–20; he joined the Hibernian Society in 1813.[314] Hope seems not to have maintained a circulating library in Philadelphia as he had in Dublin in 1796. Peter Benson joined the Hibernian Society in 1790 and auctioned books in Philadelphia 1796–1800.[315]

By the time of the Union Hugh Gaine and Samuel Loudon had been established in New York as prominent Irish printers, booksellers, and newspaper publishers for many years. Although they had been born in New York after their father had emigrated from Ireland in 1756, Thomas and James Swords were also influential members of the New York book trade 1786–1832.[316] Undoubtedly, these four helped to attract the sixteen Irish bookmen, several of them United Irishmen, who came to New York after the breakdown of the Irish book trade and the failure of the rebellion of 1798. One of these was John Chambers, cited repeatedly in this study as the printer of the Dublin editions of Boswell's *Life of Johnson*, and Sir John Hawkins's *Life of Johnson*, as one of the publishers of Gibbon's *Miscellaneous Works* in 1796, and as the printer of William Guthrie's popular *Modern Geography* and the outstanding four-volume reprint of Smollett's *Don Quixote* in 1796. Chambers was also one of Mathew Carey's main Dublin suppliers as late as 1803. A United Irishman, Chambers added a political to the economic motivation for leaving Dublin, and he worked primarily as a stationer in the New York book trade 1805–19.[317] He also published two works in 1817 and 1819 and wrote his own pamphlet with a fellow Irish bookman W. J. Duane in 1818 the *Settlement of Emigrants from Ireland*. A fellow United Irishman, Samuel Neilson had published the *Northern Star* in Belfast 1792–97 but was forced to flee to New York in 1798 where he planned a newspaper on Irish interests with contributions by many who had been out in '98. Neilson failed in his venture and died in Poughkeepsie, New York, in 1803.[318] His biography was published in 1804 in New York by another recent emigrant from the Irish book trade Bernard Dornin. Formerly a United Irishman working with John Magee on the *Dublin Evening Post* and in Magee's bookshop, John Daly Burk was in Boston by 1796 publishing the *Polar Star and Boston Daily Advertiser*, Boston's first daily, and in New York by 1798 publishing the *Time-Piece*, a republican tri-weekly formerly edited by the poet Philip Freneau. Like his fellow Irish republican publishers Mathew Lyon and William Duane, Burk made many enemies among the Federalists and ran afoul of the Alien and Sedition Acts. His second career in New York as a playwright and historian flourished in Petersburg, Virginia, in the few years remaining to him before his death in a duel in 1808, and it is his literary work that got him into the *Dictionary of American Biography*.[319]

Another United Irishman and also member of a noted Catholic literary family in Ireland, Thomas O'Conor was in the New York group of Irish bookmen by 1801. O'Conor's grandfather Charles O'Conor of Belanagare and his uncle Rev. Charles O'Conor have appeared several times in this study as commentators on Gibbon, Goldsmith, and Johnson. Thomas O'Conor was active as a publisher of several newspapers and magazines in New York and as an author in his own right during the American war with Britain 1812–15. His own achievement was a modest one, but his son Charles earned recognition in the *Dictionary of American Biography* as a jurist. O'Conor had two other refugees from the Irish book trade as partners in publishing ventures. In 1812 he joined Stephen Wall in publishing the *Military Monitor and American Register* and Edward Gillespy in publishing the *New York Shamrock and Hibernian Chronicle* and other works; Gillespy had been in New York publishing the

Shamrock and several Catholic works since 1810;[320] one of the latter was the *Catholic Question in America* written by Gillespy's fellow emigrant from Ireland William Sampson. Though these enterprises were based in New York, their Irish proprietors advertised regularly in the Philadelphia *Aurora* published by their countrymen. A key member of this New York republican group was John Doyle, who after working as a printer in Dublin where his father had been a United Irishman, emigrated first to Philadelphia in 1817 and to New York the next year. After 1823 Doyle's bookshop in New York was a rendezvous for Irishmen who had participated in the rebellions of 1798 and 1803.[321] The notorious Walter "Watty" Cox was the last of the United Irishmen to work in the New York book trade. The Dublin publisher of the *Union Star* 1798–1800 and the *Irish Magazine* 1807–15, Cox put in two stints in the New York book trade 1801–02 and 1816–21 where he published a periodical *The Exile* and at least three other works.[322]

Other Irish bookmen in the New York book trade seem to have been less politically oriented, or at least they are not identified with the United Irishmen. Matthew Field from Dublin published a number of Catholic works in New York 1817–32[323] but never attained the prominence that his son Joseph M. Field (1810–56), the actor and journalist, and his grandchild Kate Field (1838–96), the author and lecturer, would obtain along with recognition in the *Dictionary of American Biography*. Four other Irish bookmen in this New York group were active in the Society of the Friendly Sons of St. Patrick. Hugh Smith and Gulian M'Evers were book auctioneers like the colorful Robert Bell, Smith in New York 1786–89, and M'Evers 1802–05.[324] Michael Boyle was a bookseller and stationer in New York during the same years as M'Evers, while John Montgomery was a contemporary of John Doyle and Matthew Field as a bookseller and book-binder.[325] A book illustrator who had come from the Irish book trade to work with New York publishers was Thomas Kelly, who after engraving for publishers in New York, Boston, and Philadelphia died in New York in 1841.[326]

The third American book trade center that lured printers and booksellers from Ireland in significant numbers around the turn of the century was Baltimore. Bernard Dornin has already appeared in this study as one of Mathew Carey's several Dublin suppliers, as one of the Dublin publishers of Sterne's *Letters* in 1788, and as the proprietor of a circulating library in Dublin. Dornin and his oldest son were in New York by 1803 where one of their first reprints was Goldsmith's *Roman History*, a Dublin favorite, but moved to Baltimore in 1809 to deal exclusively in Catholic books, mostly reprints.[327] Dornin's son was operating a bookshop in Poughkeepsie, New York, by 1805, and there was another Dornin bookshop in Edenton, North Carolina.[328] Another son Thomas Aloysius Dornin left the family business at an early age to enter the United States Navy where his feats as a flag officer earned him a place in the *Dictionary of American Biography*. In America Dornin continued his close personal and professional relationships with Patrick Byrne and Mathew Carey, and he had much of his printing done during his New York sojourn by a former Cork printer Thomas Kirk and most of his printing during his Baltimore sojourn by the Irish printers Dobbin and Murphy. Dornin ended his career in Philadelphia where he sold Catholic books in 1817 and 1818 to Mathew Carey. Like Dornin two members of the Rice bookselling clan in Dublin had supplied Carey with Dublin reprints before emigrating themselves to America. James Rice was a member of the Baltimore book trade 1792–1805 where he published most of his twenty-three books with Henry and Patrick Rice of Philadelphia, formerly of Dublin, probably his kinsmen. His brother John did not join him in Baltimore until 1803 and then published only five works before dying in 1805.[329] John Rice has appeared in this study as the publisher with others of reprints of Boswell's *Life of Johnson*, both in its abridged and unabridged forms, Goldsmith's *Roman History*, all in 1792, and from 1796 Gibbon's *Miscellaneous Works* and Goldsmith's *History of England*. The *Bradshaw Collection* credits John Rice with twenty-one other publications, including important reprints of Richard Sheridan, Edmund Burke, Peter Pindar, August Kotzebue, and Joseph Priestley, several of these with Patrick Byrne, who would emigrate two years ahead of Rice. In addition to these works, the *National Union Catalog* lists fourteen publications, including reprints of two novels by Ann Radcliffe, Fanny Burney's *Evelina*, and Monk Lewis's *Tales of Wonder*, the latter with Bernard Dornin and John Stockdale, both of whom would emigrate to America, too.

Like the Rice family, the Dobbin family of Cockhanagh, near Monaghan, supplied more than one member to the Baltimore book trade. The eldest brother Archibald Dobbin was at work in the Baltimore book trade when he died in 1808.[330] After completing his printing apprenticeship in Ireland in 1793, the second brother Thomas Dobbin emigrated to Baltimore in 1794 and was soon joint publisher of the *Baltimore Telegraph* and the *City Gazette*. Among the works that he printed before his death in 1808 was a reprint of Gibbon's *Decline and Fall of the Roman Empire* and a reprint of Robert Burns's *Poems*.[331] Another United Irishman out in '98, the third brother George Dobbin after taking his brother's printing apprenticeship in Armagh emigrated to Baltimore in 1798 and, though a Presbyterian, reprinted from a total production of seventy-nine 1802–14 a number of Catholic books for Bernard Dornin and three newspapers. His partner in the printing and bookselling business during the years 1802–7 was his brother Thomas, with whom he reprinted important plays by Colman, Cumberland, and Kotzebue, Pope's *Essay on Man*, and novels of Lady Morgan; during the years 1807–14 his partner was Thomas Murphy, a Presbyterian from Dublin who was involved with four newspapers.[332] In 1809 Dobbin and Murphy claimed to have "the greatest assortment and quantity of job-type in the United States."[333] George Dobbin's widow Catherine Dobbin continued the partnership with Murphy and one of her husband's newspapers until at least 1817, and it was during these years that one of their employees printed the *Star-Spangled Banner* for the first time.[334] The elder son of George and Catherine Dobbin, Robert Dobbin took over both the printing business and Baltimore's best known newspaper *The American*, which his parents had published.[335] The younger son George Washington Dobbin (1809–91) was a jurist and civic leader in Baltimore.[336]

Like the Dobbin family, the Keatinge family of Dublin supplied three of its members to the Baltimore book trade. George and Henry Keatinge and George's son George were in Baltimore by 1794 when George senior announced in a newspaper that he had been trained in Dublin as a printer. His catalogue in 1796 listed among others reprints of *Robinson Crusoe* and Parson Weems's best-selling *Life of Washington*, later to be best known for the cherry tree episode. The Keatinge brothers combined many skills; both were printers and booksellers, and George senior was also a bookbinder and stationer, and Henry a music publisher. Young George Keatinge after publishing the Westminster, Maryland, *Observer*, was publishing his Baltimore newspaper as late as

1827.[337] The most prominent of the several Irish book trade families to enter the Baltimore book trade was the family headed by the same Patrick Byrne, who contributed so significantly to the Dublin and Philadelphia book trades. Maintaining his Philadelphia firm 1801–14, the senior Byrne also established a shop specializing in law books in Baltimore in 1806. His sons William and Patrick took over their father's business, but William Byrne who died prematurely seems to have had his own bookshop by 1805 and young Patrick his by 1810.[338]

Five other Irish printers or booksellers were contemporaries in Baltimore of the five Irish book trade families, Dornin, Rice, Dobbin, Keatinge, and Byrne. The most important of these was George Douglas, formerly a Londonderry printer, bookseller, and newspaper publisher. In Londonderry Douglas had published the *Londonderry Journal* 1772–96 and such works as Henry Grattan's *Speech for a Declaration of the Rights of Ireland* in 1782 and a reprint of Tom Paine's *Rights of Man* in 1791 and subscribed for ten sets for his customers of James Mullalla's *View of Irish Affairs* in 1795. By 1797 he was in Philadelphia where he published from the tenth Dublin edition Grattan's *Present State of Ireland* with James and Mathew Carey. After brief stays in Philadelphia and Petersburg, Virginia, where he issued a catalogue of 825 titles, Douglas moved to Baltimore where he published most of his thirty works in America. As usual with Irish booksellers whether in Ireland or in America most of Douglas's productions were reprints including important works by Daniel Defoe, Alexander Pope, Tom Paine, and August Kotzebue; at least one of these, *Forensic Eloquence, Sketches of Trials in Ireland for High Treason, including the Speeches of Mr. Curran* was sold in Philadelphia according to the *Aurora* for 25 August 1894 by Douglas's fellow Irish booksellers Patrick Byrne and Edward Hudson. He must have especially valued his reprint of *Curran's Speeches* because in announcing a new publishing venture in New York in 1812 he cited as proof of his qualifications the *Londonderry Journal* and *Curran's Speeches*. In the *Aurora* for 17 March 1812 Douglas said that he and "a number of Irish gentlemen" were establishing a newspaper the *Western Star and Harp of Erin* in New York that would be addressed primarily to Irish emigrants "who now form a very considerable portion of the population of these states." This venture lasted for only two years, and Douglas was back in Baltimore. Michael Duffey after a brief stint in Pennsylvania as a newspaper publisher was in Baltimore by 1798 when he printed the *Catholic Catechism*, and he continued as a printer until at least 1801.[339] Alexander Boland, "printer of Ireland," died in Baltimore in 1808 at the age of forty-eight.[340] Samuel M'Crea from Strabane, County Tyrone, was a printer, bookseller, and newspaper publisher in Baltimore from 1800 until 1807 when he died at the age of thirty-eight.[341] Somewhat later but still early enough to have witnessed the disastrous effect of the Union on the Irish book trade, Bernard Murray came from Dublin to work as a stationer and bookseller in Baltimore 1816–19.[342]

Of the sixty-two Irish bookmen in the third wave of emigration to the United States about the turn of the century, most continued their bookmaking careers in the three publishing centers of Philadelphia, New York, and Baltimore. At least three, however, went elsewhere along the Atlantic Seaboard, and four headed west for new opportunities. John Moriarty emigrated from Ireland to Salem, Massachusetts, where Barnard Macanulty had preceded him, and operated a bookshop from 1795 until his early death in 1797.[343] With press experience in both Dublin and London, Stephen Cullen Carpenter published the *Charleston Courier* (South Carolina) from 1803 until 1806 when he moved north to publish first the *People's Friend and Daily Advertiser* in New York and then the *Monthly Register and Review* in 1811 in Philadelphia.[344] His own works were published in London in six volumes, and these along with his attainment as a publisher won notice in the *Dictionary of American Biography*. Jailed in Cork for his participation in the '98, Dennis Driscol had published the *Cork Gazette* 1796–97 and newspapers in New York, Philadelphia, and Baltimore 1800–3 before journeying south to Augusta, Georgia, to publish the *Augusta Chronicle* from 1803 until his death in 1811. His statement in the *Augusta Chronicle* for 4 July 1810 was the kind of statement that might have been made by any number of Irish bookmen in the third wave: "The editor of the *Augusta Chronicle* having been these eighteen years past, both in the Old and the New Country, fighting the battles of Republicanism, perceives that his hairs are growing grey in the service."[345]

Joseph Charless has already been cited for his outstanding publishing career in St. Louis after some early years in Philadelphia working with his mentor Mathew Carey. Charless's work was continued by his sons Edward and Robert and a stepson.[346]

Similarly, after printing for the William Duanes in Philadelphia, James Wilson headed west to publish the *Western Herald and Steubenville Gazette* in Ohio 1815–38 and other works. Winning fame and fortune in publishing, banking, railroads, and government, Wilson fathered seven sons, five of whom achieved eminence; two continued Wilson's several publishing interests, two were Civil War generals, and one a leading Presbyterian clergyman and the father of Woodrow Wilson. President Wilson, valuing his Irish heritage from his grandfather, once told the Sons of Saint Patrick in New York: "I myself am happy that there runs in my veins a very considerable strain of Irish blood .... There is something delightful in me that every now and then takes the strain off my Scotch conscience and affords me periods of most enjoyable irresponsibility.[347] Moses Dawson and the only unmarried woman among the 101 Irish book craftsment in the United States Mary Carroll also headed west. Dawson was in Dublin as late as 1814 printing the *Grand Exhibition*, but he was a member of the Cincinnati book trade by 1823 and the "notorious" publisher of a democratic newspaper the *Cincinnati Advertiser*. Dawson supported both William Henry Harrison, whose biography he published, and Andrew Jackson, who described Dawson on 17 October 1844 as "my old friend."[348] Mary Carroll emigrated from Ireland at the age of fourteen and was a bookseller in New Orleans until her death in 1833.[349]

When the Irish reprint industry disintegrated at the end of the eighteenth century, a significant number of its practitioners emigrated to America so that they could continue to reprint British books; in so doing they kept the Irish reprint tradition alive and helped to make the American book trade largely a reprint industry like the one from whence they came. That the publishing industry in the United States for the first third of the nineteenth century was devoted to reprints of British works is certainly clear. Copyright protection had been available to American writers since 1791, but few availed themselves of it. Of thirteen thousand books published in the United States during the first decade after the copyright law was enacted, only 556 books were copyrighted in Pennsylvania, Massachusetts, New York, Virginia and Maine.[350] Pennsylvania had only eighty registrations for copyright during the period 1790–94, and six of these works were published by Mathew Carey.[351] During the period 1800–9 only one-tenth of the books printed in Massachusetts were by American authors.[352] As late as 1820 70 percent of the books published in America were reprints of British editions, most of which were still under copyright.[353] The popular novel by Sir Walter Scott that sold for the equivalent of $7.50 in Britain in a three-volume edition sold in the United States for two dollars in a two-volume reprint.[354]

The Irish booksellers were not the sole cause of the American reprint industry, but they made an important contribution to it. Their number contributed to the great increase in the number of printers, for example, in the two publishing centers Philadelphia and New York. Philadelphia printers increased in number from fifty-three in 1791, to eighty-one in 1800, to 168 in 1810, and to 207 in 1820. New York printers increased in number from twenty-six in 1790, to fifty-six in 1800, to ninety-five in 1810, and to 164 in 1820.[355] These increases came at the expense of the Dublin printers who dropped in number from fifty-three in 1787, the same number as in Philadelphia in 1791, to twenty-seven in 1800.[356] No printer left the Dublin for the London book trade during this period, though a number of engravers did;[357] those who left Dublin went to the United States to do what they had been doing. To be sure, printers and booksellers especially from Scotland, England, and Germany also entered the American book trade during these years, but they did not come from a reprint tradition. The Irish book trade contributed not only numbers but leadership to the American book trade. Mathew Carey is the outstanding example, but fifteen others also made the *Dictionary of American Biography*, and Patrick Byrne, among the most successful of the Dublin and Philadelphia booksellers, is not included. The founding of the American Company of Booksellers in 1802 undoubtedly reflected the influence of the Stationer's Company in London, but it also reflected the Guild of St. Luke the Evangelist in Dublin. Assisted by his fellow Irish booksellers William Duane and Patrick Byrne, Mathew Carey took the initiative in setting up the organization, and he was elected one of its two officers. The other officer, its president as the oldest printer and bookseller in the United States, was Hugh Gaine, formerly of the Belfast book trade. In addition to Carey and Gaine, other members of the Board of Directors of the Company were the Swords brothers of New York, sons of an Irish emigrant and founders of the New York Association of Booksellers in 1802.[358] Although the company did not achieve the success its founder hoped for, it sought to organize the booksellers, improve the standards and profits, and of special importance, "to cease importation of books of which there are good United States editions at a discount."[359] Undoubtedly, Byrne, Carey, Duane, Gaine, and other Irish booksellers in the Company had made the same argument in Ireland.

Though the House of Carey, the leading American publishing firm in the early nineteenth century, was firmly opposed to copyright protection in the United States for British writers, it usually did not indulge in unauthorized reprinting practices of the American book trade as a whole with its large Irish contingent. Since Carey's dealings with British writers and publishers are known, they may be contrasted with the usual American practice. Like their Irish models, American publishers had agents in London to send them copies as soon as they were published or better yet sheets from printing houses. In contrast, Mathew Carey, his sons Henry and Edward Carey, and his son-in-law Isaac Lea usually had their London agent John Miller pay London publishers for publication rights in America. At first Miller paid the London publisher, but later the Careys had Miller deal directly with the British author. The novels of Sir Walter Scott, who was the British writer most in demand in America, provide good examples. The Careys and Isaac Lea were Scott's authorized publishers in America, and they paid Scott an average of seventy-five pounds a novel.[360] As in pre-Union Ireland, however, American publishers pirated one another's editions. Henry Carey boasted in 1823 that the Carey edition of Scott's *Quentin Durward* was out so fast "the Pirates may print it as soon as they please"; he went on to say, nevertheless, that the pirate edition would "be out in about 48 hours after they have one of our Copies."[361] Even though the Careys usually paid for publication rights, American publishers had such a bad reputation in Britain for pirating that the Careys sometimes fell under the general opprobrium. Sir Walter Scott's publisher Archibald Constable accused the Careys and other Philadelphia firms of reprinting a Scott novel from sheets stolen from the printing house in Edinburgh by a journeyman printer.[362] Several years later during his tour of America the popular British novelist Captain Marryat observed that if Scott had obtained a copyright in America, "It would have been worth to him by this time £100,000."[363] Constable's complaint echoes that of Samuel Richardson's in 1753 against the Dublin pirates of his *Sir Charles Grandison*. The Carey's virtue paid off, however, since by 1839 their books had a market value of $150,000, with the upstart Harpers their only rival.[364]

Even though the Careys, unlike most American publishers, were willing to pay British writers or publishers for reprinting privileges in America, they were adamantly opposed to international copyright as almost all their colleagues were, and H. C. Carey, son of Mathew Carey and a leading publisher and economist, would lead the fight against international copyright at mid-century.[365] H. C. Carey's arguments against international copyright in his often reprinted *Letters on International Copyright* of 1853 draw heavily on what the Union and the Extension of Copyright to Ireland had done to his Irish relatives in the Irish book trade. British copyright law after half a century has "almost annihilated both the producers and the consumers of books" in Ireland; "Ireland not only produces no books but furnishes no market for those produced by others."[366] In arguments reminiscent of the arguments of the eighteenth-century Irish book trade Carey accuses British publishers and writers of trying to monopolize ideas and the expression of these ideas that are the common property of mankind. The claims by British authors "to pecuniary reward have been much exaggerated,"[367] and Carey's favorite example is Charles Dickens. Americans protect their own writers, and if British writers want protection in America, they should emigrate to America. The new British Copyright Law of 1842 that British writers and publishers want extended to the United States gives them a monopoly for forty-two years. The result in Britain has been books that are overpriced and a populace that reads few books. In America books are cheap and demand for them is high. With international copyright books would go up significantly in price, and popular literacy would suffer. American progress and British decline are tied to the price of books. Dickens has more readers in the United States than he does at home, and American demand helps British demand. The arguments of Carey and others were successful, and reprinting in America of British books was free to continue until 1891. Naturally, British authors and publishers continued to complain, and the *London Critic*'s response two years after Carey's pamphlet is a good example. The *Critic* did not object to reprinting British books in America, but pleaded with American publishers:

"Only pay for them when they don't legitimately belong to you. Mental culture is a good thing, but honesty is a better; and however extensive the 'reading empire,' to which the American publishers minister, may become, they never can be honest men until they have wiped off the debt which they owe to the authors of this country."[368]

Born in the United States but with roots deep in the Irish book trade, H. C. Carey reflected the attitudes of eighteenth-century Irish booksellers at home and abroad. These were the views though rarely stated as such that the 101 Irish booksellers brought to America, and most of them acted on these views as they participated in the United States reprint industry that they had so heavily influenced. There was a significant difference, however, between the two national book trades on the question of copyright. Not bound by British law, the Irish book trade acknowledged copyright protection for no one, native or foreigner. On the other hand, the American book trade was required by law to pay native authors for their copyrights. But H. C. Carey spoke for both in acknowledging no obligation to British writers or publishers, even though Carey himself did tend to pay British writers or publishers for publication rights in America.

9
Three Dublin–Philadelphia Booksellers

This study has chronicled the three movements of at least 101 Irish book tradesmen from the Irish to the American book trade. From each of these three phases of emigration a bookseller's career should be examined in detail to show how he continued in America the reprint tradition in which he had been trained and worked in Ireland. For the first phase before the American Revolution Robert Bell provides an interesting example, for the second phase after the American Revolution William Spotswood, and for the main wave of sixty-two Irish booksellers about the turn of the century Patrick Byrne. Clearly, Mathew Carey is the outstanding figure of the second phase as he is of the Irish-American book trade as a whole, but his career has been well documented, and his massive bibliography has just been published. Robert Bell is better known than Spotswood or Byrne since he earned a place in the *Dictionary of American Biography*, but his career in the Dublin book trade needs to be documented.[369] William Spotswood's brief career in Boston has been identified,[370] but not his transfer from the Dublin to the Philadelphia book trade. Patrick Byrne representing the third wave published at least 370 works, mostly reprints, in Dublin and Philadelphia but is known primarily as a United Irishman.[371] Probably Bell did not cross the paths of the younger two since he left Dublin in 1767 for Philadelphia where he died in 1784 before the other two arrived. Spotswood arrived in Philadelphia the year of Bell's death after having spent at least fourteen years in the Dublin book trade. In Dublin Spotswood must have known Byrne, whose career began in 1779, and they were part of the large Irish book trade community in Philadelphia from 1801 until Spotswood's death in 1805; Spotswood printed at least one work for Byrne in 1803. Though Spotswood's views on reprints of the English writers appear not to have been recorded, his practice of reprinting London editions in great profusion in Dublin, Philadelphia, and Boston makes clear that he agreed with the vigorous defenses that Bell and Byrne gave of Irish reprinting practices.

Bell's years in the Dublin book trade 1759–67 were important because he developed a rationale for Irish reprinting practices and several roles as a bookman that he would continue in his outstanding career as printer, bookseller, auctioneer, and circulating library proprietor in Philadelphia 1767–84. As cited in the first and third chapters Bell proclaimed in 1767 in Dublin and again in 1771 in Philadelphia the right of Irish booksellers whether in Ireland or America to reprint London editions at will without paying the copyright holder. His statements are probably the most definitive ones made by Irish booksellers in either Ireland or America, and his influence in America was considerable. Irish newspapers reveal the young Bell as an auctioneer of books, as a bookseller, as a publisher, but not as a printer. He auctioned off at least the library of the Rev. Dr. James Duchal in 1761, the library of Howard Parry in 1762, and the library of a gentleman going abroad in 1766.[372] Bell's own stock consisting of 691 titles, predominately Dublin reprints but a few London and Glasgow editions, was auctioned off by Thomas Armitage in 1767, the year of Bell's departure for Philadelphia.[373] There is no evidence that he was a printer in Dublin, though he had been one in Scotland, and he certainly would become a leading printer in Philadelphia, but he had several works printed for him. In addition to two volumes of Sterne's *Tristram Shandy* in 1762, as noted in chapter four, the original Dublin edition of the *Whole Works of Sir James Ware concerning Ireland*, as revised and improved by Walter Harris 1739–46 was reprinted for Bell and John Fleming in 1764. Bell and others issued a reprint of Paul Hiffernan's tragedy *The Earl of Warwick* in 1767, and Bell reprinted Alexander Donaldson's *Some Thoughts on the State of Literary Property* in 1767 with his own preface and a defense of the Dublin reprints.

Irish newspapers reveal more about young Bell as a bookseller. Bell's list in Sleater's *Public Gazetteer* for 21 June 1760 consists of sixty-two works, mostly Dublin reprints of English writers. Bell's big year was his last in Dublin, 1767, in which he not only published his manifesto about the right to reprint the English writers without permission but also worked more aggressively as a bookseller. On 19 May 1767 in Sleater's *Gazetteer* he listed with five other Dublin booksellers a number of Dublin reprints of English writers. In keeping with his additions to Donaldson's pamphlet Bell prefaced his list with a statement against Dublin booksellers who were importing London editions: "In order to encourage the Printing Business in this Kingdom (which some of the Junto [a group of Dublin booksellers] endeavour to suppress by importation and contracting for Books printed in London with their Names) there are now in the Press several Works of the most established Reputation, which will be sold proportionately under Value with the above." Bell's bookselling activities also took him outside Dublin in 1767. The *Leinster Journal* for 1 July 1767 lists Bell's notice that he has come from Dublin to sell books in Kilkenny for several days specifically to "Lovers of Literary Entertainment and Amusement." Bell's notice then quotes from the *Citizen of the World* by Oliver Goldsmith, one of the authors to be reprinted by Bell in Philadelphia: "In proportion as Society refines, Books must ever become more necessary. In a Polite Age almost every Person becomes a Reader."

Robert Bell had made an earlier move in 1759 from Scotland, where he had learned some of the book arts, and in 1767 he made the move to Philadelphia where he would become one of the best known bookmen of his time. There is no evidence that Bell printed any work in Dublin, but in Philadelphia he became the twelfth leading printer in America during the period 1764–83 with two hundred works. Two of his fellow emigres from the Irish book trade, John Dunlap in Philadelphia and Hugh Gaine in New york, ranked second and sixth respectively.[374] Bell was the third leading printer of political pamphlets 1764–76 with seventeen, though, following the Irish reprint tradition, twelve of these were reprints. These seventeen pamphlets were reprinted by others forty times 1764–76 so that Bell was second only to Edes and Gill of Boston as the printer whose pamphlets were most often reprinted in America or abroad. Most of his prominence as a pamphleteer was due to *Common Sense* by his employee Tom Paine, which may have sold as many as 150,000 copies in 1776 in its twenty-nine editions.[375] As with other Irish booksellers, whether in Ireland or America, most of Bell's large publishing list consists of reprints, many of them of significant English writings. Bell's defense of his reprints of Blackstone's *Commentaries*, Hume's *History of England* and Adam Ferguson's *Essay on the History of Civil Society* in 1771 has been cited in chapter three. While at work on these reprints Bell reported in the *Pennsylvania Gazette* for 15 August 1771 that he would sell his reprint of Blackstone's *Commentaries* for $8 as opposed to $26 for the London edition. Another work he was reprinting at the same time William Robertson's *History of the Reign of Charles V*, he would sell for $4.25 rather than $15 for the London edition; Hugh Gaine subscribed for twelve sets. Bell's argument is the argument of Irish booksellers everywhere that buyers can save money on the cheap reprints and that the money stays at home. It is the patriotic duty of readers in Philadelphia to buy American reprints, and their purchases "will render an essential service to this community, by encouraging native manufactures."

A number of the works Bell had sold in his Dublin shop he reprinted in Philadelphia. Examples include Lady Mary Wortley Montagu's *Letters*, Samuel Johnson's *Rasselas*, Goldsmith's *Traveller*, all in 1768, Defoe's *Robinson Crusoe* in 1776, James Thomson's *Seasons*, Edward Young's *Night Thoughts*, and Milton's major poems, all in 1777; Bell's were the first American reprints of Johnson's *Rasselas* and Milton's *Paradise Lost*. For his reprint of Lord Chesterfield's *Principles of Politeness* in 1778, Bell took the preliminary matter from the Dublin reprint of Chesterfield's *Letters*,[376] one of whose Dublin publishers was William Spotswood, soon to join the Philadelphia book trade. Another interesting reprint was of Thomas Leland's *History of Ireland* which Bell reprinted in 1774 with the other two leading Irish printers in America John Dunlap and Hugh Gaine. Carl and Jessica Bridenbaugh find that Bell "more than anyone else in these years laid the solid foundations for book publishing in America."[377]

Bell had auctioned books in Dublin, and he was widely known in Philadelphia as a colorful and voluble auctioneer of books. Along with the many catalogues for his book shop he published numerous book auction catalogues, and his auctions are regularly advertised in the *Pennsylvania Gazette* and elsewhere. Contemporaries said of Bell, "It was as good as a play to attend his sales at auction."[378] Bell's *Illuminations for Legislators, and for Sentimentalists*, published in the year of his death, argues for anyone's right to auction books in much the same way that he had argued in Dublin and in Philadelphia for the right to reprint London editions without the permission of the copyright holder. Also in 1784 in his *Address to Every Free-Man; But Especially to the Free Citizens of Pennsylvania, concerning, a Tyrannical Embargo, now laid upon the Free-Sale of Books by Auction*, Bell complains of his arrest for conducting unauthorized book auctions; book auctions should not be limited to those auctioneers appointed by the state. The *Pennsylvania Gazette* shows that Bell operated a circulating library in addition to his auctioneering and publishing activities. Although other Irish booksellers in America such as Bernard Dornin, Thomas Hope, and William Spotswood had operated circulating libraries in Dublin, Bell must have taken it up in Philadelphia as still another supplement to his income. Bell's many book trade activities in Philadelphia flourished, and in 1774 his son James came from Dublin to join his father's firm.[379]

William Spotswood and his wife Hannah left the Dublin book trade to join the Philadelphia book trade in 1784, the year of Robert Bell's death. Spotswood has been noted briefly as the proprietor of the Universal Circulating Library in Dublin, as a publisher of Goldsmith and Sterne, and as one of the second wave of Irish booksellers to emigrate to America. For fourteen years 1770–84, Spotswood worked in Dublin as printer, bookseller, publisher, lottery keeper, circulating library proprietor, and as newspaper publisher. Of at least eighteen titles that bear his name in the imprint 1772–84, all but four are reprints of London editions. Spotswood printed seven of these, all reprints except a translation of Sallustius by an Irishman Hugh Maffett. Noteworthy among the ten reprints, in addition to Sterne's *Letters* and the three works by Goldsmith previously cited, are David Garrick's *Lethe*, two editions of Lord Chesterfield's *Letters* in 1774 and 1775, and Chesterfield's *Miscellaneous Works* in 1777; Spotswood was one of thirty-six Dublin booksellers for whom the latter was reprinted. Spotswood also served as the printer to the Antiquarian Society in Dublin 1782–83, and in this capacity he printed Charles Vallancey's massive *Collectanea de Rebus Hibernicis*.[380] In addition to these eighteen titles Spotswood also published the *Dublin Chronicle* with R. Stewart in 1770.[381]

Although Spotswood does not seem to have advertised his books for sale in the Dublin newspapers as he advertised his books for hire, he is listed as a bookseller in the subscription list for the 1777 Dublin reprint of Goldsmith's *History of the World and Animated Nature* described in chapter seven. Like many Irish booksellers, whether in Dublin or Philadelphia, he also sold lottery tickets in his shop first in College Green and then at Essex Gate in Dublin. He must have been successful in this work since as late as 1783, a year before his transfer from the Dublin to the Philadelphia book trade, he purchased the lottery office of one of the most prosperous booksellers Luke White.[382]

During his first two years in the Philadelphia book trade Spotswood was closely allied with two former colleagues in the Dublin book trade Mathew Carey and Christopher Talbot in publishing four periodicals, the *Complete Counting-House Companion*, the *Pennsylvania Evening Herald*, the *American Museum*, and the *Columbian Magazine*. By 1787 Talbot had withdrawn from all four, the energetic Carey had taken over the *American Museum*, and Spotswood had hired the brilliant lawyer and future statesman Alexander Dallas as editor of the *Pennsylvania Herald*. The newspaper under the guidance of Spotswood and Dallas included considerable literary material and also reported at length the deliberations at the Constitutional Convention of 1787. Spotswood was forced to discharge Dallas because he antagonized Federalist leaders and readers by giving full coverage to arguments by the opposition. Unwilling to lose Dallas's services, Spotswood then replaced his Irish editor of the *Columbian Magazine* John O'Connor with Dallas. Often recognized, along with Mathew Carey's *American Museum* as the most important magazine published in America in the eighteenth century, the *Columbian Magazine* had a longer run than any previous magazine and a larger circulation, and it was also the first to pay writers.[383] Patterned after the Dublin book trade's two principal magazines, *Exshaw's* and the *Hibernian*, which were in turn imitating the *Gentleman's Magazine*, the *Columbian Magazine* consists mostly of reprinted materials like its Irish models. Nevertheless, Spotswood and his most famous editor Francis Hopkinson and A. J. Dallas solicited original contributions from leading writers like Jeremy Belknap, Charles Brockden Brown, Noah Webster, and three future presidents of the United States, Thomas Jefferson, James Madison, and John Quincy Adams; the complete set of the *Columbian Magazine* 1787–92 was in Jefferson's library. Each issue in addition to prose fiction and essays also contains a verse section entitled the

"Columbian Parnassiad" during the three years of Spotswood's proprietorship. Although Spotswood hired an Irish editor John O'Connor briefly in 1787, the magazine had little of specifically Irish interest during that year, a letter in Latin from an Irishman in the June issue and a brief report on Irish emigration in the October issue.

Spotswood's ideas about his *Magazine* are revealed in his correspondence with Jeremy Belknap and Belknap's correspondence with Ebenezer Hazard, the Postmaster-General. Spotswood's first choice for editor in 1787 was Jeremy Belknap, who declined the offer but agreed to write for a guinea each a number of biographies under the rubric of the "American Plutarch." His novel the *Foresters* appeared in serial form in the magazine in 1787 before it was published as a book. Spotswood wrote to Belknap on 25 February 1788 that the American Plutarch "should interest readers on all parts of the continent."[384] A few months later Spotswood told Belknap that though he valued his new American citizenship highly, he did not want the *Columbian Magazine* to become involved in American political struggles because of the problems he had faced with Dallas's editorship of the *Pennsylvania Herald*. Belknap had apparently urged Spotswood to take over the editorship himself, but Spotswood replied on 4 December 1788: "Your favorable opinion with respect to my undertaking the editorship I am obliged by; but I am too sensible of my own deficiency in the necessary requisites to hazard such an undertaking."[385] Nevertheless, Spotswood seems to have served for several months as editor in 1789 and 1790, but by this time the magazine was in serious financial straits, and Spotswood sold it in 1790 to one of his former employees William Young. Although 1,500 copies of the magazine were sold each month, Spotswood was obliged to subsidize the publication from his own pocket, and William Free estimates the annual loss was 125–450 pounds.[386] Looking back over his many contacts with the magazine, Jeremy Belknap wrote to Ebenezer Hazard on 20 March 1793 after the collapse of the magazine: "Spotswood is the only one of the old proprietors of the *Columbian Magazine* in whose correspondence I had any pleasure. I think him a clever fellow."[387] Belknap observed with approval at the end of the year that Spotswood was moving his printing equipment to Boston where he would be "an addition to the number of good citizens."[388]

Publishing magazines and newspapers was but one of Spotswood's many interests. During his twenty-one years as an Irish bookseller in America, fifteen in Philadelphia and six in Boston, he was involved as printer or publisher or both with 280 publications.[389] Spotswood had shown considerable interest in original writings for his *Columbian Magazine*, and he offered Jeremy Belknap even before the copyright law of 1790 "paper, printing, and binding, and the profits on the sales to be mutually divided" for the *Foresters* previously published in serial form in the *Columbian Magazine*.[390] This interest in American writings was unusual for Spotswood, however; his long publications list shows that he essentially continued the Dublin reprint tradition in which he had worked for fourteen years. His one publication in the first year of his Philadelphia sojourn, a reprint of Charles Macklin's comedy the *True-Born Irishman*, sets the tone of much of what he would do in the next twenty-one years. Spotswood's American production consists largely of reprints of London editions, many of them plays, novels, verse, and letters. Elizabeth Nelson Adams finds that a fourth of the 120 works Spotswood published in Boston 1794–1800 were British plays,[391] and this is essentially true of his larger Philadelphia production. Spotswood reprinted well-known plays by John Burgoyne, Richard Cumberland, John O'Keefe, Charles Macklin, and Richard Sheridan in addition to a number of ephemeral ones. Spotswood had done three reprints of Lord Chesterfield's *Works* in Dublin, and he catered to a comparable demand for Chesterfield in Philadelphia and Boston. In 1789 he reprinted Chesterfield's *Accomplished Gentleman* and in his *New Complete American Letter Writer* Chesterfield's *Principles of Politeness*; the latter work he reprinted in a volume with aphorisms of John Lavater and La Rochefoucauld in 1792. After his move to Boston in 1794 he reprinted the *Gentleman's Pocket Library* containing many of Chesterfield's witticisms, a work also sold in Philadelphia by two of Spotswood's former colleagues in the Dublin book trade Henry and Patrick Rice, with whom Spotswood often collaborated in America. To meet the demand in Philadelphia for the verse satires of John Wolcot, better known as Peter Pindar, Spotswood in 1789 reprinted in separate volumes Peter Pindar's *Odes*, his *Subjects for Painters*, his *Lousiad*, and his *Works*, the last two with John Rice, also formerly of the Dublin book trade. Spotswood regularly advertised in the *Pennsylvania Gazette*, and in several issues in October 1789 he and John Rice had large advertisements for Pindar's *Poetical Works*: "After the rapid sale, and universal approbation, which the productions of this humorous and satiric author have obtained among all ranks of people in Great Britain and Ireland, it would be needless to trouble the public with any new encomiums"; consistent with the Dublin tradition the price of the reprint is "less than one quarter of the London price." The next year Spotswood reprinted Pindar's *Subjects for Painters* and *Odes* and again in 1792–94 Pindar's *Works*, this time with Henry and Patrick Rice.

In Dublin Spotswood had lent the novels of Richardson and Fielding from his circulating library, and in Philadelphia in 1786 he reprinted Richardson's three novels and Fielding's *Joseph Andrews* and *Tom Jones*, and he added Fielding's comedy the *Fathers* in Boston in 1975. Also in Dublin Spotswood had reprinted Sterne's *Letters* and lent the *Beauties of Sterne* from his circulating library, and in Philadelphia he reprinted the *Beauties of Sterne* in 1789. Another of Spotswood's authors in Dublin had been Goldsmith, three of whose works he had reprinted in addition to the English version of the *Comic Romance of Monsieur Scarron* widely attributed to Goldsmith. In Philadelphia he reprinted Goldsmith's popular children's story *Goody Two-Shoes* as had two Irish predecessors in America Hugh Gaine and Robert Bell, and as part of a volume containing Mrs. Burke's *Ela*, Goldsmith's *Deserted Village*. Other British poems of note that Spotswood reprinted were Pope's *Essay on Man* both in 1788 and in 1805, Christopher Smart's *Poems* in 1791, and Isaac Watts's *Poems and Hymns* in 1793

Needless to say, not all Spotswood's production was of literary significance. The Evans–Bristol–Shaw bibliographies contain many books for children, and Spotswood's many advertisements in the *Pennsylvania Gazette* and the *Gazette of the United States* often mention children's books, but these were almost invariably reprints of London editions, many of them children's classics like Fielding's *Tom Thumb*, Thomas Day's *Children's Miscellany* and *History of Little Jack*, and Goldsmith's *Goody Two-Shoes*. In his advertisement in the *Gazette of the United States* for 21 March 1802 after he had returned to Philadelphia from Boston, Spotswood mentioned several thousand books for children, Spotswood's moves from Philadelphia in 1794 to Boston and back to Philadelphia in 1801 suggest that he was not wholly successful as a printer and bookseller, and such a conclusion is also suggested by the short duration of the four periodicals with which he was associated. In Philadelphia and Boston he does not seem to have established a circulating library or a lottery office as he had done in Dublin and as many successful booksellers in the United States did. Nevertheless, his three surviving catalogues show a growth in his trade from thirty titles in 1785 to four hundred in 1794 to one thousand in 1795.[392] He was successful, too, in training apprentices, and at least two of these became outstanding printer–booksellers in Philadelphia, William Young and one member of the influential Conrad family, both of whom Spotswood mentioned to Jeremy Belknap on 9 October 1788.[393] He also left a successor in his wife Hannah, who sold printing equipment in 1806 and in 1807 to Mathew Carey from her shop at 17 Chestnut, Philadelphia.[394] His main achievement was probably the *Columbian Magazine*.

Spotswood and Patrick Byrne overlapped in the Philadelphia book trade 1801–5. Of the sixty-two Irish book tradesmen who transferred to the American book trade at about the time of the extension of the British Copyright Law to Ireland, Byrne left the most complete record of his career in Dublin 1779–1801 and in Philadelphia 1801–14. Byrne has been cited more often in this study than any Irish bookseller in Ireland or America. He has appeared first as a publisher of twenty-two reprints of works by or about the eight major authors and as the publisher along with William Porter and James Moore of the massive *Parliamentary Register: or History of the Proceedings and Debates of the House of Commons of Ireland* in eighteen volumes 1781–1800 and of the *Universal Magazine and Review or Repository of Literature* 1789–93. Along with Robert Bell he has also appeared as one of the most spirited apologists, for the Dublin reprints, especially in his defense in the *Dublin Journal* for 13 July 1784 of his unauthorized reprinting of Thomas Sheridan's *Dictionary* and his arguments the next year against copyright in his *Account Settled! or A Balance Struck Between the Irish Propositions and the English Resolutions*. His third role has been that of supplier of Irish editions in large numbers to the American market, primarily to Mathew Carey in Philadelphia 1787–1801, but probably to others, too.

Patrick Byrne published at least 292 titles in Dublin 1779–1801 and 78 in Philadelphia 1801–14, and he published a number of these in more than one edition. In the *Dublin Journal* for 16

September 1780, Byrne announced himself as a bookseller, stationer, and buyer of libraries, at 35 College Green, Dublin, and by 1785 he was also a lottery keeper at 108 Grafton Street. Many of the sixty-eight original works that he published, however, list him as a printer. All these works are pamphlets except for James Mullala's *Political History of Ireland* in 1793 and the *Parliamentary Register*, and all on Irish affairs; almost all are listed in the *Bradshaw Catalogue*, which credits Byrne with 110 works.[395] Since Byrne was both a Roman Catholic and in his last decade in Dublin a United Irishman, a number of the pamphlets are concerned with the campaign for Catholic emancipation, and several, including two by Wolfe Tone promote the interests of the United Irishmen. In 1792 alone Byrne published ten pamphlets on behalf of Catholic Emancipation, including one by Wolfe Tone and one by Richard Burke, son of the great statesman, several of whose works Byrne reprinted.

Like his colleagues in the Irish book trade, Byrne devoted most of his efforts towards reprinting English writers, and of his total Dublin production of 292, 216 are reprints.[396] Undoubtedly, many, probably most, of these reprints were piracies from the perspective of British writers and publishers. As noted in chapter one, in response to Thomas Sheridan's charge that Byrne had pirated his *Dictionary* in 1784, Byrne had proclaimed his right to reprint a British work "without the Author's immediate consent"; Byrne presumably had done the same with Sheridan's *Grammar*, which he reprinted both in 1781 and 1784, and with many other works. His ability to undersell the London editions consistently probably reflects the absence of copyright payment. Nevertheless, there is evidence for a few works that Byrne either paid the copyright holder or had some kind of agreement with the copyright holder, normally the London publisher. An interesting example is a work by Edmund Burke published by Byrne in a Dublin edition and by John Debrett in a separate London edition. Burke apparently authorized editions of his *Letter to Sir Hercules Langrishe* in 1792 by both Byrne and Debrett, although he preferred Debrett's more correct edition. He complained to his son c. 8 March 1792: "Byrnes publication of my Letter to Sir H L was so blundering as to vex me. He makes me say, & that at a Critical point, the direct reverse of my Sense." Burke further lamented that in his second edition, and Byrne published two thousand copies in the two editions, Byrne had "chosen to amend it into a Blunder."[397] Whether Burke authorized Byrne's reprinting 1792–93 of his *Works* in the J. Dodsley London edition is unknown. Byrne may have made arrangements with John Debrett on other occasions. Byrne reprinted five of Debrett's pamphlets during the controversy over Irish and British commerce 1785–87. The imprint of Samuel Parr's *Preface to Bellendenus* published by Debrett in 1788 lists Byrne as the seller in Dublin; after his move to Philadelphia in 1801 Byrne would obtain this book for Thomas Jefferson.[398] In 1797 Byrne reprinted Debrett's edition of Thomas Erskine's *View of the Causes and Consequences of the Present War with France*, which went through thirty-six editions in 1797.

The reprinting of law books, which would become Byrne's specialty in Philadelphia, began during Byrne's last decade in the Dublin book trade. Of the twenty-four books he reprinted on English higher court proceedings at least two were printed jointly with the London publisher. Byrne's 1794 edition of William Ridgeway's *Reports of Cases in King's Bench and Chancery, 1733–45* is printed from the same type as the London edition by Charles Dilly. Byrne's 1795 edition of Thomas Peake's *Cases determined at nisi prius, in the Court of King's Bench*, 1790–94 has the name of R. Brooke, the London publisher of the work the same year, in the imprint. In 1796 Byrne reprinted Blackstone's *Commentaries*, the work that had occasioned Robert Bell's famous manifesto of 1771 in Philadelphia. Another of these twenty-four law books Lord Raymond's *Reports of Cases argued and adjudged in the Courts of King's Bench and Common Pleas* Byrne after his transfer to the Philadelphia book trade would provide from his Dublin warehouse for his most famous customer in the United States President Thomas Jefferson; Jefferson on several occasions instructed his agent to buy Dublin editions of English law books because they were cheaper. In 1805 in Philadelphia Byrne would also obtain for Jefferson from his Dublin warehouse William Enfield's *History of Philosophy* and Charles Home's *History of England*, both of which Byrne reprinted in Dublin in 1792 along with Lord Raymond's *Cases*. Seven other reprints by Byrne at this time in Dublin were also in Thomas Jefferson's library.

Byrne did not limit his reprinting of English writers to the twenty-two works by or about the eight masters of this study; he published fifty-nine additional literary works first published in

London. Besides the two satires on James Boswell by John Wolcot (Peter Pindar) previously cited, Byrne reprinted eleven other comic poems by Peter Pindar. He was especially active in reprinting new plays that were popular on the London stage during the last two decades of the century. He reprinted thirty-four comedies, including five each by James Cobb and John O'Keeffe, four by Frederick Reynolds, three each by George Colman and Richard Cumberland, and two each by Elizabeth Inchbald, Thomas Morton, and William Shield. Such popular novels as Matthew Lewis's *Monk*, John Moore's *Zeluco*, and Ann Radcliffe's *Romance of the Forest* and the *Italian* were also represented. Not only was John Moore represented as a novelist but as a writer of three well-known travel books about England, France, and Italy. Byrne reprinted five works by Thomas Paine, six by Edmund Burke, and three by Joseph Priestley, all writers of literary significance though writing primarily on political affairs; Byrne would continue to publish Priestley in Philadelphia. Byrne's thirty other reprints of political writings were mostly ephemerae.

Byrne reached a peak in 1792 when he reprinted twenty-seven works and issued eleven original pamphlets on Irish affairs. The next year represented a strong year, too, with nineteen reprints and six original pamphlets and a book on Irish affairs; this was also the year of his admission to St. Luke's Guild as the first Roman Catholic bookseller. In 1794 there were nine reprints and one original pamphlet and in 1795 ten reprints and one pamphlet. There was something of a recovery in 1796 with thirteen reprints but no pamphlets. The next year, however, dropped to five reprints, and the year of the great rebellion only two. Byrne's publishing list in the *Dublin Evening Post* for 15 September 1798 announces his withdrawal from the book trade. His departure from the book business was delayed, for though he published nothing in 1799, he published in 1800 a reprint of John Walker's *Academic Speaker* and reprinted plays by James Cobb, George Colman, and August Kotzebue. In spite of the diminished production these last years in the Dublin book trade were prosperous ones for Byrne, and as he would report often in 1802 in the Philadelphia *Aurora*, he was able to store books at the end of the century in his Dublin warehouses that he would be able to draw on in the future. In the traumatic year of 1798 he was paid £1,663.6s.7d. by one of his Philadelphia customers Mathew Carey, and Carey still owed Byrne £584.15s.7d., as noted in chapter three. Byrne also had income in 1798 from selling real estate, probably his house and business in preparation for leaving the country.[399]

This last decade of Byrne's career in the Dublin book trade was the period of his heavy involvement with the Dublin Society of United Irishmen, which he joined along with thirteen other booksellers and printers. Though Byrne, like John Chambers and John Stockdale, who also left the Dublin book trade and the United Irishmen for the American book trade, was regarded as a dangerous radical, he claimed to be a businessman rather than a political figure. When chided by Lord Clonmell, Chief Justice of the King's Bench and one of the library owners of this study, for publishing Archibald Hamilton's Rowan's report of his trial as a United Irishman in 1794, Byrne said: "I have but one principle in trade which is to make money of it, and that if there were two publications giving different features to the trial I would publish both."[400] In spite of this disclaimer Byrne's republican sympathies were well known, and on 10 May 1798 he introduced two rebel leaders John and Henry Sheares to one of his customers Captain John Armstrong, who Byrne thought might be willing to lead a rebellion in Dublin. Armstrong revealed the plot to his superiors in the British Army, and the Sheares brothers were executed, and Byrne was imprisoned in Newgate on 21 May 1798.[401] His imprisonment was soon commuted to banishment by King George III,[402] though Byrne did not leave Dublin until late in 1801 after selling Sterne's *Works* and other reprints from his shop in Dublin to Mathew Carey in Philadelphia in July and receiving payment of £581.5s.6d. from Carey in September.

Though forced to leave Dublin because of his republican leanings, Byrne, like most of his sixty-one colleagues at the turn of the century, might have left anyway because of the Union and the extension of copyright to Ireland with its inevitably disastrous effect on the Irish book trade. Patrick Byrne and his family, including two grown sons Patrick and William who would enter the book business in Baltimore, were in Philadelphia by 5 October 1801 when Byrne and Mathew Carey borrowed two thousand Spanish milled dollars from a fellow Irish bookseller in America Hugh Gaine, Byrne presumably to set up his shop in Philadelphia.[403] On 30 December 1801 Byrne made the first of hundreds of announcements over the next thirteen years in the

Aurora about books available in his Law and Miscellaneous Book Store. His first advertisement stressed law books but also lists histories, classics, novels, and plays. The one and only book published by Byrne in 1801 was a reprint of George Colman's comedy the *Poor Gentleman*, printed twice by another ex-Dublin printer Joseph Charless for Byrne;[404] in Dublin Byrne had reprinted three other comedies by Colman. Byrne primarily was selling Dublin rather than American reprints, however, and he reported in the *Aurora* of 28 April 1802 that he was importing Dublin editions from his warehouse in Dublin, "which is more extensively stocked than any in Ireland." His Dublin editions of British law books sell for one fourth of the London price; Vesey's *Reports*, for example, sells for $4.50 in Byrne's Dublin reprint rather than for the equivalent of $15.00 in the London edition. He boasts, too, and this is probably an exaggeration, that "A review of the imprints of law books, published in Dublin during the last twenty years, will shew that they were either exclusively or in partnership printed by him." It was Dublin editions of British law books that President Thomas Jefferson especially wanted from Byrne; Jefferson had seventy-five Irish editions in his library of which twenty-four were reprints of British law books. Byrne filled a large order for Jefferson in February 1805 from his Dublin warehouses; most of these Byrne had reprinted in Dublin during the years 1786–92.[405] On 23 December 1802, in the *Aurora* Byrne indicated the magnitude of his imports from Dublin: "Byrne within the last two years has brought books into this country from his warehouses in Dublin, the duties of which have amounted to 10,000 Dollars."

Byrne was not content to limit his book business in 1802 to importing the Dublin reprints that he had published himself in Dublin and stored in his warehouses there. He also published his catalogue and his own American reprints of thirteen London editions. Six of these were reprints of British law books, to one of which, Sir John Willes's *Reports of Adjudged Cases in the Court of Common Pleas*, Thomas Jefferson, among others, subscribed. He also reprinted Aesop's *Fables* with three fellow Irish booksellers in Philadelphia, Mathew Carey, Henry and Patrick Rice. Reprints of important British works in 1802 include Hugh Blair's profoundly influential *Lectures on Rhetoric*, William Godwin's novel *Caleb Williams, the Poems of Ossian*, and Monk Lewis's *Adelmorn the Outlaw*; Byrne had reprinted the latter's *Monk* in Dublin in 1796. The productions of 1803 were essentially of the same type, reprints of English writers, most of them law books. Joseph Priestley's *Lectures on History*, printed for Byrne in 1803 by his fellow Irish emigré William Spotswood, however, represents a change. Byrne had reprinted the work in 1788 and 1791 in Dublin, but now he claims the American copyright. Since Priestley, like Byrne, had emigrated to the United States, he was now protected by American copyright law, and presumably Byrne paid him for the five original works that Byrne published in 1803.

In the *Aurora* for 14 May 1804, Byrne announced that his son-in-law Edward Hudson had joined his firm. Credited by the Irish poet Thomas Moore for making known to him the "rich mine of our country's melodies," Hudson had been imprisoned for his involvement in the Irish Rebellion of 1798. Thomas Moore visited Hudson in Philadelphia and described to his mother on 13 June 1804 Patrick Byrne as "a very rich bookseller" who had taken Hudson into partnership.[406] With Hudson, Byrne reprinted two collections of cases argued in the Court of Common Pleas and the Court of King's Bench in 1804, but then Hudson left Byrne's firm to take up dentistry in which he had been trained in Dublin, and his achievement in this field earned him a place in the *Dictionary of American Biography*. Byrne published only eight books in 1804 and three in 1805, but as he did every year in the *Aurora* advertised hundreds of other books for sale, law books primarily, but also novels, plays, and classics, and works on Irish affairs. Low productivity and the loss of his partner may have made Byrne restless, and on 2 February 1805 he announced his willingness to sell out or exchange his vast book stock for land or houses in any one of the state capitals, Byrne's business also included the selling of lottery tickets, paper, stationery supplies, and on occasion cotton from South Carolina. Apparently no one made the kind of offer Byrne wanted, and he not only retained his Philadelphia bookshop, which had occupied three locations in Philadelphia, but by 8 August 1805 had opened up a new shop in Baltimore with his sons Patrick and William. Nevertheless, he was still interested in divesting himself of his miscellaneous book stock and offered it for sale on 17 May 1806, or in exchange "for printing, bookbinding, house, lot or land."

From 1806 until 1809 Byrne listed himself as a law bookseller. He continued to reprint London editions of law collections and also to import reprints from his Dublin warehouses, but in 1806 he began to publish American law books, and on 3 February 1806, he announced his purchase of the copyright for the important series of American law reports by A. J. Dallas, now a leading lawyer but formerly editor for two of William Spotswood's periodicals. The magnitude of Byrne's trade in law books is shown by his advertisement in the *Aurora* for 2 February 1807 that he was able to supply one thousand sets each of massive legal works like Dallas's *Reports*, for which Byrne owned the copyright, and his own reprints of Sir Edward Hyde East's *Crown Law* and Sir Edmund Saunders's *Reports of the Court of King's Bench*. This full column advertisement which appears often in 1807 also contains testimonials to Byrne's typography. As a Dublin bookseller Byrne had supplied Mathew Carey in Philadelphia with several thousand pounds worth of Dublin reprints 1788–1801, and as Carey's colleague in Philadelphia he continued to supply Carey with both Dublin reprints and his own reprints, many of these law books. On 29 May 1805 Byrne sold Carey $1,032.66 worth of law books, and the Carey accounts show there were numerous sales for lesser amounts. In New York Bernard Dornin, formerly Byrne's colleague in Dublin, sold Byrne's law books in 1807 and William Falconer in 1805.[407]

In Byrne's latter years in the Philadelphia book trade he returned to the general book business with which he had started the American phase of his career in 1801. Throughout 1809 in addition to law books he was selling medical books, novels, and lottery tickets for institutions in New York, Philadelphia, and Baltimore. He continued this general book business in 1810 and on 17 April 1810 advertised fourteen books for Roman Catholic readers. The same year in the *Aurora* for October 5th he described himself as having a "distinguished Lottery Office and eminent Law Book Store." During the period 1810–12 Byrne published three works by Thomas Cooper, for which he must have paid copyright. All three works, Cooper's legal opinions, his edition in Latin with his translation of Justinian's *Institutes*, and his *Introductory Lecture at Carlisle College* (now Dickinson) were in Thomas Jefferson's library probably furnished for him by Byrne, who had provided so many Dublin editions for Jefferson. Byrne's last publication was an American legal work Hugh Brackenridge's *Law Miscellanies* in 1814. Byrne's business with Mathew Carey continued up until Byrne's death in 1814, but in these latter years

Carey's sales to Byrne much exceeded his purchases. The Carey accounts show that in November 1808 Byrne owed Carey $1,779.37, and a month before his death Byrne still owed Carey $107.92

Robert Bell, William Spotswood, and Patrick Byrne, then, were trained and employed in the Dublin reprint trade during three different periods, Bell 1759–67, Spotswood, 1770–84, and Byrne 1779–1801. Like nearly a hundred of their fellows in the Dublin book trade, they transferred to the American book trade as part of the three waves of emigration, before the American Revolution, after the American Revolution, and in response to the threat or fact of the Union and its disaster for the Irish reprints. Byrne in Dublin was more successful than Bell or Spotswood, but all three were able to maintain themselves in the Dublin book trade over a period of years. All three were successful in the American book trade where, as they had been accustomed to do in Dublin, they involved themselves primarily in reprinting English writers, Bell in Philadelphia 1767–84, Spotswood in Philadelphia and Boston, 1784–1805, and Byrne in Philadelphia and Baltimore 1801–14. All three reprinted a number of significant English writers in Dublin and Philadelphia, Bell fewer than Spotswood and Byrne since his career in Dublin was shorter, but he made up for it in Philadelphia. Thus all three represent the two sequential roles played by most of the Irish-American booksellers in the dissemination of English literature, culture, and learning: first as publishers and sellers of reprints, or sometimes apprentices, in Ireland itself, secondly as importers of Irish reprints and practitioners in the American book trade of the Irish reprint tradition.

10
A Final Estimate

Booksellers in Ireland through their cheap reprints contributed significantly to extending British literature, learning, and culture to people in Ireland, Britain, and the United States of America who either could not or would not pay for the expensive London editions. There was a demand for cheap books in the English-speaking world, and the Irish booksellers catered to this demand with marked success. Since they usually paid no copyright and used cheaper materials, they sold their reprints for much less than the London editions, and they got them into circulation almost as fast. During the latter decades of the century booksellers in Ireland were able to take most of the market in their native land, to export at least some reprints surreptitiously to Britain, and as the century neared its end to send a substantial portion of their total production to the United States. Foreign sales were enhanced by the *Dublin Catalogues* of 1786 and 1791, which enabled foreign booksellers to order reprints of the English writers from Dublin booksellers.

Their clientele at home was mainly the landed and professional classes. Owners of private libraries, patrons of the several types of community libraries, buyers of subscription editions, eighteenth-century owners of the numerous copies of Irish reprints that survive today, all point to this conclusion. Evidence of a broader audience in Ireland itself is harder to find, certain Roman Catholic reprints published by subscription, a few book clubs with working-class members, and schoolchildren in two dioceses. The few Catholic reprints that list subscribers by occupation identify some buyers as skilled tradesmen and small businessmen, and some of these could afford to belong to the commercial lending libraries. By the end of the century after the relaxation of the penal laws there were significant numbers of Roman Catholics in the Irish book trade itself, starting with the leading Dublin–Philadelphia bookseller of this study Patrick Byrne. The efforts of the London book trade during much of the eighteenth century to keep Irish reprints out of Britain and to get the British Copyright Law extended to Ireland suggest a British audience, but documentation is scattered and sometimes ambiguous. The Irish Customs House books, the Mathew Carey accounts and letters, American subscribers to Irish reprints, and the testimony of Irish booksellers in the Irish Parliament 1795–96 point to a large clientele in the United States by the end of the century, possibly greater in number than the home audience, as the Irish booksellers told Parliament in 1796. Reprints in America by former members of the Irish reprint trade account for even more American readers.

The impact of the Irish reprint industry on the United States book trade was enormous. The Irish book trade was a training ground for at least 101 booksellers, printers, bookbinders, stationers, engravers, and auctioneers who joined the American book trade, and undoubtedly many more, judging from the profusion of Irish names in American book trade directories and the anonymous Irish emigrants listed as printers on ship passenger lists. Such a massive transfer from one national book trade to another is unique in the annals of publishing. These transplanted Irish bookmen imported the Irish reprints as did many other American booksellers not of Irish origin until the Act of Union put an end to the reprints. Before the Union, but especially after the Union when the Irish reprints were no longer available, Irish booksellers in America issued their own reprints of English writers and helped to make the early nineteenth-century American book trade a reprint industry far surpassing its Irish model. As it had been with their mentors back in Ireland, it was more profitable to reprint London editions than to publish original works by native authors. American authors were protected by copyright, and there were also few of them; most of the Irish-American booksellers out of necessity and habit reprinted London editions. The Irish book trade trained the giant of early nineteenth-century publishing in the United States, Mathew Carey, and fifteen others whose significant achievements in publishing and related fields earned them places in the *Dictionary of American Biography*. It also sent over one of its leading printer–booksellers, Patrick Byrne. Although only the book firm established by Mathew Carey lasted to the present day, twenty others were continued by family members,[408] and others were founded by a new generation of Irish booksellers as the nineteenth century wore on. Usually regarded as the two most important American magazines before 1800, the *American Musuem* and the *Columbian Magazine* were both published from Irish models by Irish-trained booksellers in Philadelphia, Mathew Carey and William Spotswood.

Of the 101 Irish bookmen joining the American book trade between 1750 and 1820, forty-three published newspapers or other periodicals, most more than one and James Carey, nine.[409] Among these forty-three, Adams, Charless, George Dobbin, Gaine, Loudon, and Lyon had sons born in the United States who continued to publish newspapers, James Lyon publishing no fewer than fifteen. By and large these were republican newspapers strongly opposed to conservative government and traditions, whether British Toryism or American Federalism. The republicanism was re-enforced by the Roman Catholicism of many of these Irish booksellers who had fought political and religious oppression in Ireland as United Irishmen or in some other guise and continued to fight it in the United States. Their newspapers offered them unusual opportunities for influencing public opinion, and the domination of the Jefferson–Jackson political tradition in the first third of the nineteenth century may include among its many causes Irish editorial labors. Their periodicals also enabled them to publicize the reprints of English writers most of them were issuing, as they had learned to do from such mentors in Ireland as John Exshaw, James Potts, and Thomas Walker, and others who both published reprints of English writers and the periodicals to advertise and review them.

In discussing the impact of unauthorized reprints on any society at any time, the impact on authorship is crucial. This effect is generally perceived in any society as a disastrous one. It is difficult to see that any of the eight British authors of this study were harmed much by Irish reprints of their works, and a spot-check suggests a comparable conclusion about eight other major British writers of the time, Berkeley, Blackstone, Burke, Lord Chesterfield, Hume, Pope, William Robertson, and Swift. With the exception of Samuel Richardson, who did his own printing, all sold the copyrights of their many works to their London publishers for at least adequate sums, and the histories of Edward Gibbon, Oliver Goldsmith, and Tobias Smollett brought them and their London publishers handsome sums. Since the authors sold their copyrights, only the London publishers would have benefited from Irish royalties. The Irish reprints undoubtedly gave all eight authors extra publicity that probably translated itself into additional sales of the London editions and hence additional profits for the London publishers, in spite of the complaints of the London booksellers against what they regarded as Irish piracies. The additional publicity may well have strengthened the author's bargaining positions when they sold copyrights of later works. There is no evidence that six of the eight thought they had been victimized by the Irish booksellers and some evidence from Boswell, Gibbon, and Smollett that they were flattered by the Irish reprints of their works. Though Boswell and Johnson were certainly in favor of limited copyright, they were strongly opposed to the perpetual copyright that the London book trade insisted upon, and Boswell published a book against it. Goldsmith and Richardson clearly thought they were victims of the Dublin pirates. Nevertheless, the Dublin pirates, especially of Richardson's *Sir Charles Grandison*, gave Richardson's novels considerable publicity that probably made up for losses Richardson suffered because of the Dublin pirated editions.

Goldsmith was apprehensive about the booksellers in his native land, and in 1759 he tried hard to sell the London edition of his *Enquiry into the Present State of Polite Learning in Europe* in Ireland. Yet the profession of letters offered Goldsmith a good living in London. Since Dublin booksellers rarely paid for an original work, it is unlikely that Goldsmith could have been a professional writer in Dublin. Like Edmund Burke, Hugh Kelly, Edmond Malone, Arthur Murphy, the three Sheridans, and many others, he had to emigrate to establish a literary career. The argument given by the few Dublin booksellers who defended their reprints, that Irish booksellers could not pay what the London book trade could pay for copyright, was almost certainly true for the Irish book trade as a whole. Possibly John Archer, Patrick Byrne, the Faulkners, and Luke White wre exceptions, but no eighteenth-century Irish book firm had the financial resources to survive very long into the nineteenth century; one of these more affluent booksellers, Thomas Todd Faulkner, successor to his famous uncle, claimed in his newspaper in April 1785 during the controversy over the commercial regulations of 1785 that the London book trade could pay writers "such a price as could not possibly be afforded by any person of that line of business in this kingdom." Few if any Dublin booksellers could have paid Goldsmith the £840 he got from his London publishers, Griffin and Nourse, for the copyright of the *History of the Earth and Animated Nature* in 1774, and not many could have paid the five hundred pounds he got for his *History of England* in 1771. The Dublin reprint of the *History of England* may have helped embolden Goldsmith to sell the copyright of the later work for the higher sum. Thomas Faulkner in the same article observed that just as Scots writers like Smollett took their books to London to get a better price than they would get in Scotland, so Irish writers would do the same. Faulkner's observation was confirmed thirty-three years later by three Dublin historians who asserted dogmatically that "no author has yet, or perhaps ever will" avail himself of the opportunity to be published in Dublin. Like the three Dublin historians, Irish authors took their works to London to be published, a choice to be continued by Irish writers throughout the nineteenth century. Examples are legion: Maria Edgeworth, Samuel Lover, Lady Morgan, C. R. Maturin, J. S. Lefanu, C. J. Lever, and many others. Goldsmith, Burke, Richard Sheridan, like gifted Irishmen in every age, were highly successful in London, and it is doubtful that they lost much income because of the Dublin reprints.

The London book trade proclaimed loud and long that it was irreparably damaged by the Irish book pirating industry. Undoubtedly, the London publishers lost sales in Ireland, Britain, and the Americas, and they fought the Irish reprint trade tooth and nail from about 1734 until the Union when British Copyright Law was extended to Ireland. But increased publicity because of the Irish reprints must have made up for some of the lost sales, and certainly the London publishers benefited hugely from the earning power of such Irish writers as Goldsmith, Arthur Murphy, and Richard Sheridan. They also learned from the Irish reprints that there was a sizeable audience in the English-speaking world for cheap books. Once their claims to perpetual copyright were dismissed by the courts such of their number as the Bells, the Cookes, and the Harrisons were able to earn large profits from their own reprints of older books. The London book trade ultimately suffered far more from the pupils than from the masters, since it was the American reprint industry in the nineteenth century with its large Irish contingent that took far more of the London trade's profits than booksellers in Ireland would ever have dreamed of.

The impact on the Irish reprint of the Irish economy itself was mixed. Without their reprints of the English writers, few Irish booksellers could have survived in the eighteenth century. Ireland was small, poor, and ignorant, and there were not enough Irish writers to keep many printers and booksellers in business or the resources to publish original works from manuscript. Because of its clientele at home and abroad, the Irish reprint industry in its peak decades was large and profitable enough to provide employment for hundreds of printers, booksellers, bookbinders, auctioneers, engravers, and workers in such related industries as paper and leather. The argument by the few Irish booksellers who bothered to defend unauthorized reprinting that they offered considerable employment was certainly sound. By the same token, however, the basis for such employment was a shaky one, and the British and American reprints, the increased paper duty, and the extension of British Copyright Law to Ireland with the Union, along with the exodus from Dublin of many readers from the governing class, combined to destroy the reprint industry. The unhappy result for Ireland was the loss of many of its book craftsmen and skilled workers in related fields to America and a few to the London book trade. Ireland's loss in this area, as in so many others, was America's gain, and the Irish book craftsmen found new and better opportunities in a larger and richer country. But at home many people were thrown out of work, and the loss of cheap books reduced educational opportunities.

Although Irish booksellers through their cheap reprints made a significant contribution to the extension of British culture, learning, and literature both at home and abroad, their contribution to bibliography, textual criticism, or the book arts was far more modest. Irish booksellers tended to reproduce the first London edition, warts and all, as fast and as cheaply as possible. To cash in on the demand generated by the London edition they ordinarily did not wait for a second London edition correcting the errata of the first, and evidence of editors and correctors of the press is hard to locate. There were certainly outstanding exceptions, however. Among the Irish reprints of works by the eight authors that show changes in text or format beyond changes in pagination, page size, and type are the following, all published in Dublin except for the Belfast edition of Goldsmith's *Poems* in 1775: the 1752 edition of Johnson's *Rambler*, the 1762 edition of Johnson's *Idler*, the 1766 edition of Johnson's *Shakespeare*, the 1775 and 1798 editions of Johnson's *Dictionary*, the 1756 abridged edition of Richardson's *Clarissa*, the 1775 edition of Goldsmith's *Poems*, the 1777 editions of Goldsmith's *Poems and Plays* and his *History of the Earth and Animated Nature*, the 1775–76 edition of Smollett's *Select Works*, and collected editions of Sterne's *Tristram Shandy* 1760–67 and his *Sermons* 1760–66. The modest bibliographical and textual interest of the Irish reprints is matched by a modest contribution to the arts of bookmaking. Exceptions are the well-printed Dublin editions of such massive works as Goldsmith's *History of the Earth and Animated Nature*, Johnson's *Lives of the Poets* 1779–81, the several editions of Gibbon's *Decline and Fall of the Roman Empire* 1776–89, and the 1796 reprint of Smollett's translation of *Don Quixote*. Copies of many of these were attractively bound, and they survive today in libraries throughout the world as testimony to eighteenth-century Irish bookbinding skills.

Eighteenth-century Dublin was richly supplied with newspapers and magazines, many of which existed in part because their proprietors needed them to advertise and review works of the English writers they were reprinting from the London editions. John Exshaw, George Faulkner, the James Hoeys, James Potts, William Sleater, and Thomas Walker were leading publishers both of periodicals and reprints of the English writers, and there were many lesser lights who combined the two roles. Although Faulkner, the Hoeys, and Sleater had rivals for their newspaper, Exshaw, Potts, and Walker had none for their magazines; all other magazines lasted only a few years. John Exshaw reprinted all eight major English writers described in this study, and for most of them several works; his total production was fifty-five, including twenty-four reprints of Goldsmith alone. Exshaw devoted substantial portions of his *Gentleman's and London Magazine* 1760–1800 to advertising, reviewing, and otherwise promoting these eight English writers and other major English writers of this period whose works he was reprinting. The two proprietors of the *Hibernian Magazine* 1771–1800 James Potts and Thomas Walker also reprinted all eight of the major writers for a total of seventy reprints, and they, too, used reviews and commentary in their *Magazine* to encourage their readers to buy their reprints of the eight writers and other significant authors. On a lesser scale the same can be said of the newspapers of Faulkner, the Hoeys, and Sleater, but these booksellers and their newspapers flourished prior to the peak decades of the Dublin book trade 1780–1800 when consumption of Dublin reprints in America was comparable to home consumption. For example, some Dublin readers must have read the summary and critique of Goldsmith's *She stoops to Conquer* in the April 1773 issues of Exshaw's *Magazine* and James Potts's *Hibernian Magazine* and then purchased the 1773 Dublin reprint of Goldsmith's comedy by Exshaw and Potts. Some of these readers probably discussed the play and its reviews in the coffeehouses and clubs of Dublin, Cork, and Belfast. When the Union ended the Dublin reprints of the English authors, the periodicals for the most part ended too, so that the three Dublin historians Warburton, Whitelaw, and Walsh could observe several years after the Union that all intellectual ferment was dead. The reprint industry, the periodicals, and intellectual exchange all flourished together.

The main beneficiaries of the Irish booksellers were two. Readers in Ireland, Britain, and America benefited from the cheap reprints of the major English writers and then the cheap British and American reprints modelled after them. The American book trade gained over one hundred Irish printers, booksellers, and engravers, many of whom with their heirs would become not only leaders in the American book trade but leaders in American society. Although English authors and publishers were not beneficiaries of the Irish booksellers and their reprinting practices in Ireland and America, probably they were not significantly harmed by the reprints. Booksellers in Ireland flourished during the latter decades of the eighteenth century because of their reprints of English writers, but then the combination of the new London and American reprints, the paper duty, and the Union, all at about the same time, destroyed their livelihood. Ireland thus became the chief loser. Its people were thrown out of work and its educational opportunities were reduced. It is doubtful, however, that booksellers in Ireland had any other option in the eighteenth century except to reprint the English writers. They did what they had to do not only to survive but to prosper for a generation, and the momentum was great enough to allow their trade to limp along through the nineteenth century until the Gaelic revival produced new writers and a revived Irish book trade. Perhaps booksellers in Ireland received some vicarious satisfaction as their former colleagues across the Atlantic continued reprinting practices no longer allowed in Ireland, and also contributed significantly to the development of a larger and more important publishing industry.

Notes

1. *Journals of the House of Commons of Great Britain, 1732–1737*, XXII, 412.

2. *Journals of the House of Commons of Great Britain, 1732–1737*, XXIII, 380

3. See F. G. James, "Irish Smuggling in the Eighteenth Century," *Irish Historical Studies*, 12 (1960–61), 249–317; L. M. Cullen, "The Smuggling Trade in Ireland in the Eighteenth Century," *Proceedings of the Royal Irish Academy*, 67 (1968–69), pt. C., 149–76.

4. Eiluned Rees and G. Walters "Pennant and the Pirates, *National Library of Wales Journal*, 15 (1967–68), 427; Eiluned Rees, "Developments in the Book Trade in Eighteenth-Century Wales," *The Library*, 5th ser., 24 (1969), 41–42.

5. Alexander Donaldson, Some *Thoughts on the State of Literary Property, Humbly Submitted to the Consideration of the Public* (London: Alexander Donaldson, 1764), pp. 7–11.

6. Robert E. Ward, *Prince of Dublin Printers, The Letters of George Faulkner* (Lexington: University Press of Kentucky, 1972), p. 56.

7. *A Letter from A Gentleman in Edinburgh, to his Friend in London; Concerning Literary Property* ([Edinburgh?], 1769), pp. 11, 15–16.

8. Carey to G. Hill, 15 Sept. 1796, Carey Letter Books, Box 4, B45, Lea-Febiger Collection, Historical Society of Pennsylvania,

9. *A Modest Plea for the Property of Copy Right* (London: Edward & Charles Dilly, 1774), pp. 28, 37.

10. *Journals of the House of Commons of the Kingdom of Ireland*, 19 vols. (Dublin: George Grierson and Abraham Bradley King, 1796–1800), XI, 2nd pt., ccccliiii.

11. *Journals of the House of Commons of Great Britain*, 1785, XL, 865.

12. *Historical Manuscripts Commission, Fourteenth Report* (1825), Appendix 9, 185

13. Charles Haliday Collection of Pamphlets Relating to Ireland, Box 271, Royal Irish Academy, Dublin.

14. Carey Letter Books, 22 Oct. 1788, Box 1, B45.

15. *The Correspondence of Johnathan Swift*, ed. Harold Williams, 5 vols. (Oxford: Clarendon Press, 1965), IV, 494.

16. *The Letters of Philip Dormer Stanhope, Fourth Earl of Chesterfield*, ed. Bonamy Dobrée, 6 vols. (London: Eyre & Spottiswoode, 1932), IV, 1219–20.

17. Benjamin Franklin, *Works*, ed. Jared Sparks, 10 vols. (Boston: Hilliard Gray & Co., 1837–40), X, 161.

18. *The Correspondence of Daniel O'Connell*, ed. Maurice R. O'Connell, 8 vols. (Shannon: Irish University Press, 1972–80), I, 14–16.

19. *The Early Life, Correspondence and Writings of the Rt. Hon. Edmund Burke*, ed. Arthur P. I. Samuels (Cambridge, Cambridge University Press, 1923), pp. 269–74.

20. Robert Munter, *The History of the Irish Newspaper*, 1685–1760 (Cambridge: Cambridge University Press, 1967), p. 18.

21. Numbers taken from James W. Phillips, "A Bibliograpical Inquiry into Printing and Bookselling in Dublin from 1670 to 1800," unpublished doctoral dissertation for Trinity College, Dublin, 1952, pp. 45, 67, 88.

22. I am especially indebted to Dr. Hugh Amory of the Houghton Library, Harvard University, for his stress on the importance of the *Dublin Catalogue* for the Dublin booksellers' international trade.

23. "Address to the Public," in Richardson's *History of Sir Charles Grandison*, 2nd ed. (London: Printed for S. Richardson, 1754), VI, 416–17. Robert and Catherine Ward defend Faulkner in "Literary Piracy in the Eighteenth Century Book Trade: the Cases of George Faulkner and Alexander Donaldson," *Factotum*, 17 (1983), 27–28.

24. Giles Barber, "Books from the old world and for the new the British international trade in books in the eighteenth century," *Studies on Voltaire and the Eighteenth Century*, 151 (1976), 213–18.

25. Irish Customs House Books on Exports and Imports, 1764–1823, MSS. 353–76, National Library of Ireland.

26. Dublin newspaper reports about attacks on sellers of British goods were sometimes reported in British newspapers. The *Edinburgh Advertiser* for 20–23 July 1784, for example, reported that a Dublin woolen draper had been tarred and feathered for selling English goods.

27. *The Monthly Miscellany, or Irish Review and Register*, 1 (April, 1796), 43–45.

28. K. H. Connell, *The Population of Ireland*, 1750–1845 (Oxford: Clarendon Press, 1950), pp. 4, 25

29. Donald H. Akenson, *The Irish Education Experiment* (London: Routledge & Kegan Paul, 1970), pp. 376–77.

30. *History of the City of Dublin*, 3 vols (London: T. Cadell and W. Davies, 1818), II, 1168–69.

31. *Letters of George Faulkner*, p. 52.

32. *Horace Walpole's Correspondence with George Montagu*, ed. W. S. Lewis and Ralph S. Brown (New Haven: Yale University Press, 1941), II, 11, 17, 20.

33. *A View of the Natural, Political, & Commercial Circumstances of Ireland* (London: T. Cadell & W. Davies, 1809), p. 230.

34. "Essay on the Natural Advantages of Ireland, the Manufactures to which they are adapted and the best means of improving those manufactures," *Transactions of the Royal Irish Academy*, 9 (1803), 371.

35. Munter, p. 87.

36. See list in Appendix 1. I am indebted to F. J. G. Robinson and P. J. Wallis, *Book Subscription Lists, A Revised Guide* (Newcastle upon Tyne: Harold Hills and Son, Lmt., 1975), which for the years 1730–60 lists subscription volumes by title and by number of subscriptions, pp. 14–36. I have used the numbers from this source unless a spot check has shown significant differences. For the years 1761–1800 Robinson and Wallis give titles but not numbers of subscribers, pp. 37–51. For these years I have supplied the numbers myself where I have been able to locate the volumes; for the most part the volumes in my list come from the National Library of Ireland, Dublin. P. O. Suilleabhain's "Catholic Books Printed in Ireland 1740–1820 Containing Lists of Subscribers," *Collectanea Hibernica*, 6–7 (1963–64), 231–33, has not been suitable for my purpose because the numbers given are of subscribers rather than number of subscriptions. For example, Challoner's *Morality of the Bible* has 780 subscribers but 1958 subscriptions, one bookseller subscribing for five hundred copies.

37. Campbell's *Survey* (Dublin: W. Whitestone, 1778), p. 400.

38. John Nichols, *Illustrations of the Literary History of the Eighteenth Century*, 8 vols. (London: Nichols and Bentley, 1817–58), VII, 841.

39. Ms. 2288, National Library of Ireland, Dublin.

40. "Printers of the Mind: Some Notes on Bibliographical Theories and Printing-House Practices," *Studies in Bibliography*, 22 (1969), 1–75.

41. Patricia Hernlund, "William Strahan's Ledgers: Standard Charges for Printing, 1738–1785," *Studies in Bibliography*, 20 (1967), p. 104.

42. *The English Common Reader, A Social History of the Mass Reading Public 1800–1900* (Chicago: University of Chicago Press, 1957), p. 50.

43. Hellmut Lehmann-Haupt, In Collaboration with Lawrence C. Wroth and Rollo G. Silver, *The Book in America*, 2nd ed. (New York: R. R. Bowker, 1951), p. 40.

44. *A Catalogue of the Greater Portion of the Library of the Late Edmond

Malone (London: Wright and Murphy, 1818); the 1775 Dublin edition of Johnson's *Dictionary* which lists Malone among the subscribers is not in this catalogue.

45. *A Tour in Ireland in 1775*, 2nd ed. (Dublin: Sheppard et al., 1776), p. 34.

46. Marian S. Carson and Marshall W. S. Swan, "John Bioren: Printer to Philadelphia Publishers," *PBSA*, 43 (1949), 324–26.

47. Carey Letter Books, 1788–94, Box 1, B45.

48. *Sale Catalogues of Libraries of Eminent Persons*, ed. A. N. L. Munby, 12 vols. (London: Mansell, 1971–75) identify few Irish reprints in the many eighteenth-century British libraries included.

49. I discuss 198 private libraries in "Private Libraries in Eighteenth-Century Ireland," *Library Quarterly*, 44 (1974), 231–47. I have added libraries of Lord Clonbrook, John Singleton, James Martin, and anonymous gentlemen c. 1781 and 1828, all MS. catalogues in the National Library of Ireland. Place of publication is identified in almost all the 203 catalogues.

50. Other peers won their honors through distinction in law or government and are included with these groups.

51. J. Barrett, Brinkley, Cox, Elrington, Hales, J. Kearney, Kelburn, Lawson, Pococke, and J. Walker.

52. The best source for information about eighteenth-century Irish Roman Catholic priests is the Irish Catholic journal *Reportorium Novum* in the first four volumes beginning in 1955. Another helpful source is MS.1548 in the National Library of Ireland, an extensive compilation by Malachy Moran in 1910 of data on Irish Catholic priests of the period 1735–1835.

53. A. Browne, C. K. Bushe, Caldwell, Egan, John Foster, J. L. Foster, O'Connell, W. C. Smyth, Stuart, Sullivan, the Earl of Clonmell, and Viscount Avonmore.

54. Browne, C. K. Bushe, Caldwell, Day, Hellen, O'Connell, W. C. Smyth, and the Earl of Clonmell.

55. *General Advertiser*, 13 January 1737; 10 September 1754; *Pue's Occurrences*, 12 January 1762; *Hibernian Journal*, 28 November 1774, 10 April 1775; *Sleater's Public Gazetteer*, 23 February 1765; *Dublin Evening Post*, 24 October 1778.

56. *Hibernian Journal*, 17 November 1775, 13 September 1782, 23 April 1784, 28 June 1784; *Freeman's Journal*, 8 November 1779.

57. *Hibernian Journal*, 20 March 1778, 20 November 1779, 11 April 1780; 6 March 1782, 4 January 1792, 19 June 1793, 29 November 1793, 13 January 1794, 3 October 1794, 2 November 1796, 6 January 1797, 1799 *passim*; *Dublin Evening Post*, 15 January 1786, 18 April 1786.

58. *Hibernian Journal* 4 January 1792, 7 July 1794, 19 January 1795; 15 January 1796, 23 October 1796; 23 October 1797; 1799 passim.; *Dublin Evening Post*, 18 April 1786, 27 May 1786.

59. Richard Robert Madden, *The History of Irish Periodical Literature*, 2 vols. (London: T. C. Newby, 1867), II, 160–63; Ian Maxted, *The London Book Trades, 1775–1800, A Preliminary Checklist of Members* (Folkestone, Kent: Dawson, 1977), p. 69

60. *Freeman's Journal*, 23 November 1784; *Dublin Evening Post*, 23 September 1786; *Hibernian Journal*, 14 April 1794.

61. *A Catalogue of Books belonging to the Dublin Library Society* (Dublin: C. Downes, 1792, 1806); a subscriber list is included.

62. Arthur Houston, *Danial O'Connell: His Early Life and Journal, 1795 to 1802* (London: Sir Isaac Pitman and Sons, Ltd., 1906), pp. 129–30.

63. *Catalogue of Books of the Cork Library Society* (Cork, 1808).

64. Paul Kaufman, "Community Lending Libraries in Eighteenth-Century Ireland and Wales, *Library Quarterly*, 33 (1963), 300–01.

65. *A Catalogue of the Books Belonging to the Belfast Society for Promoting Knowledge* (Belfast: M'Caw, Stevenson, and Orr, 1888), pp. 9–11, 16, 30–34.

66. The Armagh borrowing record is unique in Ireland, and it must be ranked with the Bristol Library Society and the Innerpeffray Public Library, Perthshire, Scotland, which Paul Kaufman claims are the only eighteenth-century British libraries whose borrowing records survive (*Libraries and Their Users: Collected Papers in Library History*; London: Library Association, 1969; p.154).

67. MS. H. II.3, Armagh Public Library, Armagh, Northern Ireland.

68. MS. H. II.12, Armagh Public Library, Armagh, Northern Ireland.

69. Maureen Wall, "The Catholic Merchants, Manufacturers, and Traders of Dublin", 1778–1782, *Reportorium Novum*, 2 No. 2 (1960), 298–323.

70. MS. D. O. D. 553, Record Office of Northern Ireland, Belfast.

71. *The Drennan Letters*, 1776–1819, ed. D. A. Chart (Belfast: His Majesty's Stationery Office, 1931).

72. See, for example, the following: Kenneth W. Porter, *The Jackson and the Lees, Two Generations of Massachusetts Merchants, 1765–1844*, 2 vols. (Cambridge, Mass.: Harvard University Press, 1937); William T. Baxter, *The House of Hancock, Business in Boston, 1724–1775* (Cambridge, Mass.: Harvard University Press, 1945); James B. Hedges, *The Browns of Providence Plantations, Colonial Years* (Cambridge, Mass.: Harvard University Press, 1952); Worthington C. Ford, *The Commerce of Rhode Island, 1726–1800*, 2 vols. (Boston: Massachusetts Historical Society, 1915); I. W. Stuart, *The Life of Jonathan Trumbull, Sen.* (Boston: Crocker and Brewster, 1859); Virginia D. Harrington, *The New York Merchant on the Eve of the Revolution* (New York: Columbia University Press, 1935); *The Beekman Mercantile Papers, 1746–1799*, 3 vols. (New York: New York Historical Society, 1956); Francis G. James, "Irish Colonial Trade in the Eighteenth Century," *William and Mary Quarterly*, 3rd ser., 20 (1963),

574–84; Hennig Cohen, *The South Carolina Gazette, 1732–1775* (Columbia, S. C.: University of South Carolina Press, 1953); Bryan Edwards, *The History, Civil and Commercial, of the British West Indies*, 5 vols. (London, G. and W. B. Whittaker, 1819).

73. *The Papers of Benjamin Franklin*, ed. Leonard Labaree, William B. Willcox, et al. (New Haven, Yale University Press, 1959–), XI, 190.

74. For discussions of colonial book imports see the following: Daniel K. Boorstin, *The Americans, The Colonial Experience* (New York: Random House, 1958); Carl Bridenbaugh, *Cities in Revolt, Urban Life in America, 1743–1776* (New York: Knopf, 1955) Elizabeth Cometti, "Some Early Best Sellers in Piedmont, North Carolina," *Journal of Southern History*, 16 (1950), 324–37; Michael Kraus, *The Atlantic Civilization: Eighteenth-Century Origins* (Ithaca, N. Y.: Cornell University Press, 1949); Hellmut Lehmann-Haupt, et al., *The Book in America*, 2nd ed. (New York: R. R. Bowker, 1951); George L. McKay, *American Book Auction Catalogues, 1713–1934* (New York: New York Public Library, 1937); Louis Shores, *Origins of the American College Library* (New York: Barnes and Noble, 1935); Frederick B. Tolles, *James Logan and the Culture of Provincial America* (Boston: Little, Brown, 1957).

75. *Franklin Papers*, III, 165.

76. David Hall to John Balfour, 20 November 1764, David Hall Letter Book, American Philosophical Society; Peter Parker, "The Philadelphia Printer: A Study of an Eighteenth-Century Businessman," *Business History Review*, 40 (1966), 34.

77. Worthington C. Ford, "Henry Knox, Bookseller, 1771–1774," *Proceedings of the Mssachusetts Historical Society*, 61 (1927–28), 255–56, 269; Henry Knox Papers, Massachusetts Historical Society; Lawrence C. Wroth, Part I in Hellmut Lehmann-Haupt, et al., *The Book in America*, 2nd ed. (New York: R. R. Bowker Company, 1951), p. 53.

78. See complete list in Appendix 2. Although at least 101 Irish bookmen joined the American book trade, only twenty, fifteen of them engravers, joined the London book trade according to Ian Maxted in his *London Book Trades, 1775–1800, A Preliminary Checklist of Members* (Folkestone, Kent: Dawson, 1977).

79. G. Thomas Tanselle, "Some Statistics on American Printing, 1764–1783," *The Press & the American Revolution*, ed. Bernard Bailyn and John B. Hench (Worcester, Mass.: American Antiquarian Society, 1980), p. 339.

80. Robert B. Winans, *A Descriptive Checklist of Book Catalogues Separately Printed in America, 1693–1800* (Worcester, Mass.: American Antiquarian Society, 1981).

81. *Printed Specimens, with conditions annexed, for reprint in America, by subscription, octavo editions of David Hume's History of England, Sir William Blackstone's Commentaries on the laws of England, and Adam Ferguson's Essay on*

the history of civil society (Philadelphia: Robert Bell, 1771), Pt. V, 1–6.

82. Of the many publication on Lyon the most notable are the DAB article, J. Fairfax McLaughlin's *Matthew Lyon* (New York: W. H. Crawford, 1900), and Aleine Austin's *Matthew Lyon* (University Park, Pa. and London: Pennsylvania State University Press, 1981); there is a good summary in John Tebbel's *History of Book Publishing in the United States*, 4 vols. (New York: R. R. Bowker, 1972–81), I, 82.

83. Austin, p. 134.

84. Austin, p. 76; McLaughlin, pp. 80, 412; Douglas C. McMurtrie, *The Beginning of Printing in the District of Columbia* (Somerville, N. J.: privately printed, 1933), p. 276; Clarence S. Brigham, *History and Bibliography of American Newspapers, 1690–1820*, 2 vols. (Worcester, Mass. American Antiquarian Society, 1947), II, 1447.

85. Winans, p. 110; Isaiah Thomas, *The History of Printing in America*, 2 vols., (Albany, N. Y., J. Munsell, 1874), I, 251–52, 300–1; George L. McKay, *A Register of Artists, Engravers, Booksellers, Bookbinders, Printers and Publishers in New York City, 1633–1820* (New York: New York Public Library, 1942), pp. 29–30; Alfred L. Lorenz, *Hugh Gaine, A Colonial Printer–Editor's Odyssey to Loyalism* (Carbondale, Illinois: Southern Illinois University Press, 1972), p. 134; Tanselle, p. 339.

86. All reprints by Irish booksellers in America are taken from Charles Evans, *American Bibliography: A Chronoligical Dictionary of All Books, Pamphlets and Periodical Publications Printed in the United States of America from the Genesis of Printing in 1639 down to and Including the Year 1820*, 13 vols. (Chicago, Univ. of Chicago Press, 1903–34; Worcester, Mass., American Antiquarian Society, 1955), Roger P. Bristol, *Supplement to Charles Evans' American Bibliography* (Charlottesville, Va., Univ. Press of Virginia, 1970), and Ralph R. Shaw, Richard H. Shoemaker, Francis P. Newton, *American Bibliography, A Preliminary Checklist 1801 to 1819*, 23 vols. (New York: Scarecrow Press, 1958–83.

87. Thomas, pp. 252, 300–1; Tebbel, *History of Book Publishing*, I, 96; Stephen B. Weeks, "The Pre-Revolutionary Printers of North Carolina: Davis, Steuart, and Boyd," *The North Carolina Booklet*, 15 (1915), 116–21.

88. Thomas, p. 312; Brigham, II, 1446; *Register of ... Printers and Publishers in New York City*, p. 45.

89. *Register of... Printers and Publishers in New York City*, p. 70; John J. Lenehan, "The Society of the Friendly Sons of St. Patrick in the City of New York," *Journal of the American-Irish Historical Society*, 8 (1908–09), 188.

90. Thomas H. Murray, "Some Voices from ye Olden Time," *Journal of the American-Irish Historical Society*, 4 (1904), 61.

91. R. J. Dickson, *Ulster Emigration to Colonial America, 1718–1775* (London: Routledge and Kegan Paul, 1966), pp. 23, 34, 59, 64.

92. Douglas C. McMurtrie, *A History of Printing in the United States* (New York: R. R. Bowker, 1936), pp. 244–48; Dorothy Lawson Hawkins,

"James Adams, the First Printer of Delaware," *Papers of the Bibliographical Society of America*, 28 (1934), 28–63.

93. McCulloch, p. 232; H. Glenn and Maude O. Brown, "A Directory of the Book-Arts and Book Trade in Philadelphia to 1820 including Painters and Engravers," *Bulletin of the New York Public Library*, 53 (1949), 389, and 54 (1950), 143, hereafter cited as "Philadelphia Book Trade Directory."

94. Cited in Rita S. Gottesman, *The Arts and Crafts in New York, 1726–1776 and The Arts and Crafts in New York, 1777–1799* (New York: New York Historical Society, 1938, 1954), pp. 244, 283.

95. McCulloch, pp. 224–25; "Philadelphia Book Trade Directory," *BNYPL*, 53 (1949), 390.

96. McCulloch, p. 126; "Philadelphia Book Tade Directory," *BNYPL*, 54 (1950), 35.

97. "Philadelphia Book Trade Directory," *BNYPL*, 53 (1949), 622; Ellis P. Oberholtzer, *The Literary History of Philadelphia* (Philadelphia: George W. Jacobs and Co., 1906), p. 86; Lyon N. Richardson, *A History of Early American Magazines, 1741–1789* (New York: Thomas Nelson and Sons, 1931), p. 154.

98. Thomas, I, 268; *Boston Printers, Publishers, and Booksellers: 1640–1800*, ed. Benjamin Franklin V (Boston: G. K. Hall, 1980), p. 361; Sidney L. Gulick, "A Chestefield Bibliography to 1800," *PBSA*, 29 (1935), 26.

99. Thomas, II, 191.

100. Irish Customs House Books on Exports and Imports, 1764–1823, MSS.353–76, National Library of Ireland.

101. *The Parliamentary Register: or History of the Proceedings and Debates of the House of Commons of Ireland, 1781–1800*, 18 vols. (Dublin: P. Byrne, W. Porter, J. Moore, 1784–1800), V, 403–7, 424.

102. *Report of the Lords of the Committee of Council, appointed for the consideration of all matters relating to Trade and Foreign Plantations* (1785), Lecky Collection of Documents on the proposed Commercial Regulations of 1785, Library, Trinity College, Dublin.

103. *Observations on the Commerce of the American States*, 2nd ed. (London: J. Debrett, 1784), p. 33.

104. *A Brief Examination of Lord Sheffield's Observations on the Commerce of the United States* (Philadelphia: M. Carey, 1791), p. 39.

105. For a good sample see Carey's *Autobiography* (Brooklyn, N. Y.: E. L. Schwaab, 1942); the DAB and DNB articles; Earl L. Bradsher, *Mathew Carey, Editor, Author, and Publisher* (New York: Columbia University Press, 1912); the best and most recent short discussion is in Tebbel, *History of Book Publishing* I, 106–17. William Clarkin's *Mathew Carey: A Bibliography of His Publications 1785–1824* (New York: Garland, 1984) offers the best evidence of Carey's achievement.

106. Carey Letter Books, Box 15, B45.

107. Mathew Carey Accounts, VII, 2344, American Antiquarian Society, Worcester, Massachusetts.
108. Carey Accounts, XV, 5992; Carey Letter Books, 1792–97, Box I, B45.
109. Carey Letter Books.
110. Carey Accounts, VII, 2408; Bradsher, p. 15; Carey Letter Books, 1793–94, Box III, B45.
111. See *Mason Locke Weems, His Works and Ways*, ed. Paul Leicester Ford and Emily Ellsworth Ford Skeel, 3 vols. (New York: privately printed, 1929).
112. "Philadelphia Book Trade Directory," *BNYPL*, 54 (1950), 129, 133; Carey, p. 21; Wilfrid Parsons, *Early Catholic Americana, 1729–1830* (New York: Macmillan and Co., 1939), pp. x-xi, 16.
113. William J. Free, *The Columbian Magazine and American Literary Nationalism* (The Hague: Mouton, 1968), pp. 29–31; Brigham, II, 889; Luther Livingston, *Livingston and his Press at Passy* (New York: Grolier Club, 1914), p. 161; Carey Letter Books, John Chambers to M. Carey, 26 March 1794.
114. "Philadelphia Book Trade Directory," *BNYPB*, 53 (1949), 296; Michael E. Hennessy, "Men of Irish Blood who have attained distinction in American Journalism," *Journal of the American Irish Historical Society*, 3 (1900), 68; Brigham, II, 905.
115. "Philadelphia Book Trade Directory," *BNYPL*, 53 (1949), 340; Joseph M. Finotti, *Bibliographia Catholica Americana* (New York: Catholic Publication House, 1872), p. 291; E. Millicent Sowerby, *Catalogue of the Library of Thomas Jefferson*, 5 vols. (Washington D.C.: Library of Congress, 1952), I, 236–39.
116. "Philadelphia Book Trade Directory," *BNYPL*, 53 (1949), 340; Finotti, p. 291; Brigham, II, 1388; Mathew Carey Letter Books, 1792–97; Box I, B45, and 1793–94, Box III, B45; *Wilmington Chronicle*, 22 October 1795; Brigham, II, 1388.
117. "Philadelphia Book Trade Directory," *BNYPL*, 53 (1949), 340; Finotti, p. 291; *A Catalogue of the Bradshaw Collection of Irish Books in the University Library, Cambridge*, 3 vols. (Cambridge: Cambridge University Library, 1916), I, 465, III, 1410; Walter G. Strickland, *A Dictionary of Irish Artists*, 2 vols. (Dublin and London: Maunsel and Co., 1913), I, 155; Mathew Carey Letter Books, 1785–96, B46, 1788–94, Box I, B45; R. B. McDowell, "The Personnel of the Dublin Society of United Irishmen, 1791–94," *Irish Historical Studies*, 2 (1940–41), 25.
118. "Philadelphia Book Trade Directory," *BNYPL*, 53 (1949), 619; John H. Campbell, *History of the Friendly Sons of St. Patrick and of the Hibernian Society for the Relief of Emigrants from Ireland* (Philadelphia: Hibernian Society, 1892), p. 123, hereafter cited as *Hibernian Society*.
119. "Philadelphia Book Trade Directory," *BNYPL*, 54 (1950), 36; Winans, p. 95; Hibernian Society, p. 511.

120. "Philadelphia Book Trade Directory,"*BNYPL*, 53 (1949), 223, 294; Hibernian Society, p. 317; Wroth in Lehmann-Haupt, p. 59.
121. "Philadelphia Book Trade Directory," *BNYPL*, 53 (1949), 389; Francis Von A. Cabeen, "The Society of the Sons of St. Tammany of Philadelphia," *Pennsylvania Magazine of History and Biography*, 26 (1902), 343.
122, "Philadelphia Book Trade Directory," *BNYPL*, 54 (1950), 28; *Hibernian Society*, p. 129.
123. "Philadelphia Book Trade Directory," *BNYPL*, 54 (1950), 27; *Bradshaw Collection*, I, 433; *Dublin Evening Post*, 23 October 1779; Brigham, II, 899, 900, 921.
124. Harriet Silvester Tapley, *Salem Imprints, 1768–1825* (Salem, Massachusetts: Essex Institute, 1927), pp. 102, 188–95; *Library of Thomas Jefferson*, IV, 496–97.
125. Marcus A. McCorison, *Vermont Imprints*, 1778–1820 (Worcester, Massachusetts: American Antiquarian Society, 1963), p. 508; Brigham, II, 911.
126. Tebbel, *History of Book Publishing*, I, 326; *Register of ... Printers and Publishers in New York City*, p. 41.
127. Winans, pp. 80–85, 101, 108–10, 143, 152.
128. George G. Raddin, Jr., *Hocquet Caritat and the Early New York Literary Scene* (Dover, New Jersey: Dover Advance Press, 1953), p. 85.
129. Mathew Carey to Thomas Allen, Carey Letter Books, 1794–95, B45, Box 3.
130. Lewis M. Stark and Maud D. Cole, *Checklist of Additions to Evans' American Bibliography in the Rare Books Division of the New York Public Library* (New York: New York Public Library, 1960), p. 65.
131. Winans, pp. 109–10; *United States Gazette*, 14 July 1796, 27 May 1800.
132. *The Parliamentary Register*, XVI (1796), 73.
133. Stuart C. Sherman, "Leman Thomas Rede's Bibliotheca Americana," *William and Mary Quarterly*, 3rd ser., 4 (1947), 348.
134. Two Dublin booksellers named John Rice emigrated to the United States, one to Philadelphia in the second phase and the other to Baltimore in the third phase to be discussed in chapter eight.
135. *Journals of the House of Commons of the Kingdom of Ireland*, XVI, 193.
136. "Essay on the Natural Advantages of Ireland, the Manufactures in Ireland to which they are adapted and the best means of improving those Manufactures," *Transactions of the Royal Irish Academy*, IX (1803), 405–6.
137. *NCBEL* lists no Irish editions of Richardson's novels, but I have examined these copies: the 1741 editions of *Pamela* at NLI and the 1742 *Pamela* at TCD; the 1748–49 *Clarissa* at TCD and the 1756 abridged *Clarissa* at NLI; the 1753 *Sir Charles Grandison* at Yale and NLI, and the 1780 edition at Yale. See Appendix 4 for publishers. *NUC* lists other

editions of *Clarissa* in 1765 and 1792, and of *Sir Charles Grandison* in 1765.

138. William S. Clark, *The Irish Stage in the Country Towns, 1720 to 1800* (Oxford: Clarendon Press, 1965), pp. 308–9.

139. *NCBEL* lists no Irish editions of Fielding's novels, but I have examined these copies: the 1742 *Joseph Andrews* at NLI and TCD, the 1747 edition at NLI, TCD, and Yale, the 1754 at TCD, the 1767 by Smith, Ewing, and Faulkner at NLI and TCD, and the 1767 by Chamberlaine and Potts at Yale; the two editions of the 1749 *Tom Jones* at Yale, the 2nd 1749 edition and the 1750 edition at TCD, the 1759 at NLI and Yale, the 1766 at NLI and Yale, the 1767 at Yale, the 1786 at TCD; the 1752 *Amelia* by Smith at Yale and the second 1752 edition by Risk et al. at TCD and Yale. See Appendix 4 for publishers. Additions in *NUC* include the 1741 *Shamela*, the [1794] *Tom Jones*. The University of Michigan does not own the 1777 *Amelia* credited to it in *NUC*. Cambridge University lists the Henshall *Joseph Andrews* [1794].

140. Richard R. Madden, *The United Irishmen*, 12 vols. (New York: Catholic Publication Society, 1916), XII, 197.

141. The only other copy known to me is the University of Chicago copy listed in the *National Union Catalog*. No Dublin subscription edition of *Clarissa* is listed in F. J. G. Robinson and P. J. Wallis, *Book Subscription Lists, A Revised Guide*.

142. Carey Accounts.

143. *Autobiography and Correspondence of Mary Granville, Mrs. Delany*, ed. Lady Llanover, 3 vols. (London: Richard Bentley, 1861), II, 569.

144. William H. Curran, *Life of John Philpott Curran*, 2 vols., 2nd ed. (Edinburgh: Archibald Constable, 1822), II, 352.

145. The figures were 2,000 for the first edition, 3,000 for the second, and 1,500 for the third according to Fred W. Boege, *Smollett's Reputation as a Novelist* (Princeton: Princeton University Press, 1947), p. 2.

146. *NCBEL* lists most but not all the Irish editions of Smollett's works. I have examined the following copies: the 1748 *Roderick Random* at NLI, the 1749 at Yale, the 1755 at NLI, the 1775 at NLI, the 1794 at NLI; the 1751 *Peregrine Pickle* at NLI and Yale, the 1768 at Yale, the 1775 at NLI, the 1787 at TCD, the 1791 abridged edition at NLI; the 1753 *Ferdinand Count Fathom* at Yale and NLI, the 1772 at TCD: the 1763 *Sir Launcelot Greaves* at NLI, the 1775 at Yale; the 1771 *Humphry Clinker* at NLI, TCD, and Yale, the 1781 at NLI and Yale; the 1796 *Don Quixote* at Yale. See Appendix 4 for publishers. *NUC* lists other editions of *Roderick Random* in 1768 and 1773, of *Sir Launcelot Greaves* in 1767, of *Humphry Clinker* in 1784, 1790, and 1793, of *Don Quixote* in 1765, and *Select Works* in 1775–76. Cambridge University lists a 1772 *Roderick Random* and a 1763 *Peregrine Pickle*.

147. Smith begins his corrections from the errata list with *profligate* in the Dublin edition, II, 146, instead of the error *prostitute* in the London

edition, III, 238. This is the sixth error, and Smith corrects the seventh and then jumps to the eleventh and twelfth errors, which he corrects.

148. Hugh Amory observes that the 1749 Dublin reprint descends from a copy of the first London edition "with cancellanda B 9, 10 in Vol. 1 and B 4, 5 in Vol. 2 in place" ("*Tom Jones* Plus and Minus: Towards a Practical Text," *Harvard Library Bulletin*, 25 (1977), 102). Smith must have found these cancellanda in the sheets from the London printing house and then corrected them when he got a copy of the London edition.

149. James Grant Raymond, *The Life of Thomas Dermody*, 2 vols. (London: W. Miller, 1806), I, 11; Thomas Dermody, *Poems, Moral and Descriptive* (London: Vernor and Hood, 1800).

150. Henry Knox Papers, Massachusetts Historical Society.

151. Although George Cockburn (fl. 1747–70) was from an old Scots landed family, he was employed in London when *Tom Jones* came out as Commissioner and Comptroller of the Navy; see Thomas H. Cockburn-Hood, *The House of Cockburn of that Ilk, and the Cadets thereof* (Edinburgh: privately printed, 1888), pp. 158–59.

152. *The Correspondence of Emily, Duchess of Leinster (1731–1814)*, ed. Brian Fitzgerald, 3 vols. (Dublin: Stationery Office, 1949–57), I, 104.

153. Mathew Carey Accounts, American Antiquarian Society.

154. The controversy is best described in T. C. Duncan Eaves and Ben D. Kimpel, *Samuel Richardson, A Biography* (Oxford: Clarendon Press, 1971), pp. 377–84. Robert and Catherine Ward take Faulkner's part in the quarrel; see chapter 1, n. 23.

155. Carey Accounts.

156. *NCBEL* lists most but not all the Irish editions of Sterne's works. I have examined the following copies: the 1760 *Tristram Shandy* at NLI and TCD, the 1761 at Yale, the 1765 both of vols. 1–4 and 5–8 at Yale, the 1767 of vol. 9 at Yale, the full set 1760–67 at TCD and Yale, the 1776 at TCD, the 1779 at NLI and Yale, the 1780 at Yale, the 1795 at TCD; the 1766 and 1775 *Letters* at Yale, the 1776 eds. at NLI, TCD, and Yale; the 1760 *Sermons* at NLI and Yale, the 1761 and 1766 at Yale, the 1785 at NLI; the 1768 1st ed. of *A Sentimental Journey* at NLI and the 2nd ed. at TCD, the 1769 at NLI, the 1775 and 1789 at NLI and TCD; the 1770 *Works* at NLI and TCD, the 1774 at NLI and Yale, the 1775 at NLI, the 1779 at Yale, the 1780 and 1794 at NLI; the 1788 *Beauties of Sterne* at TCD. See Appendix 4 for publishers. *NUC* lists a 1784 edition of *Beauties of Sterne*.

157. The first edition of *Tristram Shandy* gives the date 1760 but no place of publication. Kenneth Monkman's argument is generally accepted that it was printed in York and half the copies sold there and half in London by the Dodsley brothers, who on 8 March 1760 bought the copyright from Sterne for £250; see Monkman, "The Bibliography of the Early

Editions of *Tristram Shandy*," *The Library*, 5th ser., 25 (1959), 11–39.
158. "Towards a Sterne Bibliography," *The Winged Skull, Papers from the Laurence Sterne Bicentenary Conference*, ed. Arthur H. Cash and John M. Stedmond (Kent, Ohio: Kent State University Press, 1971), p. 295.
159. *Letters of Laurence Sterne*, ed. Lewis P. Curtis (Oxford: Clarendon Press, 1935), pp. 137–38.
160. *A Series of letters between Mrs. Elizabeth Carter and Miss Catherine Talbot 1741–70; to which are added letters from Mrs. Elizabeth Carter to Mrs. Vesey, 1763–87*, ed. M. Pennington, 4 vols. (London: F., C., and J. Rivington, 1809), III, 334.
161. Mathew Carey Accounts.
162. *Autobiography*, III, 593, 588.
163. *The Complete Works of the late Rev. Philip Skelton, Rector of Fintona, to which is prefixed, Burdy's Life of the Author*, ed. Robert Lynam (London: Richard Baynes, 1824), I, cxlvi.
164. *The Triumvirate: or, the Authentic Memoirs of A. B. and C.*, 2 vols. (London: W. Johnston, 1764), I, xiv-xvi.
165. Bradford Papers, Historical Society of Pennsylvania.
166. *Posthumous works of a late celebrated genius, deceased* (Dublin: J. Exshaw, et al., 1770), pp. 19, 173.
167. Mathew Carey Accounts.
168. *Robert Addison's Library*, ed. William J. Cameron and George McKnight (Hamilton, Ontario: McMaster University, 1967).
169. Bradford Papers, Historical Society of Pennsylvania.
170. Mathew Carey Accounts.
171. Mathew Carey Accounts.
172. Mathew Carey Accounts; Carey Letter Books.
173. *The Aurora* (Philadelphia), 31 August 1796.
174. Mathew Carey Accounts.
175. Mark Elstob, *A Trip to Kilkenny, From Durham, by Way of Whitehaven and Dublin* (Stockton, Durham: R. Christopher, 1778), pp. 114–15.
176. Mathew Carey Accounts.
177. *Boswell's Life of Johnson, Together with Boswell's Journal of a Tour to the Hebrides and Johnson's Diary of a Journey into North Wales*, ed. G. B. Hill, rev. L. F. Powell, 6 vols. (Oxford: Clarendon Press, 1934–50), I, 348.
178. *Letters of Samuel Johnson*, ed. R. W. Chapman, 3 vols. (Oxford: Clarendon Press, 1952), I, 398–99.
179. *NCBEL* lists most of the Dublin reprints of Johnson's works but not all. I have examined the following copies: the 1738 *London* at NLI and Yale; the 1749 *Irene* at TCD and Yale; the 1752 *Rambler* at NLI and TCD, the 1785 (Heery) at TCD, the 1793 at NLI; the 1762 *Idler* at TCD and in the collection of H. W. Liebert, New Haven, Connecticut; the 1758 *Dictionary* at NLI, the 1768 and 1775 editions at NLI, TCD, Univ. of N. C. (CH), and Yale; the 1798 at NLI, TCD, and Washington and

Lee Univ.; the 1759 *Rasselas* at NLI, TCD, and Yale, the 1777 and 1787 editions at NLI; the 1766 *Shakespeare* at NLI, the 1771 at TCD, the 1791 (2) and 1794 editions at TCD; the 1775 *Journey to the Western Islands of Scotland* by Leathley et al. at NLI, TCD, Yale, and in the Liebert collection, the 1775 Pope ed. at TCD and Liebert, the 1775 Walker ed. at NLI, TCD, and Liebert, the 1775 Williams ed. at NLI, TCD, and Liebert; the 1777 *Political Tracts* at NLI and Yale; the 1782 *Beauties of Johnson* at NLI, TCD, and Yale; the 1785 *Prayers and Meditations* at NLI, the 1796 at TCD; the 1785 *Poems* at NLI and Yale; the 1788 *Letters* at NLI and Yale; the 1779 *Lives of the Poets* at TCD and Liebert, the 1779–81 at NLI, TCD, Yale and Univ. of N. C. (CH), the 1793–1802 at NLI, TCD, and the Dublin Public Library, the 1795 in Liebert; the 1793 *Works* at NLI and Yale. See Appendix 4 for details of publication. *NUC* lists other editions of the *Dictionary* in 1764, of the *Lives of the Poets* in 1780–81, variants of the 1785 *Rambler* printed for Thomas Walker and for William Sleater, and *Rasselas* c. 1795.

180. *Yale Edition of the Works of Samuel Johnson, The Rambler*, ed. W. J. Bate and Albrecht B. Strauss (New Haven: Yale University Press, 1969), p. xxxi.

181. Ward, p. 77.

182. Mathew Carey Accounts.

183. See Genevieve Yost, "The Reconstruction of the Library of Norborne Berkeley, Baron de Botetourt, Governor of Virginia 1768–1779," *PBSA*, 36 (1942), 97–123.

184. *Catalogue of the Cashel Diocesan Library* (Boston: G. K. Hall and Company, 1973).

185. Henry Knox Papers.

186. *Library of Thomas Jefferson*, V, 133–34.

187. *A Catalogue of the Library at Fonmon Castle, Glamorgan*, ed. Margaret Evans (Cardiff: The Library, University College, Cardiff, 1969).

188. Warburton, et al., II, 1158.

189. Carey Letter Books, Box 3, B45; Carey Accounts.

190. Bradford Papers, Historical Society of Pennsylvania.

191. *Robert Addison's Library*.

192. Boswell is the only one of the eight major writers whose bibliography in *NCBEL*, compiled by Frederick A. Pottle, the leading Boswell scholar of our time, is complete. I have examined the following copies of Dublin editions: the 1768 3rd ed. of *An Account of Corsica* at NLI, TCD, the 1768 4th ed. at TCD, Yale; the 1768 *Letters of Lady Jane Douglas* at Yale; the 1785 *Journal of a Tour to the Hebrides* at NLI, Yale; the 1792 abridged *Life of Johnson* at NLI, Yale; the 1792 *Life of Johnson* at NLI, TCD, Yale (2). See Appendix 4 for details of publication. Pottle describes a copy of the 5th Dublin edition of *Corsica* in private hands in *Literary Career of James Boswell* (Oxford, 1929), p. 59; Cambridge University also lists this edition.

193. See my article "James Boswell and the Irish Press, 1767–1795," *Bulletin of the New York Public Library*, 73 (1969), 581–98.
194. See my discussion in "A New Letter by James Boswell," *Studies in Scottish Literature*, 8 (1970), 118–22.
195. *Letters of James Boswell*, ed. Chauncey Brewster Tinker, 2 vols. (Oxford: Clarendon Press, 1924), I, 171.
196. Edward Dilly to Boswell, 27 July 1767 (MS. Yale, C 1061).
197. *Letters of James Boswell*, I, 163.
198. James Boswell, *Decision of the Court of Session upon the Question of Literary Property* (Edinburgh: Alexander Donaldson, 1774)
199. *Parliamentary Register*, XIII, 130.
200. Still the best of the many discussions of the case is A. Francis Steuart, *The Douglas Cause* (Glasgow and Edinburgh: W. Hodge and Co., 1909); Frederick A. Pottle gives the definitive statement about Boswell's participation in *James Boswell, the Earlier Years, 1740–1769* (New York: McGraw-Hill, 1966), pp. 311–17, 339–41.
201. MS Yale, C 610.
202. Pope is not identified in H. R. Plomer, G. H. Bushnell, and E. R. McC. Dix, *A Dictionary of the Printers and Booksellers Who Were at Work in England, Scotland and Ireland from 1726 to 1775* (Oxford: Bibliographical Society, 1932), and I find nothing about him in the Dublin newspapers. *NCBEL*, II, 1132, identifies the Pope edition as a London reprint of the Williams Dublin edition. The Harvard copy, the only one listed in the *National Union Catalog*, is identified as an unauthorized London reprint.
203. Carey Accounts.
204. O'Conor Papers, MSS. B.1.2, Royal Irish Academy, Dublin.
205. Joyce Hemlow, *A Catalogue of the Burney Family Correspondence, 1749–1878* (New York: New York Public Library, 1971), p. 24.
206. *Letters of James Boswell*, II, 330.
207. O'Conor Papers, Gilbert Collection, Dublin Public Library (Pearse Street), and Royal Irish Academy, Dublin.
208. *The Correspondence and other Papers of James Boswell Relating to the Making of the Life of Johnson*, ed. Marshall Waingrow (New York: McGraw-Hill Book Company, [1969]), p. 124.
209. Maurice Craig, *Irish Bookbindings, 1600–1800* (London: Cassell and Company, 1954), Plate 55.
210. The 1779 edition is not listed in the *National Union Catalog*, but I have examined a copy at Trinity College, Dublin, originally purchased by William FitzGerald (1749–1804), 3rd Duke of Leinster. The only authority for a second edition is a Falkner Grierson Catalogue (Dublin) of eighteenth-century books for 1966 that identifies a second edition "with text completely reset and many variant readings from the first edition." The University of North Carolina (Chapel Hill) set that I have seen has the same pagination as the first edition; it is listed in the *National*

Union Catalog, Vol. 282, p. 419, as a third Irish edition, but this is not in the imprint.

211. Mathew Carey Accounts.

212. I am indebted to Herman W. Liebert, Director Emeritus of the Beinicke Rare Book Library at Yale, for calling my attention to this edition in his own collection.

213. Mathew Carey Accounts.

214. Mathew Carey Accounts.

215. Waingrow, p. 390; Frederick A. Pottle, *The Literary Career of James Boswell* (Oxford: Clarendon Press, 1929), p. 167.

216. Waingrow, p. 393.

217. Ian Maxted, *The London Book Trades, 1775–1800, A Preliminary Checklist of Members* (Folkestone, Kent: Dawson, 1977), p. 82.

218. Waingrow, pp. 495–96.

219. Houston, pp. 139, 143–44, 146–47, 151, 154.

220. William Henry Curran, *Sketches of the Irish Bar* (London; H. Colburn, 1855), I, 78.

221. *Miscellaneous Sketches; or Hints for Essays* (London; G. C. & J. Robinson, 1798), I, 69, 81.

222. Houston, pp. 147–48, 164, 175, 180, 183.

223. O'Conor-Walker Correspondence, MSS. Gilbert Collection No. 203, Dublin Public Library (Pearse Street).

224. Peter Burrowes Papers, MSS. 23K53, Royal Irish Academy, Dublin.

225. *Miscellaneous Sketches*, I, 82–84.

226. *The Collected Letters of Oliver Goldsmith*, ed. Katherine C. Balderston (Cambridge: Cambridge University Press, 1928), pp. 34–35, 47, 52, 56.

227. In October 1976 Richard A. Nicholson, antiquarian bookseller of Chester, listed a Dublin edition by Dillon Chamberlaine in 1759, but I have been unable to trace it.

228. *NCBEL* lists most of the Dublin editions of Goldsmith's works but not all. I have examined the following copies: the 1762 *Citizen of the World* at NLI, TCD, Yale, the 1769 at NLI, Yale, the 1775 at NLI, TCD; the 1767 *Essays* at Yale, the 1772 at NLI, TCD, Yale, the 1793 at NLI, the 1766 1st Dublin ed. of the *Vicar of Wakefield* at NLI, TCD, Yale, the 2nd at Yale, the Corke ed. at NLI, Yale, the 1767 at Yale, the 1767 Mein ed. at Yale, the 1791, 1793, 1794, eds, at TCD, the 1797 ed in French at TCD and Yale; the 1768 *Good Natur'd Man* at NLI, Yale, the 1770 at Yale, the 1784 at Dublin Public Library, NLI, Yale; the 1773 Belfast *She Stoops to Conquer* at Yale, the 1773 Dublin ed. with Colles at NLI, TCD, Dublin Pub., the 1773 Dublin ed. without Colles at TCD, Yale, the 1774 at NLI, TCD, Yale, 1784 at NLI, 1785 at TCD, 1792 at NLI, Yale; 1767 *Traveller* at NLI, TCD, Yale, 1770 at Yale (2); 1770 1st ed. of the *Deserted Village* at TCD, 1770 2nd ed. at NLI, 1784 NLI; 1775 *Poems* Yale, 1801

TCD; 1776 *Haunch of Venison* NLI, TCD, Yale; 1777 *Poems and Plays* by Price et al. at Yale, TCD, the Wilson 1777 ed. at NLI, Yale, 1785 Yale; 1783 *Beauties of Goldsmith* at NLI, TCD, Yale. See Appendix 4 for publishing information. *NUC* lists other eds. of the *Vicar of Wakefield* c. 1780 and 1800. Harvard does not own the two 1793 eds. of *She Stoops to Conquer* credited to it in *NUC*.

229. "John Mein, Publisher: An Essay in Bibliographic Detection," *PBSA*, 36 (1942), 199–214.

230. Mathew Carey Accounts, American Antiquarian Society.

231. See Giles Barber, "Pendred abroad, A view of the late eighteenth-century book trade in Europe," *Studies in the Book Trade in Honour of Graham Pollard* (Oxford: Oxford Bibliographical Society, 1975), p. 246.

232. Carey Accounts.

233. Henry Knox Papers, Massachusetts Historical Society.

234. William S. Clark, *The Irish Stage in the County Towns, 1720–1800*. (Oxford: Clarendon Press, 1965), p. 313.

235. Hoover H. Jordan, *Bolt Upright; The Life of Thomas Moore*, 2 vols. (Salzburg: Institut für Englische Sprache und Literatur, Universität Salzburg, 1975), I, 172–79.

236. Henry Knox Papers.

237. W. B. Todd, "The Private Issues of The Deserted Village," *Studies in Bibliography*, 7 (1955), 239.

238. O'Conor Correspondence with Joseph Cooper Walker, MSS. Gilbert Collection, Dublin Public Library (Pearse Street).

239. Twiss, p. 87.

240. "The Private Issues of *The Deserted Village*," *SB*, 6 (1954), 26.

241. *The Correspondence of Thomas Percy and Edmond Malone*, ed. Arthur Tillotson (Baton Rouge: Louisiana State University Press, 1944), pp. 31–32.

242. Charles O'Conor wrote to J. C. Walker in June 1785 about Luke White's Dublin edition of Goldsmith's works, and James Moore advertised his in the *Dublin Evening Post* in September 1793; it was also listed in several private libraries.

243. The fullest account is in Katherine C. Balderston, *The History and Sources of Percy's Memoirs of Goldsmith*(Cambridge; Cambridge University Press, 1926), but it needs to be supplemented by Richard Harp's edition and annotation of *Thomas Percy's Life of Dr. Oliver Goldsmith* (Salzburg, Austria: Institüt fur Englische Sprache und Literatur, Universität Salzburg, 1976).

244. John Nichols and John Bowyer Nichols, *Illustrations of the Literary History of the Eighteenth-Century*, 8 vols. (London; John Nichols, 1817–58), VII, 190–91; VIII, 47–50.

245. "On Style in Writing, considered with respect to Thoughts and

Sentiments as well as Words, and indicating the Writers' peculiar and characteristic Disposition, Habit and Powers of Mind," *Transactions of the Royal Irish Academy*, 5, Pt. 2 (1794), 84–85.

246. "The Poetical Character of Doctor Goldsmith," *Transactions of the Royal Irish Academy*, 6, pt. 2 (1797), 72–73, 102.

247. Richard D. Altick, *The English Common Reader, A Social History of the Mass Reading Public, 1800–1900* (Chicago: University of Chicago Press, 1957), p. 56; J. W. Saunders, *The Profession of English Letters* (London: Routledge and Kegan Paul, 1964), p.153.

248. Ward, p. 73.

249. Mathew Carey Accounts, American Antiquarian Society.

250. John Ginger, *The Notable Man, The Life and Times of Oliver Goldsmith* (London: Hamish Hamilton, 1977), pp. 242, 315.

251. A. Lytton Sells, *Oliver Goldsmith, His Life and Works* (London: George Allen and Unwin, Ltd., 1974), p. 368.

252. *Boswell's Life of Johnson*, II, 236.

253. *NCBEL* lists most but not all the Dublin editions of Goldsmith's histories. I have examined the following sets: the 1776 *History of the Earth* at Yale, the 1777 at NLI, TCD, Yale, the 1982 at NLI; the 1765 *History of England in Letters to a Son* at NLI, TCD, Yale, the 1767 at NLI, the 1784 at NLI, Yale; the 1771 *History of England* at TCD, the 1789 ed. at NLI, the 1796 at TCD; the 1779 abridgement at NLI; the 1769 *Roman History* at TCD, the 1771 at TCD, the 1792 at TCD, the 1800 Cork ed. at NLI, TCD, the 1798 abridgement at NLI; the 1774 *Grecian History* at NLI, TCD, Yale, the 1801 at NLI. See Appendix 4 for details of publication. *NUC* lists other eds. of the *Abridgement of the History of England* in 1797, *Roman History* in 1775–76, 1786, the *Abridgement* in 1781, the *Grecian History* in 1795. Cambridge University lists a 1788 *Grecian History*.

254. Carey Accounts.

255. Martin Brenan, *Schools of Kildare and Leighlin, A.D. 1775–1835* (Dublin: Gill, 1935), p. 34.

256. Ralph M. Wardle, *Oliver Goldsmith* (Lawrence, Kansas: University of Kansas Press, 1957), p. 283.

257. *The Miscellaneous Works of Oliver Goldsmith, M.B.*, 4 vols. (London: J. Johnson, C. and J. Robinson, 1801), I, 111.

258. *British Parliamentary Papers, First Report of the Commissioners on Education in Ireland*, 12 (1825), Appendix 221, p. 553.

259. Brenan, *passim*.

260. Carey Accounts.

261. Carey Accounts.

262. Warburton et al., II, 1323.

263. *NCBEL* lists most but not all the Dublin editions of Gibbon. I have examined the following sets: the 1776 *Decline and Fall* at TCD, the 1777 at NLI, the 1781 at NLI, the 1784 at NLI, the 1788 at NLI, the 1789 at

NLI and Yale, the *Abridgement* of 1790 at NLI and TCD; the 1777 *Essai sur L'Étude de la Littèrature* at TCD; the 1779 *Vindication* at NLI, TCD, and Yale; the 1796 *Miscellaneous Works* at NLI, TCD, and Yale. See Appendix 4 for publication details. *NUC* lists other editions of the *Decline and Fall* in 1777 and 1782, the *Essay on Literature* in 1788.

264. J. E. Norton identifies a set in her own possession in *A Bibliography of the Works of Edward Gibbon* (Oxford: Oxford University Press, 1940), p. 107.

265. *Library of Edward Gibbon*, ed. Geoffrey Keynes, 2nd ed. (London: St. Paul's Bibliographies, 1980); *Letters of Edward Gibbon*, ed. J. E. Norton, 3 vols. (New York: Macmillan, 1956), II, 116

266. The only Dublin edition I have seen is in Vol. 397 of the Haliday Collection, Royal Irish Academy, Dublin, but the London edition has been reprinted in the Garland series, *Gibboniana*.

267. Craig, p. 35.

268. Nicholas Barker, "A Note on the Bibliography of Gibbon, 1776–1802," *The Library*, 5th ser., 17 (1963), 49.

269. Carey Accounts.

270. This rare edition is listed by Norton but not by *NCBEL* or in the *National Union Catalog*.

271. Norton, *Gibbon Bibliography*, p. 197.

272. *Recollections of the Table-Talk of Samuel Rogers. To Which is Added Porsoniana*, 3rd ed. (London: Edward Moxon, 1856), pp. 306–07, 333.

273. Walker to William Hayley, 22 August 1796, Walker Papers.

274. Browne, I, 37–38, 40–41, 46, II, 359.

275. *Critical and Miscellaneous Essays* (Cork: privately printed, 1850), pp. 93, 96–98.

276. Houston, pp. 230, 241.

277. *Memoirs of the Life and Writings of the late Charles O'Conor of Belanagare*, ed. Charles O'Conor (Dublin: J. Mehain, 1796), p. 311; O'Conor to J. C. Walker, 27 November 1786, O'Conor Papers, Gilbert Collection.

278. There is a good summary of these development in copyright in Sir Frank McKinnon, "Notes on the History of English Copyright," *The Oxford Companion to English Literature*, ed. Sir Paul Harvey, 4th ed. (Oxford: Clarendon Press, 1967), pp. 924–26.

279. *The English Common Reader*, pp. 54–55.

280. Clonbrock Papers, Bookseller's Account, MS. 22,177, National Library of Ireland.

281. James Phillips found only sixty-three of five hundred Irish books printed on Irish paper, p. 309.

282. *Journals of the Irish House of Commons*, XVI, 189–93.

283. *The Parliamentary Register*, XVI, 73–121.

284. "Essay on Manufactures in Ireland," pp.406–8.

285. Warburton, et al., II, 1168.

286. *A History of the City of Dublin*, 3 vols. (Dublin: James Duffy, 1861), I, 188.
287. Warburton, et al., II, 1157–58.
288. Guild of St. Luke the Evangelist, Journal of Proceedings, vol. 6 (1785–1813), MS. 12,126, National Library of Ireland.
289. *British Parliamentary Papers, House of Commons, Third Report of the Commissioners of Inquiry into the Collection and Management of the Revenue arising in Ireland* (1822), XIII, 6, and appendices 2–4, pp. 15–18.
290. Carey's *Autobiography*, p. 44; Tebbel, *History of Book Publishing*, I, 108–9.
291. Silver, *The American Printer*, p. 174.
292. Carey's *Autobiography*, p. 44; Rollo G. Silver, "Mathew Carey's Proofreaders," *Studies in Bibliography*, 17 (1964), 123–33.
293. "Bernard Dornin, America's First Catholic Bookseller," *Books in America's Past; Essays Honoring Rudolph H. Gjelsness* (Charlottesville: University Press of Virginia, 1966), pp. 111.
294. *Book Pirating in Taiwan* (Philadelphia: University of Pennsylvania Press, 1969), p. vii.
295. "Bernard Dornin," pp. 108–9.
296. Tebbel, *History of Book Publishing*, I, 208.
297. Mathew Carey (1760–1839), Isaac Lea (1792–1886), Henry Charles Carey (1793–1879), Abraham Hart (1810–85), Henry Charles Lea (1825–1909), Matthew Carey Lea (1827–97), Henry Carey Baird (1825–1912).
298. See David Kaser, *Joseph Charless, Printer in the Western Country* (Philadelphia: University of Pennsylvania Press, 1963).
299. "Philadelphia Book Trade Directory," *BNYPL*, 53 (1949), 291; J. Havergal Sheppard, "Colonel John Binns," *Journal of the American-Irish Historical Society*, 22 (1930–31), 55–56.
300. "Philadelphia Book Trade Directory," *BNYPL*, 53 (1949), 394; *Hibernian Society*, pp. 398–99; James Morton Smith, *Freedom's Fetters, The Alien and Sedition Laws and American Civil Liberties* (Ithaca, N. Y.: Cornell University Press, 1956), pp. 277–306; John Tebbel, *The Compact History of the American Newspaper* (New York: Hawthorn Books, 1963), p. 78. Alan C. Clark, "William Duane," *Records of* the *Columbia Historical Society*, 9 (1906), 14–62.
301. *Library of Thomas Jefferson*, I, 273–74; III, 3–11.
302. Alan C. Clark, p. 26; William Duane *Report of the Extraordinary Transactions which took place at Philadelphia in February 1799; in consequence of a memorial from certain natives of Ireland to Congress praying a repeal of the Alien bill* (Philadelphia: William Duane, 1799).
303. Mary Elizabeth Clark, *Peter Porcupine in America; The Career of William Cobbett, 1792–1800* (Philadelphia: Times and News Publishing, 1939), pp. 176–77.

304. Wilfrid Parsons, "Early Catholic Publishers of Philadelphia," *Catholic Historical Review*, 24 (1938–39), 150–51; Tebbel, *History of Book Publishing*, I, 528–29.
305. "Philadelphia Book Trade Directory," *BNYPL*, 53 (1949), 397; Finotti, pp. 266–67.
306. "Philadelphia Book Trade Directory," *BNYPL*, 54 (1950), 131. R. B. McDowell, "The Personnel of the Dublin Society of United Irishmen, 1791–94," *Irish Historical Studies*, 2 (1940–41), 48. *NUC* lists addresses by Henry Grattan in 1797 and 1800, three editions of speeches by J. P. Curran 1805–11, speeches 1799–1800 by Robert Orr, James Napper Tandy, and W. J. MacNeven and also the latter's *Ramble through Switzerland* in 1803, Sir Richard Musgrave's *Memoirs of the Irish Rebellions* in two editions 1801–02, two reports in 1800 of Irish Parliamentary debates on the Union, trials for high treason in 1798 and 1802 in Ireland, and O'Conor's *History of the Irish Catholics* in 1813.
307. "Philadelphia Book Trade Directory," *BNYPL*, 53 (1949), 224; *Bradshaw Collection*, III, 1467; David McNeely Stauffer, *American Engravers upon Copper and Steel*, 2 vols. (New York: Grolier Club, 1907), I, 17–18; II, 22–23.
308. "Philadelphia Book Trade Directory," *BNYPL*, 53 (1949), 493–94; Stauffer, I, 133–35; II, 242–46.
309. "Philadelphia Book Trade Directory," *BNYPL*, 53 (1949), 621; Maxted, p. 160.
310. "Philadelphia Book Trade Directory," *BNYPL*, 53 (1949), 339; *Hibernian Society*, p. 339.
311. "Philadelphia Book Trade Directory," *BNYPL*, 54 (1950), 31; Winans, pp. 179–80; Hibernian Society, p. 501.
312. "Philadelphia Book Trade Directory," *BNYPL*, 54 (1950), 142; *Hibernian Society*, pp. 544–45; R. Carlyle Buley, *The Old Northwest, Pioneer Period, 1815–1840*, 2 vols. (Bloomington: Indiana University Press, 1951), II, 513; Brigham, II, 892.
313. "Philadelphia Book Trade Directory," *BNYPL*, 54 (1950), 142; *Hibernian Society*, p. 544.
314. "Philadelphia Book Trade Directory," *BNYPL*, 53 (1949), 493; *Hibernian Society*, p. 432; Brigham, II, 1432.
315. "Philadelphia Book Trade Directory," *BNYPL*, 53 (1949), 223; *Hibernian Society*, p. 317.
316. Charles E. Butler, "T. and J. Swords, Publishers," *BNYPL*, 58 (1954), 89–93.
317. M. Pollard, "John Chambers, Printer and United Irishman," *The Irish Book*, 3 (1964), 1–22; "*Register of … Printers and Publishers in New York City*, p. 17; *New York Evening Post*, 18 April 1807.
318. Richard Robert Madden, *Irish Periodical Literature*, II, 225–33, and

The United Irishmen, Their Lives and Times, 12 vols. (New York: Catholic Publication Society, 1916), IX, 73.

319. See Joseph I. Shulim, "John Daly Burk: Irish Revolutionist and American Patriot," *Transactions of the American Philosophical Society* NS, 54, Pt. 6 (1964), 2–60; *Register of ... Printers and Publishers in New York City*, p. 56; Finotti, pp. 209–12.

320. Finotti, 63, 209, 232; *Register of ... Printers and Publishers in New York City*, p. 56; Paul J. Foik, *Pioneer Catholic Journalism* (New York: United States Catholic Historical Society, 1930), pp. 12–17; *Aurora*, 20 Nov. 1811, 1 Sept. 1812.

321. Richard C. O'Connor, "John T. Doyle," *Journal of the American-Irish Historical Society*, 11 (1911–12), 141–43; Thomas Meehan, "Catholic Literary New York," *Catholic Historical Review*, 4 (1918–19), 404, and "John Doyle, Publisher," *Historical Records and Studies, Catholic Historical Society*, 10 (1917), 172–78.

322. *Register of ... Printers and Publishers in New York City*, p. 20; Seamus O'Cassidy, "Watty Cox and his Publications," *Bibliographical Society of Ireland*, 5 (1935), 19–38.

323. *Register of ... Printers and Publishers in New York City*, p. 27; Finotti, p. 21.

324. *Register of ... Printers and Publishers in New York City*, pp. 67, 46; Richard C. Murphy and Lawrence J. Mannion, *The History of the Society of the Friendly Sons of Saint Patrick in the City of New York, 1784 to 1955* (New York: J. C. Dillon, 1962), p. 537, hereafter cited as *Sons of Saint Patrick*.

325. *Register of ... Printers and Publishers in New York City*, pp. 12, 51; *Sons of Saint Patrick*, pp. 535–36.

326. Stauffer, I, 149–50; II, 265–72.

327. Kaser, "Bernard Dornin," pp. 107–28.

328. Kaser, "Bernard Dornin," pp. 114–15.

329. Rollo G. Silver, "The Baltimore Book Trade, 1800–1825," *BNYPL*, 57 (1953), 305, hereafter cited as "The Baltimore Book Trade"; *Bradshaw Collection*, I, 457–58; Mathew Carey Letter Books, 13 May, 10 September 1791.

330. "Baltimore Book Trade," p. 191; A. Rachel Minick, "A History of Printing in Maryland 1791–1800, with a Bibliography of Works Printed in the State during that Period," unpublished M.S. thesis for Faculty of Library Service, Columbia University, 1948, mimeographed by Enoch Pratt Free Library, Baltimore, 1949, p. 89.

331. "Baltimore Book Trade," p. 192; Minick, pp. 89–91; 96; Brigham, II, 1404.

332. "Baltimore Book Trade," pp. 191–92, 300; Minick, p. 73; Finotti, p. 65; Brigham II, 1403, 1459; Thomas D. Penniman, "The Early History of the *Baltimore American*," *Maryland Historical Magazine*, 28 (1933), 272–78.

333. Silver, *The American Printer*, pp. 118–19.
334. "Baltimore Book Trade," pp.191–92; Silver, *The American Printer*, pp. 119–20; Parsons, *Early Catholic Americana*, p. xix; Brigham, II, 1403.
335. Parsons, *Early Catholic Americana*, p. xix; Minick, p. 73; Tebbel, *History of Book Publishing*, I, 528.
336. *Cyclopaedia of American Biographies*, ed. John Howard Brown, 7 vols. (Boston: James H. Lamb, 1897–1903), II, 476.
337. "Baltimore Book Trade," pp. 248–49; Minick, pp. 120–21, 125, 149–50, 346; Kaser, "Bernard Dornin," p. 128; Brigham, I, 224, 270.
338. "Baltimore Book Trade," p. 185.
339. "Baltimore Book Trade," p. 193; Minick, pp. 135–37, 397, 412; Brigham, II, 1405.
340. "Baltimore Book Trade," p. 183.
341. "Baltimore Book Trade," p. 251; Brigham, I, 226.
342. "Baltimore Book Trade," pp. 300–1.
343. Tapley, pp. 187–88.
344. William L. King, *The Newspaper Press of Charleston, S. C.* (Charleston: Edward Perry Book Press, 1872), pp. 90–99.
345. Earl L. Bell and Kenneth C. Crabbe, *The Augusta Chronicle, Indomitable Voice of Dixie, 1785–1960* (Athens, Georgia: University of Georgia Press, 1960) pp. 20–23; Brigham, II, 1405; Madden, *Irish Periodical Literature*, II, 181.
346. Kaser, *Joseph Charless*, pp. 25, 136.
347. Henry Wilkinson Bragdon, *Woodrow Wilson, The Academic Years* (Cambridge, Massachusetts: Belknap Press of Harvard University Press, 1967), p. 4; Francis P. Weisenburger, "The Middle Western Antecedents of Woodrow Wilson," *Mississippi Valley Historical Review*, 23 (1936–37), 375–90.
348. *Bradshaw Collection*, I, 513, No. 2994; Walter Sutton *The Western Book Trade: Cincinnati as a Nineteenth-Century Publishing and Book Trade Center* (Columbus, Ohio: Ohio State University Press, 1961), p. 319; *Correspondence of Andrew Jackson*, ed. John Spencer Bassett, 7 vols. (Washington, D. C.: Carnegie Institution, 1926–35), VI, 325. Frederic Hudson, *Journalism in the United States, from 1690 to 1872* (New York: Haskell House, 1873, repr. 1968), p. 199.
347. Roger McCutcheon, "Books and Booksellers in New Orelans, 1730–1830," *Louisiana Historical Quarterly*, 20 (1937), 616; Kaser, *Book Pirating in Taiwan*, p. 7.
350. Frederick R. Goff, "The First Decade of the Federal Act for Copyright, 1790–1800," *Essays Honoring Lawrence C. Wroth* (Portland, Maine: Anthoensen Press, 1951), p. 102.
351. Goff, pp. 113–28.
352. Silver, *The American Printer*, p. 113.
353. Tebbel, *History of Book Publishing*, I, 221.

354. Tebbel, *History of Book Publishing*, I, 210.
355. Silver, *The American Printer*, p. 141.
356. Phillips, p. 67
357. Ian Maxted in his *London Book Trades* lists fifteen Irish engravers in the London book trade, four booksellers, and one printer George Keating, but Keating had departed for London by 1784 (pp. 127–28).
358. Tebbel, *History of Book Publishing*, I, 215–16
359. H. Glenn Brown, "Philadelphia Contributions to the Book Arts and Book Trade, 1796–1810," *PBSA*, 37 (1943), 288–89; *Aurora*, 26 March 1802.
360. David Kaser, *Messrs. Carey and Lea of Philadelphia, A Study in the History of the Booktrade* (Philadelphia: University of Pennsylvania Press, 1957), p. 109.
361. Kaser, *Messrs. Carey and Lea*, p. 108.
362. Kaser, *Messrs. Carey and Lea*, p. 102.
363. Quoted in James D. Hart, *The Popular Book, A History of America's Literary Taste* (New York: Oxford University Press, 1950), p. 75.
364. Kaser, *Messrs. Carey and Lea*, p. 63.
365. Tebbel, *History of Book Publishing*, I, 599–60.
366. H. C. Carey, *Letters on International Copyright* (Philadelphia: A Hart, late Carey and Hart, 1853), p. 32.
367. H. C. Carey, p. 44.
368. Quoted in Tebbel, *History of Book Publishing*, I, 225.
369. In addition to the DAB article a one-line notice appears in Plomer, p. 376, and brief descriptions in Tebbel's *History of Book Publishing*, I, 54–55, 96, and Carl and Jessica Bridenbaugh, *Rebels and Gentlemen: Philadelphia in the Age of Franklin* (New York: Reynal and Hitchcock, 1942), but Tebbel and the Bridenbaughs note only Bell's Scots background.
370. *Boston Printers*, pp. 460–61, but Spotswood is not identified as Irish, pp. 460–61; Plomer, p. 403, has five lines.
371. Most recently in R. B. McDowell, *Ireland in the Age of Imperialism and Revolution, 1760–1801* (Oxford: Clarendon Press, 1979), pp. 387, 525, 602.
372. Sleater's *Public Gazetteer*, 28 November 1761; auction catalogues in National Library of Ireland.
373. Auction catalogue in National Library of Ireland.
374. Tanselle, p. 339
375. Tanselle, pp. 353–54.
376. Gulick, 45.
377. *Rebels and Gentlemen*, p. 86.
378. McCulloch, p. 219.
379. McCulloch, p. 232.
380. Eight of these are identified in the *Bradshaw Catalogue*, I, 342; the four of Goldsmith and Sterne are in their respective chapters; five are in

the *National Union Catalog, Pre-1956 Imprints*, and the *Complete Country-Dancer* in the *Catalogue of the Books and Manuscripts of Sir John T. Gilbert* (Dublin: Browne and Nolan, 1918).

381. Plomer, p. 403.

382. Mem. 236830, Bk. 352, p. 105 (1783); Mem. 236831, Bk. 352, p. 106 (1783); Registry of Deeds, Dublin.

383. William J. Free, *The Columbian Magazine and American Literary Nationalism* (Hague: Mouton, 1968), p. 14. Neither Free nor Lyon N. Richardson in his lengthy discussion of the magazine in his *History of Early American Magazines*, is aware of Spotswood's background in the Dublin book trade.

384. *Belknap Papers, Collections of the Massachusetts Historical Society*, 6th ser., 4 (1891), 391.

385. *Belknap Papers*, 6th ser., 4 (1891), 429.

386. Free, p. 21.

387. *Belknap Papers*, 5th ser., 2 (1877), 325.

388. *Belknap Papers*, 5th ser., 2 (1877), 345–56.

389. As listed in the Evans–Bristol Bibliography 1784–1800 and the Shaw–Shoemaker Bibliography 1801–5.

390. Rollo G. Silver, *The American Printer, 1787–1825* (Charlottesville, Va.: University Press of Virginia, 1967), pp. 98–99.

391. *Boston Printers*, p. 460.

392. Winans, No. 108, 193, 208.

393. *Belknap Papers*, 6th ser., 4 (1891), 421.

394. Rollo G. Silver, "The Costs of Mathew Carey's Printing Equipment," *Studies in Bibliography*, 19 (1966), 95; "Philadelphia Book Trade Directory," *BNYPL*, 54 (1950), 129.

395. *Bradshaw Collection*, I, 388–404.

396. See Appendix 3 for reprints by Byrne alone or with others in Dublin 1779–1801; there are undoubtedly others that I have not found.

397. *The Correspondence of Edmund Burke*, ed. Thomas W. Copeland, et al., 9 vols. (Cambridge and Chicago: Cambridge University Press, 1958–70), VII, 94–95.

398. *Library of Thomas Jefferson*, III, 141–42.

399. Mem. 334560, Bk. 512, p. 395 (1798), Registry of Deeds, Dublin.

400. Sir John Gilbert, "The Streets of Dublin," *Irish Quarterly Review*, 3 (1853), 48.

401. Gilbert, pp. 46–50; R. B. McDowell, *Ireland in the Age of Imperialism*, pp. 387, 602.

402. R. B. McDowell, "The Personnel of the Dublin Society of United Irishmen, 1791–94," *Irish Historical Studies*, 2 (1940–41), 24.

403. Carey Accounts, Vol. 21, p. 922.

404. Byrne's Philadelphia publications are in the *American Bibliography* of Shaw and Shoemaker.

405. *Library of Thomas Jefferson*, I, 165; II, 44, 192; III, 141–42; IV, 159.
406. *The Letters Of Thomas Moore*, ed. Wilfred S. Dowden, 2 vols. (Oxford: Clarendon Press, 1964), I, 66–68; "Philadelphia Book Trade Directory," *BNYPL*, 53 (1949), 493.
407. *New York Evening Post*, 19 Jan. 1807, 12 Nov. 1805.
408. Adams, Bell, Binns, Brown, Byrne, Campbell, Charless, Cummiskey, Dobbin, Dornin, Duane, Dunlap, Field, Gaine, Keatinge, Loudon, Lyon, the two Rice families, Spotswood.
409. Adams, Binns, Brooks, Andrew Brown Sr., Andrew Brown, Jr., Burk, James Carey, Mathew Carey, Carpenter, Charless, Cox, Cuming, Dawson, George Dobbin, Thomas Dobbin, Douglas, Driscol, William Duane, William John Duane, John Dunlap, Duffey, Gaine, Gillespie, Henry, Hope, Howe, George Keatinge I and II, Kirk, Loudon, Lyon, M'Crea, Mitchell, Murphy, Nicola, O'Connor, O'Connor, Parker, Spotswood, Steuart, Talbot, Wall, James Wilson.
410. Warburton, et al., II, 1158.

Appendix 1

Irish Editions published by Subscription 1730–1801

All figures starred are from F.J.G. Robinson and P.J. Wallis, *Book Subscription Lists, A Revised Guide* (Newcastle upon Tyne: Harold Hill and Son, Ltd., 1975).
All other figures are mine.

1. *Life of James Freney*, 1754 26*
2. Joseph Little, *The humbugged turned humbugger*, 1750 61*
3. Thomas Vernon, *Cases argued and adjudged in Chancery*, 1730 63*
4. William Cavendish, *A new method … to dress horses*, 1740 68*
5. Fynes Moryson, *History of Ireland*, 1599–1603, 1735 69*
6. W. Beawes, *Lex Mercatoria*, 1773 82
7. Conyers Middleton, *History of the life of … Cicero*, 1741 86*
8. John Locke, *Paraphrase and notes on the epistles of St. Paul*, 1738 90*
9. *The State Letters of Henry, Earl of Clarendon*, 1765 95
10. Dalrymple's *Essay towards a general history of feudal property*, 1759 101*
11. Gilbert Burnet, *Life of William Bedell, Bishop of Kilmore*, 1736 105
12. Swift's *Work*, 9 vols., 1758 112
13. G. E. Howard's *Works*, 1782 112
14. Peter Browne, *Sermons*, 1749 124*
15. John Ozell, *Works of Rabelais*, 1738 128*
16. John Gay, *Poems on Several Occasions*, 1730 130*
17. Charles Varley, *A Treatise in Agriculture*, 1765 130
18. M. Archdall, *Monasticum Hibernicum*, 1786 134
19. Joseph Rogers, *Essay on epidemic diseases*, 1734 134*
20. Francis Bernard, *Fifty-one Moral Discourses*, 1740 140*
21. John Singleton, *General Description of the West-Indian Islands*, 1776 150

22. Burnet's *History of the Reformation of the Church of England*, 1733 153*
23. Le Sage, *Gil Blas*, 1730 156*
24. Samuel Clarke, *Sermons*, 1734 158*
25. Richard Barton, *Analogy of Divine Wisdom*, 1750 163*
26. Philip Miller, *The Gardener's Dictionary*, 1732 168*
27. Eaton's *Abridgement of Astronomy and Natural Philosophy*, [1795] 169
28. Isaac Newton, *Observations upon prophecies of Daniel*, 1733 169*
29. Thome Alveres de Andrade, *Sufferings of our Lord Jesus Christ*, 1754 180*
30. Thomas De Burgo, *Hibernia Dominicana*, 1762 183
31. Joseph Hillary, *Poems*, [1794] 184
32. G. E. Howard, *Treatise of the Exchequer and Revenue of Ireland*, 1776 192
33. Samuel Clarke, *Sermons*, 1738 192*
34. *The Pettycoat, a poem*, 1738 193*
35. Edmund Borlase, *History of the Irish Rebellion*, 1743 193*
36. Elizabeth Carter, *Works of Epictetus*, 1758 194*
37. John Hornihold, *Sacraments Explain'd*, 1746 200*
38. King's *Protestants of Ireland under King James's Government*, 1768 209
39. L'Abbe Grou, *The School of Christ*, 1801 210
40. John Sterling, *Bombarino*, 1768 214
41. Eustace Budgell, *Memoirs ... of the Boyles*, 1754 220*
42. G. E. Howard, *Treatise of the Exchequer and Revenue of Ireland*, 1759 227*
43. Robert Egan, *The General Exchange*, 1781 220
44. Hanway's *Historical Account of British Trade over the Caspian Sea*, 1754 231*
45. Alban Butler, *Moveable Feasts ... of the Catholic Church*, 1755 233
46. John Brickell, *Natural History of North Carolina*, 1737 234*
47. Morel's *Devotions to Jesus Christ in the Holy Sacrament*, 1795 234
48. Edward Lee, *The Statute Law of Ireland*, 1734 235*
49. *The Whole Proceedings of the Siege of Drogheda*, 1736 238*
50. W. Knowler, *The Earl of Strafford's Letters and despatches*, 1740 243*
51. Edward Spratt, *New Book of Constitutions ... of the Masons*, 1751 248*
52. H. Boyd's translation of Dante's *Inferno*, 1785 260
53. Harris's *Life and Reign of William Henry, Prince of Orange*, 1749 260*
54. John Hornihold, *The Decalogue Explain'd*, 1751 270*
55. Pope's *Works*, 1736 270*

56. Nicholas Tindall, *History of England*, 1747 274*
57. William Preston's *Poems*, 1793 276
58. Henry Brooke's *Poems*, 1792 277
59. *Flora's Banquet, A Collection of Poems*, 1782 280
60. [C. Walmesley], *General History of the Christian Church*, 1790 280
61. Trydell's *Essays on the Theory and Practice of Music*, 1766 281
62. W. Harris, *Works of Sir James Ware concerning Ireland*, 1745 282*
63. Anyas Bushe, *Socrates, A Dramatic Poem*, 1759 287*
64. Matthew Pilkington, *Poems*, 1730 287*
65. Fleming's *Collection of all the Irish and English Statutes*, 1741 288*
66. J. Dodd, *Essays and Poems*, 1700 289
67. Roderic O'Flaherty, *Ogygia Vindicated*, 1755 294
68. Charles Rollin, *The Roman History*,1742 296*
69. E. Walsh, *Bagatelles*, 1793 307
70. R. Pool and J. Cash, *Views of the ... Public Buildings ... in Dublin*, 1780 314
71. *Letters between Henry and Frances*, 1760 317*
72. Jane Moore, *Poems*, 1796 320
73. John Lodge, *Peerage of Ireland*, 5 vols., 1789 330
74. Silvester Gooman, *Sermons*, 1798 335
75. Giovanni de Bona, *A Guide to Heaven*, 1755 338*
76. J. Rutty, *Essay towards a Natural History of Dublin*, 1772 340
77. Parker's *Memoirs of the most remarkable military Transactions*, 1746 341*
78. John Hornihold, *The Decalogue Explain'd*, 1746 341
79. *The Volunteers Companion*, 1784 348
80. Thomas Simes, *The Military Medley*, 1767 349
81. Meade Swift, *Miscellaneous Works*, 1772 351
82. Charlotte Brooke, *Reliques of Irish Poetry*, 1789 357
83. Robert Gibson, *Treatise of Practical Surveying*, 1752 359*
84. John Dryden, *Life of St. Francis Xavier*, 1743 363*
85. Thomas Delamayne, *Love and Honour, a Dramatick Poem*, 1742 371*
86. John Keogh, *Zoologica Medicinalis Hibernica*, 1739 374*
87. Towers' *Philosophical Inquiry into the Laws of Nature*, 1750 370*
88. Steuart's *Inquiry into the Principles of Political Economy*, 1770 371
89. James Delacour, *A Prospect of Poetry*, 1770 377
90. Matthew, O'Brien, *Sermons*, 1798 387
91. James Kennedy, *Modern Elements of Numerical Arithmetic*, 1759 388*
92. Thomas Leland, *History of Ireland*, 1775 389
93. Richard Hayes, *Negociator's Magazine*, 1749 390*
94. Robert Gibson, *A Course of Experimental Philosophy*, 1755 391*
95. Robert Dickinson, *Universal Mercantile Tables*, 1783 393

96. Fenn, *Instructions in the Drawing School established by the Dublin Society*, 1769 393
97. T. Stackhouse, *Life of our Lord and Saviour, Jesus Christ*, 1758 394*
98. Segnari's *True Wisdom: or Considerations for Every Day of the Week*, 1795 396
99. Joseph Dwyer, *The Trinitarian Manual*, 1795 397
100. Downes, *All vows kept, a comedy*, 1733 399
101. John Ferrar, *View of Ancient and Modern Dublin*, 1796 399
102. Johnson's *Dictionary of the English Language*, 1775 401
103. Francis Walsh, *The Antediluvian World*, 1743 411
104. Charles Phipps, *Doctrine of Vulgar and Decimal Fractions*, 1745 417*
105. R. Hitchcock, *An Historical View of the Irish Stage*, 1788 425
106. J. Rutty, *An Essay towards a Natural History of Dublin*, 1757 426*
107. *Memoirs of Captain Peter Drake*, 1755 434*
108. H. Boyd, Poems, 1793 456
109. Samuel Richardson, *Clarissa*, 1756 458
110. Philip Francis, *Odes, Epodes of Horace*, 1742 458*
111. W. Chetwood, *Voyages … of Capt. Richard Falconar*, 1752 460*
112. Samuel Shepherd, *Sermons*, 1790 463
113. Barnard's *Life of the … Rt. Rev. Richard Challoner*, 1793 491
114. R. Manning, *A single Combat*, 1757 499
115. W. Chetwood, *Voyages … of William Owen Gwin Vaughan*, 1754 501*
116. Goldsmith's *History of the Earth and Animated Nature*, 8 vols. 1777 501
117. Charles Smith, *Antient and Present State of … Waterford*, 1746 503*
118. Thomas a Kempis, *The Imitation of Christ*, 1798 504
119. W. Chetwood, *Memoirs of Ben Jonson*, 1756 506*
120. *Theodorick, King of Denmark*, 1752 506*
121. Andrew Meagher, *The Popish Mass*, 1771 513
122. Ephraim Chambers, *Cyclopaedia*, 1740 516*
123. W. Chetwood, *A General History of the Stage*, 1749 517*
124. W. Harris, *Sir James Ware's Works Concerning Ireland*, 1739 522*
125. R. F. Robert Parson, *A Christian Directory*, 1753 527*
126. W. Wilkes, *A Letter of … advice to a young lady*, 1740 529*
127. Walter Harris, *Hibernica*, 1747 533*
128. Ephraim Chambers, *Cyclopaedia*, 1787 547
129. E. Ryan, *A Short View of the … Mosaic and Christian Codes*, 1795 556
130. F. O'Gallagher, *An Essay on the Investigation of Nature*, 1784 559
131. *Poems*, 1748 559
132. François de Feller, *The Philosophical Catechism*, 1800 568

133. Richard Barton, *Lectures in Natural Philosophy*, 1750 576*
134. John Ferrar, *History of Limerick*, 1787 577
135. David Bindon, *A Political Essay upon Commerce*, 1738 590*
136. Hill Chetwood, *Miscellanea nova et curiosa*, 1749 593*
137. George Touchet, *Historical Collections*, 1758 598*
138. Johnson's *Dictionary*, 1798 601
139. C. O'Conor's *Dissertations on ... Ireland*, 1753 607*
140. Mark West, *Sermons*, 1785 609
141. Elizabeth Haywood, *The Female Spectator*, 1746 624*
142. G. Faulkner, *An Universal History*, 7 vols., 1744 626*
143. J. Fitzgerald, *Cork Remembrancer*, 1783 636
144. T. Smollett's *Don Quixote*, 4 vols., 1796 647
145. Charles Smith, *Antient and Present State ... of Cork*, 1750 650*
146. J. Simon, *Essay towards an Historical Account of Irish Coins*, 1749 655*
147. Alban Butler, *Life of the Holy Mother St. Teresa*, 1794 669
148. John Winstanley, *Poems*, 1741 670*
149. W. J. Mickle, translation of the *Lusiad*, 1791 679
150. J. Lackman, *A History of the Cruel Sufferings of the Protestants*, 1763 689
151. Henry VIII, *Assertio Septum Sacramentorum*, 1766 699
152. Samuel Whyte, *Poems*, 1795 705
153. Laurence Whyte, *Poems*, 1740 711*
154. Samuel Burdy, *Life of Rev. Philip Skelton*, 1792 712
155. John Hornihold, *The Real Principles of Catholicks*, 1750 721*
156. Amyas Griffith, *Miscellaneous Tracts*, 1788 748
157. Joseph Middleton, *A Correct Book of Interest*, 1778 752
158. Dudley Bradstreet, *Lives*, 1757 757*
159. John Winstanley, *Poems*, 1742 757
160. John Winstanley, *Poems*, 1751 762*
161. George Hay, *The Pious Christian*, 1788 772
162. Sallust, *Catiline and Jugurthine Wars*, trans, H. Maffett, 1772 777
163. Horace's *Epistles*, Bk. II, trans. C. Carthy, 1731 790*
164. William Guthrie, *Improved System of Modern Geography*, 1789 807
165. Bayly's *Life and Death of John Fisher, Bp. of Rochester*, 1740 823*
166. *A Collection of Poems*, 1789–90 824
167. Sir John Temple, *History of the General Rebellion in Ireland*, 1766 856
168. Henrietta Battier, *Poems*, 1791 861
169. Richard Eaton, *The Book of Rates*, 1765
170. *Life and Uncommon Adventures of Dudley Bradstreet*, 1755 929*
171. W. Gahan, *Youth Instructed in the ... Christian Religion*, 1798 976
172. John Brown, *Dictionary of the Holy Bible*, 1801 1065
173. Josephus, *Works*, 1796 1083

174. Samuel Whyte, *Shamrock*, 1772 1129
175. Swift's *Works*, 4 vols., 1735 1150*
176. W. Thompson, *An Enquiry into the Natural State of Man*, 1743 1203*
177. C. Cruttwell, *New Universal Gazetteer*, 1800 1227
178. *Chronology of some Memorable Accidents*, 1743 1233
179. Shakespeare's *Dramatic Works*, ed. Ayscough, 1791 1288
180. John Anketell, *Poems*, 1793 1339
181. Swift's *Works*, 1738 1340*
182. William Fletcher, *Twenty Sermons*, 1772 1411
183. William Crawford, *History of Ireland*, 1783 1470
184. Pope's *Miscellany*, 1736 1500*
185. William Wilson, *The Post-Chaise Companion*, [1786] 1529
186. Rheims-Douai Bible, 1791 1573
187. G. Hay, *The Scripture Doctrine of Miracles Displayed*, 1789 1606
188. Thomas Bond, *A Digest of Foreign Exchanges*, 1795 1827
189. *Life and Military Actions of Eugene of Savoy*, 1737 1829*
190. Richard Challoner, *The Morality of the Bible*, 1765 1958
191. J. Harrison, *Scriptural exposition of Church Catechism*, 1738 2318*
192. James Mullalla, *View of Irish Affairs*, 1795 1622
193. D. R. O'Conor, *Works*, 1798 2673
194. Dr. Kennicott's Universal Family Bible, c. 1795 c.3000

Appendix 2

Irishmen in the American Book Trade 1750–1820

Each of the 101 names in the list is followed by his main destination, the emigration phase (expressed in numbers 1 to 3), and whether he was listed in the *Dictionary of American Biography* (DAB) or the *Dictionary of National Biography* (DNB).

Adams, James. Wilmington, Delaware, 1.
Barralet, J. J. Philadelphia, 3.
Bell, James. Philadelphia, 1.
Bell, Robert. Philadelphia, 1, DAB.
Benson, Peter. Philadelphia, 3.
Binns, Benjamin. Philadelphia, 3.
Binns, John. Philadelphia, 3, DAB.
Boland, Alexander. Baltimore, 3.
Boyle, Michael. New York, 3.
Boyd, Alexander. Philadelphia, 3.
Brooks, Philip. New York, 1.
Brown, Andrew, Sr. Philadelphia, 2.
Brown, Andrew, Jr. Philadelphia, 2.
Burk, John Daly. New York, 3, DAB.
Byrne, Patrick, Sr. Philadelphia, 3.
Byrne, Patrick, Jr. Baltimore, 3.
Byrne, William, Baltimore, 3.
Campbell, John, Philadelphia, 3.
Carey, James, Philadelphia, 2.
Carey, John, Philadelphia, 2, DNB
Carey, Mathew. Philadelphia, 2, DAB, DNB.
Carey, William P. Philadelphia, 2, DNB
Carpenter, Stephen. Charleston, South Carolina, 3, DAB.

Carroll, Mary, New Orleans, 3.
Chambers, John. New York, 3.
Charless, Joseph, St. Louis, 3, DAB
Cox, Walter. New York, 3, DNB
Cuming, Samuel. Philadelphia, 3.
Cummiskey, Eugene. Philadelphia, 3.
Dawson, Moses. Cincinnati, 3.
Dean, John. Philadelphia, 1.
Dean, Joseph. Philadelphia, 2.
Dellap, Samuel. Philadelphia, 1.
Dellap, William. Philadelphia, 1.
Dobbin, Archibald. Baltimore, 3.
Dobbin, George. Baltimore, 3.
Dobbin, Thomas. Baltimore, 3.
Dornin, Bernard, Sr. Baltimore, 3.
Dornin, Bernard, Jr. Poughkeepsie, New York, 3.
Douglas, George. New York, 3.
Doyle, John. New York, 3.
Driscol, Dennis. Augusta, Georgia, 3.
Duane, William. Philadelphia, 3, DAB.
Duane, William John. Philadelphia, 3, DAB.
Duffey, Michael. Baltimore, 3.
Dunlap, John. Philadelphia, 1, DAB.
Dunlap, William. Philadelphia, 1.
Fagan, Augustine. Philadelphia, 3.
Field, Matthew. New York, 3.
Flanagan, David. New York, 1.
Gaine, Hugh. New York, 1, DAB.
Gillespy, Edward. New York, 3.
Henry, John. Windsor, Vermont, 2, DAB.
Hope, Thomas. Philadelphia, 3.
Houston, H. H. Philadelphia, 3.
Howe, Thomas. West Indies, 1.
Humphrys, William. Philadelphia, 3.
Hudson, Edward. Philadelphia, 3, DAB
Keatinge, George, Sr. Baltimore, 3.
Keatinge, George, Jr. Baltimore, 3.
Keatinge, Henry. Baltimore, 3.
Kelly, Thomas. New York, 3.
Kirk, Thomas. New York, 2.
Loudon, Samuel. New York, 1, DAB
Lyon, Matthew. Fair Haven, Vermont, 1, DAB
Macanulty, Barnard B. Salem, Massachusetts, 2.
M'Crea, Samuel. Baltimore, 3.

Macdougall, John D. Providence, Rhode Island, 1.
M'Evers, Gulian. New York, 3.
McMahon, Bernard. Philadelphia, 3, DAB
Mitchell, William. Philadelphia, 3.
Montgomery, John. New York, 3.
Moriarty, John. Salem, 3.
Moore, Hugh. Philadelphia, 2.
Murphy, Thomas. Baltimore, 3.
Murray, Bernard. Baltimore, 3.
Neagle, James. Philadelphia, 3, DNB.
Neilson, Samuel. New York, 3.
Nicola, Lewis. Philadelphia, 1, DAB.
O'Connor, John. Philadelphia, 2.
O'Conor, Thomas. New York, 3.
Parker, John. Philadelphia, 2.
Patterson, John. Philadelphia, 2.
Poalk, Robert. Philadelphia, 3.
Reader, John. Philadelphia, 1.
Rice, Henry. Philadelphia, 2.
Rice, James. Baltimore, 2.
Rice, John. Philadelphia, 2.
Rice, John. Baltimore, 3.
Rice, Patrick. Philadelphia, 2.
Smith, Hugh. New York, 3.
Spotswood, Hannah. Philadelphia, 2.
Spotswood, William. Philadelphia, 2.
Steuart, Andrew. Wilmington, North Carolina, 1.
Stewart, Alexander. New York, 3.
Stockdale, Johm. Philadelphia, 3.
Talbot, Christopher. Philadelphia, 2.
Templeton, Oliver. New York, 3.
Wall, Stephen. New York, 3.
Wilson, James. Steubenville, Ohio, 3.
Wilson, John. Philadelphia, 3.

Appendix 3

Patrick Byrne's Reprints in Dublin 1779–1800

Seventy-seven reprints by Patrick Byrne are listed in the *Catalogue of the Bradshaw Collection of Irish Books in the University Library, Cambridge* (Cambridge: Cambridge University Library, 1916), I, 388–404. Twenty-five more are listed in the *Catalogue of the Books and Manuscripts Comprising the Library of the late Sir John T. Gilbert* (Dublin: Browne and Nolan, 1918): plays by James Cobb (5), Richard Cumberland, Alexander Franklin, Elizabeth Inchbald, John Macaulay, Edward Morris, Thomas Morton (2), Francis North, William Pearce, Frederick Reynolds (2), John Rose, and George Stevens; works by Thomas Erskine, Comte. T., Bishop Watson, John Williams, and Tate Wilkinson, and anonymous works, *Dialogue on the state of Parliament* (1783), and *Livre Rouge* (1790). Thirteen more are listed in the *Catalogue of the Library of Thomas Jefferson* (Washington, D.C.: Library of Congress, 1952): titles 387, 495, 744, 1337, 1377, 1430, 1757, 1808, 2077, 3545, 3612, 3958, 4847. Two reprints are listed in Sidney L. Gulick, "A Chesterfield Bibliography to 1800," *PBSA*, 29 (1935), 2–114, titles 137, 145. The remaining 98 reprints by Byrne, all listed in the *National Union Catalog, Pre-1956 Imprints*, are listed below since they are difficult to locate in the *Catalog*:

118. John Moore, *A view of society and manners in Italy*, 1781
119. Thomas Sheridan, *A Rhetorical Grammar of the English Language*, 1781
120. *History of Lord North's Administration*, 1782
121. *Beauties of Goldsmith*, 1783
122. Fanny Burney, *Cecilia*, 1783
123. William Combe, *Original love letters by a lady of quality*, 1784
124. Hannah More, *Sacred Dramas*, 1784
125. Thomas Sheridan, *Dictionary of the English Language*, 1784
126. James Boswell, *Tour to the Hebrides*, 1785

127. [W. Cooke] *Life of Samuel Johnson*, 1785
128. Thomas Erskine, *Rights of juries vindicated*, 1785
129. Samuel Johnson, *Prayers and Meditations*, 1785
130. Samuel Johnson, *Poetical Works*, 1785
131. John Courtenay, *Poetical review of the character of Samuel Johnson*, 1786
132. Elizabeth Inchbald, *The Widow's Row, a farce*, 1786
133. John O'Keeffe, *Peeping Tom*, 1786
134. Mrs. Piozzi, *Anecdotes of Samuel Johnson*, 1786
135. John Wolcot, *An epistle to James Boswell*, 1786
136. John Wolcot, *Bozzy and Piozzi*, 1786
137. *Beauties of Johnson*, 1787
138. Sir John Hawkins, *Life of Samuel Johnson*, 1787
139. Count Mirabeau, *Enquiries concerning lettres de cachet*, 1787
140. William Pitt, *Speech in House of Commons*, 1787
141. Henry Flood, *Speech in the House of Commons*, 1787
142. Durnford and East, *Reports of cases argued in the Court of King's Bench*, 1787
143. House of Lords, *Case of Mary Westby*, 1787
144. John Wolcot, *Instructions to a celebrated laureat*, 1787
145. John Wolcot, *The Lousiad*, 1787
146. John Wolcot, *Ode upon ode*, 1787
147. Thomas Paine, *Prospects on the Rubicon*, 1788
148. Mrs. Piozzi, *Letters to and from Samuel Johnson*, 1788
149. Joseph Priestley, *Lectures on history and general policy*, 1788
150. Laurence Sterne, *Original Letters*, 1788
151. Daniel Defoe, *Robinson Crusoe*, 1789
152. Sir John Kelyng, *Reports on cases in the Court of King's Bench*, 1789
153. Count Mirabeau, *History of the Court of Berlin*, 1789
154. John Moore, *Zeluco*, 1789
155. Joseph Towers, *Memoirs of Frederick the Third of Prussia*, 1789
156. John Walker, *The Academic Speaker*, 1789
157. John Wolcot, *Peter's Prophecy*, 1789
158. John Wolcot, *A poetical epistle to a falling minister*, 1789
159. John Wolcot, *Poetical Works of Peter Pindar*, 1789
160. Edward Gibbon, *Decline and Fall of the Roman Empire*, (abridged), 1790
161. J. C. Lavater, *Aphorisms on Man*, 1790
162. *Trial of John Stockdale for Libel*, 1790
163. Richard Cumberland, *The Observer*, 1791
164. Durnford and East, *Reports of cases in the King's Bench*, 1791 (3rd ed.)
165. Joseph Priestley, *Lectures on History*, 1791
166. *Plays of Shakespeare*, 1791
167. John Wolcot, *The Lousiad, an heroi-comic poem*, 1791

168. John Wolcot, *Poetical Works*, 1791
169. *Advice to a certain Lord High Chancellor, twelve Judges, etc*, 1792
170. James Boswell, *Life of Samuel Johnson*, 1792
171. *A Collection of Interesting Biography*, 1792
172. Joseph Priestley, *An appeal on the riots in Birmingham*, 1792
173. Ann Radcliffe, *The Romance of the Forest*, 1792
174. Samuel Richardson, *Clarissa*, 1792
175. John Wolcot, *Works of Peter Pindar*, 1792–93
176. *Reports of cases argued in Common Pleas and Exchequer*, 1792
177. Sir W. Jones, *Dissertations relating to Asia*, 1793
178. John Moore, *A journal during a residence in France*, 1793
179. Thomas Paine, *Mr. King's speech at Egham*, 1793
180. Francis Vesey, *Reports of cases argued in Chancery*, 1793
181. William Shield, *Hartford Bridge, an operatic farce*, 1793
182. William Shield, *Sprigs of Laurel, a comic opera*, 1793
183. Adam Smith, *Wealth of Nations*, 1793
184. John Taylor, *Sermons*, 1793
185. William Tidd, *Law of costs in civil actions*, 1793
186. Arthur Young, *The Example of France*, 1793
187. John O'Keeffe, *Wild Oats, a comedy*, 1794
188. Sir James Dyer, *Reports of cases 1513–82*, 1794
189. C. Stedman, *History of the … American War*, 1794
190. William Ridgeway, *Reports of cases in King's Bench, 1733–45*, 1794
191. Laurence Sterne, *Works*, 1794
192. Thomas Peake, *Cases determined at nisi prius in King's Bench*, 1795
193. Richard Cumberland, *First Love, a Comedy*, 1795
194. John Moore, *A view of the French Revolution*, 1795
195. Sir Richard Musgrave, *A Letter on the Present Situation*, 1795
196. Arthur O'Connor, *Speech in the House of Commons on the Catholic Bill*, 1795
197. John O'Keeffe, *Life's Vagaries, a Comedy*, 1795
198. John Wolcot, *Works of Peter Pindar*, 1795
199. John Wolcot, *Pindariana*, 1795
200. William Blackstone, *Commentaries*, 13th ed., 1796
201. Henry Blackstone, *Reports of cases argued in Common Pleas and Exchequer*, 1795
202. Edmund Burke, *Letter to a noble Lord*, 1796
203. *Miscellaneous Works of Edward Gibbon*, 1796
204. M. G. Lewis, *The Monk*, 1796
205. Sir Richard Musgrave, *Considerations on the Present State of England and France*, 1796
206. Joseph Reeve, *Practical discourses on the works of God*, 1796
207. Alexander Anstruther, *Reports of cases in the Court of Exchequer*, 1796

208. William Tidd, *Practice of the Court of King's Bench in personal actions*, 1796
209. John Walker, *The Academic Speaker*, 1797
210. Thomas Erskine, *A View of the Present War with France*, 1796
211. John Moore, *Views of Human nature, chiefly in England*, 1797
212. Ann Radcliffe, *The Italian*, 1797
213. Frederick Reynolds, *Cheap Living, a comedy*, 1798
214. George Colman, *The heir-at-law, a comedy*, 1800
215. Henry Blackstone, *Reports of cases argued in Common Pleas and Exchequer*, 1800
216. John Walker, *The Academic Speaker*, 1800

Appendix 4

Irish Reprints consulted for this work

Short titles are used for all works and arabic numerals for dates.

Henry Fielding

The History of the Adventures of Joseph Andrews, and of his Friend Mr. Abraham Adams. 2 vols. Dublin: Printed by S. Powell, for G. Ewing, and W. Smith in Dame-street, and G. Faulkner in Essex-street, 1742.

2nd ed. 2 vols. Dublin: Printed for G. and A. Ewing, and W. Smith in Dame-street, and G. Faulkner in Essex-street, 1747.

3rd ed. 2 vols. Dublin: Printed for G. and A. Ewing, et al., 1754.

4th ed. 2 vols. Dublin: Printed for W. and W. Smith, G.Faulkner, and T. Ewing, Booksellers, 1767.

4th ed. 2 vols. Dublin: Printed for D. Chamberlaine, and J. Potts, Booksellers, in Dame-Street, 1767.

The History of Tom Jones, A Foundling. 3 vols. Dublin: Printed for John Smith at the Philosophers-Heads on the Blind-Quay, 1749.

2nd ed. 3 vols. Dublin: Printed for John Smith, 1749.

3rd ed. 3 vols. Dublin: Printed for John Smith, 1750.

3 vols. Dublin: Printed for W. Smith, P. Wilson, J. Exshaw, and H. Bradley, 1759.

3 vols. Dublin: Printed for W. Smith, et al., 1766.

3 vols. Dublin: Printed for James Hoey, sen., James Hoey, jun., D. Chamberlaine, and James Potts, 1767.

3 vols. Dublin: Printed for R. Marchbank, 1786.

Amelia. 4 vols. in 2. Dublin: Printed for John Smith, 1752.

4 vols. in 2. Dublin: Printed for G. Risk, C. Wynne, O. Nelson, P

Wilson, J. Exshaw, J. Edsall, S. Price, M. Williamson, and H. Saunders, Booksellers, 1752.

Beauties of Fielding. Dublin: Printed by James and William Porter, 1783.

Samuel Richardson

Pamela: or Virtue Rewarded. 2 vols. Dublin: Printed by R. Reilly, for George Ewing and George Faulkner, 1741.

6th ed. 4 vols. Dublin: Printed for George Ewing, George Faulkner, and William Smith, 1741–42.

Clarissa. Or, The History of a Young Lady. 7 vols. Dublin: Printed by George Faulkner, 1748–49.

An abridgement. 2 vols. Dublin: Printed for W. Sleater, 1756.

4th ed. 7 vols. Dublin: Printed for James Potts, 1765.

The History of Sir Charles Grandison. 7 vols. London: Printed by S. Richardson, and Dublin, Re-printed and sold by the Booksellers, 1753.

[Vol. 7 imprint:] London: Printed by S. Richardson and Dublin, Re-printed by and for H. Saunders, 1754.

6th ed. 7 vols. Dublin: Printed for Thomas Walker, 1780.

Tobias Smollett

The Adventures of Roderick Random. 2nd ed. 2 vols. Dublin: Printed and Sold by Richard James, opposite Sycamore Alley in Dame-Street, 1748.

3rd ed. 2 vols. Dublin: James, 1749.

4th ed. 2 vols. Dublin: James, 1755.

9th ed. 2 vols. Dublin: Printed for the United Company of Booksellers, 1775.

2 vols. Dublin: Printed by T. Henshall, [1794].

The Adventures of Peregrine Pickle. In which are included Memoirs of a Lady of Quality. 3 vols. Dublin: Printed for Robert Main, Bookseller in Dame-Street, opposite to Fownes's-Street, 1751.

3rd ed. 4 vols. Dublin: Printed by Henry Saunders and James Potts, 1768.

4th ed. 3 vols. Dublin: Printed by the United Company of Booksellers, 1775.

8th ed. 4 vols. Dublin: Printed and sold by R. Marchbank, 1787.

Abridged ed. Dublin: Printed by T. M'Donnell, 1791.

The Adventures of Ferdinand Count Fathom. 2 vols. Dublin: Printed for R. Main, Bookseller, in Dame-street, 1753.

2 vols. Dublin: Printed by James Potts, 1772.

The Adventures o Sir Launcelot Greaves. 2nd ed. Dublin: Printed by James Hoey, jun., 1763.
3rd ed. Dublin: Printed for the United Company of Booksellers, 1775.

The Expedition of Humphry Clinker. 2 vols. Dublin: Printed for A. Leathley, J. Exshaw, H. Saunders, W. Sleater, D. Chamberlaine, J. Potts, J. Hoey, jun., J. Mitchell, J. Williams, W. Colles, T. Walker, J. A. Husband, R. Moncrieffe, W. Wilson, and D. Hay, 1771.
2 vols. Dublin: Printed for A. Leathley, D. Chamberlaine, J. Exshaw, W. Sleater, J. Potts, J. Hoey, jun., J. Williams, W. Colles, T. Walker, J. A. Husband, R. Moncrieffe, W. Wilson, and M. Hay, 1774.
2 vols. Dublin: Printed for J. Exshaw, M. Hay, W. Sleater, D. Chamberlaine, J. Potts, J. Hoey, and J. Williams, 1781.

The History of England, From the Revolution to the Death of George II. 5 vols. Dublin: Luke White, 1787.

The History and Adventures of the renowned Don Quixote. Translated from the Spanish of Miguel de Cervantes Saavedra, to which is prefixed some account of the author's life by T. Smollett. 4 vols. Dublin: J. Chambers, 1796.

Laurence Sterne

The Life and Opinions of Tristram Shandy, Gentleman. Vols. 1–2, 3rd. ed. Dublin: Printed for D. Chamberlaine, in Smock-Alley, and S. Smith, at Mr. Faulkner's in Essex Street, 1760.
Vols. 3–4. Dublin: Printed for H. Saunders, D. Chamberlaine, and S. Smith, 1761.
2nd ed. Vols. 1–4. Dublin: Printed by Henry Saunders, 1765.
Vols. 5–8. Dublin: Printed by Henry Saunders, 1765.
Vol. 9. Dublin: Printed for W. and W. Smith, J. Exshaw, H. Saunders, S. Watson, and W. Colles, 1767.
4th ed. 9 vols. in 2. Dublin: Printed by H. Saunders, 1776.
9 vols. in 3. Dublin: Printed for J. Potts, J. Williams, W. Colles, T. Walker, C. Jenkin, and L. White, 1779.
4th ed. 9 vols. in 3. Dublin: Printed for D. Chamberlaine, W. Colles, and J. Potts, 1780.
9 vols. in 3. Dublin: Printed by T. Henshall, [1795].

The Sermons of Mr. Yorick. 2 vols. Dublin: Printed for G. Faulkner, P. Wilson, H. Bradley, and W. Smith, jun., Booksellers, 1760.
2 vols. in 1. Dublin: Printed in the Year 1761.
3rd ed. 2 vols in 1. Dublin: Printed for W. and W. Smith, G. Faulkner, and H. Bradley, 1766.
2 vols. in 1. Dublin: Printed for T. Armitage, 1785.

Letters from Yorick to Eliza. Dublin: Printed for T. Armitage, 1776.

Dublin: Printed for Messrs. Chamberlaine, Williams, Wilson, Husband, Moncrieffe, Porter, and Flyn, 1775.

2 vols. in 1. Dublin: Printed by R. Stewart, Sold by the Booksellers in Dublin and Cork, 1776.

Letters of the Late Rev. Mr. Laurence Sterne, to his Most Intimate Friends. 3 vols. in 1. Dublin: Printed for J. Exshaw, W. Whitestone, W. Sleater, D. Chamberlaine, J. Potts, J. Williams, W. Watson, J. Hoey, S. Watson, W. Colles, W. Wilson, R. Moncrieffe, C. Jenkin, T. Walker, T. Armitage, T. T. Faulkner, E. Cross, M. Mills, T. Wilkinson, J. Colles, P. Wilson, W. Spotswood, and J. Beatty, 1776.

3 vols. in 1. Dublin: Printed for T. Armitage, 1776.

A Sentimental Journey Through France and Italy. By Mr. Yorick. 2 vols. in 1. Dublin: Printed for G. Faulkner, J. Hoey, Sen., J. Exshaw, and H. Saunders, 1768.

2nd ed. Dublin: Printed for G. Faulkner, W. and W. Smith, J. Hoey, Sen., P. and W. Wilson, J. Exshaw, H. Saunders, L. Flin, D. Chamberlain, W. Sleater, J. Potts, J. Williams, and W. Colles, 1769.

7th ed. 2 vols. in 1. Dublin: Printed for T. Armitage, 1775.

4 vols. [including *Letters*]. Dublin: Printed for T. T. Faulkner, W. Smith, P. Hoey, W. Wilson, J. Exshaw, C. Jenkin, L. Flin, D. Chamberlaine, W. Sleater, J. Potts, J. Williams, and W. Colles, 1780.

The Works of Laurence Sterne. 4th ed. 6 vols. Dublin: Printed for H. Saunders, D. Chamberlaine, and J. Potts, Booksellers, 1770.

7 vols. Dublin: Printed for Thomas Armitage, 1774.

5th ed. 4 vols. [*Tristram Shandy* not included]. Dublin: Printed for H. Saunders, D. Chamberlaine, and J. Potts, 1775.

8 vols. Dublin: Printed for T. Armitage, 1779.

5th ed. 7 vols. Dublin: Printed for H. Saunders, D. Chamberlaine, and J. Potts, 1780.

7 vols. Dublin: Printed by P. Byrne, 1794.

The Beauties of Sterne; Including all his Pathetic Tales, And most distinguished Observations on Life. 9th ed. Dublin: Printed by H. Colbert, No. 136, Chapel-Street, opposite Abbey-Street, 1788.

Samuel Johnson

London; a Poem. In Imitation of the Third Satire of Juvenal. Dublin: Printed by and for George Faulkner, 1738.

Irene: a Tragedy. Dublin: Printed by S. Powell, for G. and A. Ewing, J. Hoey, A. Bradley, J. Exshaw, W. Brien, and R. James, 1749.

The Rambler. 6 vols. in 3. Dublin: Printed by George Faulkner, 1752.

4 vols. 11th ed. Dublin: Printed by D. Graisberry, for Thomas Heery, 1785.

4 vols. Dublin: James Moore, 1793.

The Idler. 2 vols. in 1. Dublin: Printed for Peter Wilson, 1762.

A Dictionary of the English Language. Abridged ed. Dublin: Printed for G. and A. Ewing, 1758.

3rd ed. Dublin: Printed by W. G. Jones and Thomas Ewing, 1768.

4th ed. 2 vols. Dublin: Printed for Thomas Ewing, 1775.

8th ed. 2 vols. Dublin: Printed by R. Marchbank, 1798.

The Prince of Abissinia. A Tale. 2 vols. in 1. Dublin: Printed for G. and A. Ewing, and H. Bradley, 1759.

8th ed. Dublin: Printed by J. Kiernan, for T. Walker, 1777.

8th ed. Dublin: Printed for Sheppard and Nugent, 1787.

The Plays of William Shakespeare. 10 vols. Dublin: Printed for A. Leathley, C. Wynne, P. Wilson, H. Saunders, J. Potts, S. Watson, J. Mitchell, and J. Williams, 1766.

12 vols. Dublin: Printed for Thomas Ewing, 1771.

16 vols. Dublin: P. Wogan, P. Byrne, W. McKenzie, J. Moore, A. Grueber, W. Jones, R. White, and J. White, 1791.

16 vols. Dublin: John Exshaw, 1794.

A Journey to the Western Islands of Scotland. 2 vols. in 1. Dublin: Printed for A. Leathley, J. Exshaw, H. Saunders, D. Chamberlaine, W. Sleater, J. Potts, T. Ewing, W. Wilson, R. Moncrieffe, and C. Jenkin, 1775.

Dublin: Printed by Thomas Walker, 1775.

Dublin: Printed for J. Williams, 1775.

London: Printed for J. Pope, 1775

Political Tracts. Dublin: Printed for Whitestone, W. Watson, E. Lynch, Hoey, W. Williams, Colles, Wilson, T. Walker, C. Jenkin, Moncrieffe, Wogan, Exshaw, L. White, J. Beatty, and C. Talbot, 1777.

The Lives of the English Poets. Dublin: Printed for Messrs. Whitestone, Williams, Colles, Wilson, Lynch, Jenkin, Walker, Burnet, Hallhead, Flin, Exshaw, Beatty, and White, 1779.

3 vols. Dublin: Printed for Messrs. Whitestone, et al., 1779–81.

3 rd ed. 3 vols. Dublin: Printed for Messrs. Whitestone, et al., 1781.

London: Printed for R. Dodsley, Pall-Mall, 1795.

The Works of the poets of Great Britain and Ireland, with prefaces, biographical and critical by Samuel Johnson, 8 vols. Dublin: Printed for J. Moore, 1793–1802.

The Beauties of Johnson. Dublin: Printed for Messrs. Price, Whitestone, Walker, Moncrieffe, Gilbert, White, Mills, Beatty, Burton, Parker, and Byrne, 1782.

The Poetical Works of Samuel Johnson, LL.D. Dublin: Printed for L. White, P. Byrne, and R. Marchbank, 1785.

Prayers and Meditations, Composed by Samuel Johnson, LL.D. Dublin: Printed for Messrs. White, Byrne, and Cash, 1785.
4th ed. Dublin: Printed for H. Colbert, 1796.

Letters to and from the late Samuel Johnson. 2 vols. in 1. Dublin: Printed for Messrs. R. Moncrieffe, L. White, P. Byrne, P. Wogan, and J. Moore, 1788.

Works. 6 vols. Dublin: Printed for Luke White, 1793.

James Boswell

An Account of Corsica, The Journal of a Tour to that Island; and Memoirs of Pascal Paoli. 3rd ed. Dublin: Printed for J. Exshaw, H. Saunders, W. Sleater, D. Chamberlaine, J. Potts, and J. Williams, 1768.
4th ed. Dublin: Printed for J. Exshaw, H. Saunders, W. Sleater, D. Chamberlaine, J. Potts, J. Williams, and W. Colles, 1768.

Letters of the Right Honourable Lady Jane Douglas; to her Husband Sir John Stewart, Bart. Dublin: Printed by J. Exshaw, 1768.

The Journal of a Tour to the Hebrides, with Samuel Johnson, LL.D. Dublin: Printed for Messrs. White, Byrne, and Cash, 1785.

A Collection of Interesting Biography. Containing I. The Life of S. Johnson, LL.D. Abridged, principally, from Boswell's celebrated Memoirs of the Doctor: II. The Life of Mr. Elwes, (Abridged) by Captain Topham: III. The Life of Captain Cook (Abridged) by Dr. Kippis. The whole revised and abridged by Sir Andrew Anecdote. Dublin: Printed for P. Wogan, P. Byrne, W. Sleater, A. Grueber, J. Moore, J. Jones, R. M'Allister, W. Jones, R. White, J. Rice, and A. Porter, 1792.

The Life of Samuel Johnson, LL.D. comprehending an Account of his Studies and numerous Works, in chronological Order; a Series of his epistolary Correspondence and Conversations with many eminent Persons; and various original Pieces of his Composition, never before published. 3 vols: Dublin: Printed by John Chambers, for R. Cross, W. Wilson, P. Byrne, A. Grueber, J. Moore, J. Jones, W. M'kenzie, W. Jones, R. M'Allister, R. White, J. Rice, and G. Draper, 1792. [Vol. II was printed by John Exshaw and Vol. III by Robert Rhames for the same booksellers.]

Oliver Goldsmith

The Citizen of the World. 2 vols. Dublin: Printed for George and Alex. Ewing, 1762.

2 vols. Dublin: Printed for J. Williams, 1769.

2 vols. Dublin: Printed for the United Company of Booksellers, 1775.

Essays. 2nd ed. Dublin: Printed for J. Williams, 1767.

3rd ed. Dublin: Printed for James Williams, 1772.

3 vols. Dublin: Printed by J. Stockdale for J. Moore, 1793.

The Vicar of Wakefield. 2 vols. Dublin: Printed for W. and W. Smith, A. Leathley, J. Hoey, sen., P. Wilson, J. Exshaw, E. Watts, H. Saunders, J. Hoey, jun., J. Potts, and J. Williams, 1766.

2nd ed. 2 vols. Dublin: Printed for W. and W. Smith, et al., 1766.

2 vols. Corke: Printed by Eugene Swiney, 1766.

2 vols. Dublin: Printed for W. and W. Smith, et al., 1767.

Dublin: Printed by the United Company of Booksellers, 1791.

2 vols. Dublin: Printed by J. Stockdale, for J. Moore, 1793.

2 vols. Dublin: Printed by T. Henshall, [1794].

Le curé de Wakefield. Dublin: Printed by G. Gilbert, 1797.

The Good Natur'd Man. Dublin: Printed by J. A. Husband, for J. Hoey, sen., P. and W. Wilson, J. Exshaw, H. Saunders, W. Sleater, J. Williams, D. Chamberlaine, J. Potts, J. Mitchell, J. Sheppard, and W. Colles, 1768.

Dublin: Printed for J. Hoey, sen., et al., 1770.

Dublin: Printed for Messrs. Price, Sleater, W. Watson, Whitestone, Chamberlaine, S. Watson, Burrowes, Potts, Williams, Hoey, Wilkinson, Sheppard, Colles, Wilson, Moncrieffe, Walker, Jenkin, Exshaw, Burnet, Hillary, Wogan, Mills, White, Higly, and Beatty, 1784.

She Stoops to Conquer. Belfast: Printed by James Magee, 1773.

Dublin: Printed for Messrs. Exshaw, Saunders, Sleater, Potts, Chamberlaine, Williams, Wilson, Hoey, jun., Husband, Lynch, Vallance, Colles, Walker, Moncrieffe, Jenkin, Flin, and Hillary, 1773.

Dublin: Printed for Exshaw, et al. [excluding Colles], 1773.

Dublin: Printed by Bartholomew Corcoran, 1774.

Dublin: Prited for Messrs. Price, Sleater, W. Watson, Whitestone, Chamberlaine, S. Watson, Burrowes, Potts, Williams, Hoey, Wilkinson, Sheppard, Colles, Wilson, Moncrieffe, Walker, Jenkin, Exshaw, Burnet, Hillary, Wogan, Mills, White, Higly, and Beatty, 1784.

Dublin: Printed for Messrs. Price, et al., 1785.

Dublin: Printed by Graisberry and Campbell, for William Jones, 1792.

The Traveller, or a Prospect of Society. Dublin: Printed by George Faulkner, 1767.

Dublin: Printed by George Faulkner, 1770.

The Deserted Village. Dublin: Printed for J. Exshaw, H. Saunders, B. Grierson, J. Potts, W. Sleater, D. Chamberlaine, J. Hoey, jun., J. Williams, C. Ingham, J. Porter, and R. Moncrieffe, 1770.

2nd ed. Dublin: Printed for H. Saunders, B. Grierson, J. Potts, W. Sleater, D. Chamberlaine, J. Hoey, jun., J. Williams, C. Ingham, J. Porter, and R. Moncrieffe, 1770.

Dublin: Printed for Messrs. Price, Sleater, W. Watson, Whitestone, Chamberlaine, S. Watson, Burrowes, Potts, Williams, Hoey, Wilkinson, Sheppard, Colles, Wilson, Moncrieffe, Walker, Jenkin, Exshaw, Burnet, Hillary, Wogan, Mills, White, Higly, and Beatty, 1784.

Poems. Belfast: Printed by James Magee, 1775.

Dublin: Printed by Charles Downes, for Thomas Reilly, 1801.

The Haunch of Venison. Dublin: Printed for W. Whitestone, W. Watson, W. Sleater, J. Potts, J. Hoey, W. Colles, W. Wilson, R. Moncrieffe, G. Burnet, C. Jenkin, T. Walker, W. Hallhead, W. Spotswood, M. Mills, J. Exshaw, J. Beatty, and C. Talbot, 1776.

Poems and Plays. Dublin: Printed for Messrs. Price, Sleater, W. Watson, Whitestone, Chamberlaine, S. Watson, Burrowes, Potts, Williams, Hoey, Wilkinson, Sheppard, W. Colles, W. Wilson, Moncrieffe, Walker, Jenkin, Hallhead, Exshaw, Spotswood, Burnet, P. Wilson, Armitage, E. Cross, Hillary, Wogan, Mills, White, T. Watson, Talbot, Higly, and Beatty, 1777.

Dublin: Printed for Wm. Wilson, 1777.

A new edition corrected. Dublin: Printed for Messrs. Price, et al., 1785.

The Beauties of Goldsmith. Dublin: Printed by J. Rea, for Messrs. S. Price, Walker, Exshaw, Beatty, Wilson, Wogan, Burton, Byrne, and Cash, 1783.

An History of the Earth and Animated Nature. 8 vols. Dublin: Printed for J. Williams, 1776.

8 vols. Dublin: Printed for J. Williams, 1777.

8 vols. Dublin: Printed by J. Williams, 1782–83.

An History of England in a Series of Letters from a Nobleman to his Son.

2 vols. Dublin: Printed for J. Exshaw and H. Bradley, 1765.

2 vols. Dublin: Printed for J. Exshaw and H. Bradley, 1767.

4th ed. 2 vols. Dublin: Printed for J., Exshaw and W. Colles, 1784.

The History of England, from the Earliest Times to the Death of George II. 4 vols.

Dublin: Printed for A. Leathley, J. Exshaw, W. Wilson, H. Saunders, W. Sleater, D. Chamberlaine, J. Hoey, jun., J. Potts, J. Williams, J. Mitchell, J. A. Husband, W. Colles, T. Walker, R. Moncrieffe, and D. Hay, 1771.

4th ed. 4 vols. Dublin: Printed for W. Sleater, H. Chamberlaine, J. Potts, W. Colles, R. Moncrieffe, T. Walker, W. Wilson, J. Exshaw, and L. White, 1789.

5th ed. 4 vols. Dublin: Printed by William Porter, for W. Gilbert, P. Wogan, J. Exshaw, W. Porter, W. McKenzie, J. Moore, W. Jones, and J. Rice, 1796.

An abridgement of the History of England, from the invasion of Julius Caesar, to the death of George II. 5th ed. Dublin: Printed by James Williams, 1779.

The Roman History. 2 vols. Dublin: Printed for S. Powel, J. Exshaw, H. Saunders, B. Grierson, W. Sleater, D. Chamberlaine, J. Potts, J. Hoey, jun., J. Williams, and C. Ingham, 1769.

2 vols. Dublin: Printed for S. Powel, et al., 1771.

2 vols. Dublin: Printed for P. Wogan, J. Exshaw, W. Sleater, J. Rice, and R. White, 1792.

2 vols. Cork: Printed by J. Connor, 1800.

The Roman History, abridged for schools. Dublin: Printed for P. Wogan, 1798.

The Grecian History. 2 vols. Dublin: Printed for James Williams, 1774.

2 vols. Dublin: Printed by P. Wogan, 1801.

Edward Gibbon

The History of the Decline and Fall of the Roman Empire. 2 vols. Dublin: Printed for William Hallhead, 1776.

4th ed. 2 vols. Dublin: Printed for William Hallhead, 1777.

6 vols. Dublin: Printed for Luke White, 1777.

5th ed. 6 vols. Dublin: Printed for William Hallhead, 1781.

6th ed. 6 vols. Dublin: Printed for W. Wilson, 1784.

6 vols. [Vols. 7–12] Dublin: Printed for Luke White, 1788.

6 vols. [Vols. 1–6] Dublin: Printed for Luke White, 1789.

2 vols. Abridged ed. Dublin: Printed by William Porter, for H. Chamberlaine, P. Wogan, P. Byrne, W. Porter, W. McKenzie, J. Jones, J. Halpen, and Grueber & McAlister, 1790.

Essai sur L'Étude de la Littèrature. Dublin: Guillaume Hallhead, 1777.

A Vindication of some passages in the fifteenth and sixteenth chapters of the history and decline and fall of the Roman empire. Dublin: Printed for W. and H. Whitestone, J. Williams, W. Colles, W. Wilson, C. Jenkin, T. Walker, R.

Moncrieffe, W. Hallhead, J. Exshaw, J. Beatty, L. White, and B. Watson, 1779.

Miscellaneous Works. 3 vols. Dublin: Printed for P. Wogan, L. White, John Chambers, P. Byrne, John Milliken, James Moore, J. Rice, W. Jones, John Halpen, Peter Moore, H. Fitzpatrick, N. Kelly, and G. Folingsby, 1796.

Index